INVISIBLE ENEMIES

Disease, Social Collapse, and Survivalism

Thomas Rivers, PhD

Invisible Enemies: Disease, Social Collapse, and Survivalism
Thomas Rivers
978-0-6487660-4-9

© Manticore Press, Melbourne, Australia, 2020.

TABLE OF CONTENTS

1. APOCALYPSE NOW?

None the less, he knew that the tale he had to tell could not be one of a final victory. It could be only the record of what had had to be done, and what assuredly would have to be done again in the never-ending fight against terror and its relentless onslaughts, despite their personal afflictions, by all who, while unable to be saints but refusing to bow down to pestilences, strive their utmost to be healers. And, indeed, as he listened to the cries of joy rising from the town, Rieux remembered that such joy is always imperiled. He knew what those jubilant crowds did not know but could have learned from books: that the plague *bacillus* never dies or disappears for good; that it can lie dormant for years and years in furniture and linen chests; that it bides its time in bedrooms, cellars, trunks, and bookshelves; and that perhaps the day would come when, for the bane and the enlightening of men, it would rouse up its rats again and send them forth to die in a happy city.

- Albert Camus, *La Peste* (1947)[1]

In most cities in the West, routine daily life has come to an abrupt halt. The shops, once bustling with customers, are closed, some shop fronts are boarded up, all with notices giving the same reason for closure. The footpaths and city streets are deserted. Nothing disturbs the sound of silence, except for the intermittent shrieks of rats, fighting over the very last remnants of scattered junk food, that once these heroin-like addicts of the subterranean realm feasted on. Good Friday, 2020, in this strange world, and the churches have their doors shut too, something not seen since the 1918-19 H1N1 influenza pandemic. One is reminded of the eerie street scenes from movies such as *On the Beach* (1959) and *28 Weeks Later* (2007). But, this is the world of the 2020 *La Peste*, a time of lockdowns, closed borders, quarantines in place, and social distancing. And, we writers cannot name the cause of this malady, under punishment of ... silence!

Welcome to the world of the new disease, a malady so terrible it can only be referred to as an 'Invisible Enemy.'

Most wars come and go, but unless civilian populations are directly attacked (e.g., the World War II bombing of London) or overrun by the enemy (e.g., the fall of France in 1940), for most, life goes on in a *Groundhog Day* kind of way. However, the virus lockdown has fundamentally tipped the ordinary world that once was defined as "normal" on its head, with the curtailment of once taken-for-granted liberties such as freedom of association and freedom of movement. Thus, in most jurisdictions in the West, and much of Asia, with the interesting partial exception of Sweden (keeping borders open, limiting social gathering to 50 people, and isolating the most vulnerable),[2] people have been prosecuted for being out in public without a proscribed reason, or having conflicting reasons,[3] or not wearing face masks in public (when justified in being out).[4] UK police have been checking peoples' shopping trollies for "non-essential" items,[5] leading to 32 percent of Brits in a recent YouGov survey feeling that the police had gone too far.[6] There is more than enough material here to supply dissertation topics to budding PhD candidates on the issues of liberty and paternalism, and what limits, if any, there are to law making.[7]

The justification of these measures is that the disease has devastating ill-health effects upon vulnerable people, and is not just another seasonal flu, as many seem to argue on the internet.[8] The actual virus may start with symptoms like the common cold, with gut infections and diarrhea. But, it may progress, particularly in older people, to attack type II lung cells, cells that help move air deep into the lungs. The virus causes the immune system to "storm," attacking the lung tissue and potentially causing massive lung damage. As Benjamin Neuman, professor of Biology at Texas A&M University, explains this action differs significantly from the seasonal flu:

> [it] is more severe than seasonal influenza in part because it has many more ways to stop cells from calling out to the immune system for help. For example, one way that cells try to respond to infection is by making interferon, the alarm signaling protein [...] blocks this by a combination of camouflage,

snipping off protein markers from the cell that serve as distress beacons, and finally shredding any anti-viral instructions that the cell makes before they can be used. As a result, [...] can fester for a month, causing a little damage each day, while most people get over a case of the flu in less than a week.

At present, the transmission rate [...] is a little higher than that of the pandemic 2009 H1N1 influenza virus, but [...] is at least ten times as deadly. From the data that is available now, [...] seems a lot like severe acute respiratory syndrome (SARS), though it's less likely than SARS to be severe.[9]

Further, obesity is another risk factor, which puts down the heartless argument that it is just old people getting it, who will not be missed if dead, because there is an obesity epidemic in the West, that includes many younger people as well, including those with high blood pressure.[10] The Invisible Enemy is also now thought to attack the heart leading to heart damage, and often death, from cardiac arrest.[11]

Some authorities have questioned the alleged seriousness of the pandemic, noting that at present, the death rate is much lower than the seasonal influenza rate.[12] For example, Eran Bendavid and Jay Bhattacharya, argued in an article in *The Wall Street Journal*, that the projections of the death toll are many times too high and:

[are] based on its high estimated case fatality rate—2% to 4% of people with confirmed [...] have died, according to the World Health Organization and others. So, if 100 million Americans ultimately get the disease, two million to four million could die. We believe that estimate is deeply flawed. The true fatality rate is the portion of those *infected* who die, not the deaths from *identified* positive cases.

The latter rate is misleading because of selection bias in testing. The degree of bias is uncertain because available data are limited. But it could make the difference between an epidemic that kills 20,000 and one that kills two million. If the number of actual infections is much larger than the number of cases—orders of magnitude larger—then the true fatality rate is much lower as well. That's not only plausible but likely based on what we know so far.

Population samples from China, Italy, Iceland, and the US. provide relevant evidence. On or around Jan. 31, countries sent planes to evacuate citizens from Wuhan, China. When those planes landed, the passengers were tested [...] and quarantined. After 14 days, the percentage who tested positive was 0.9%.

7

If this was the prevalence in the greater Wuhan area on Jan. 31, then, with a population of about 20 million, greater Wuhan had 178,000 infections, about 30-fold more than the number of reported cases. The fatality rate, then, would be at least 10-fold lower than estimates based on reported cases.[13]

However, the counter that can be made is that the projected high death rates have not occurred because the lockdowns have, at present, been effective in preventing the spread of the disease.[14] On the disease mortality issue, Stephanie Pappas summarizes that a recent study of cases:

in the United States estimated a mortality rate of 10% to 27% for those ages 85 and over, 3% to 11% for those ages 65 to 84, 1% to 3% for those ages 55 to 64 and less than 1% for those ages 20 to 54. These numbers shouldn't be taken as the inevitable toll of the virus, however. The case-fatality rate is determined by dividing the number of deaths by the total number of cases. Epidemiologists believe the total number of infections […] is underestimated because people with few or mild symptoms may never see a doctor. As testing expands and scientists begin using retrospective methods to study who has antibodies […] circulating in their bloodstreams, the total number of confirmed cases will go up, and the ratio of deaths to infections will likely drop.

For example, in South Korea, which conducted more than 140,000 tests […], officials found a fatality rate of 0.6%.

However, complicating the matter, mortality numbers lag behind infection numbers simply because it takes days to weeks for severely ill people to die. […] Thus, current death rates should properly be divided by the number of known infections from the previous week or two, researchers wrote in February in *Swiss Medical Weekly*. A report published March 13 in the journal *Emerging Infectious Diseases* adjusted for this «time delay» between hospitalization and death. The authors estimated that, as of Feb. 11, the death rate […] was as high as 12% in Wuhan, 4% in Hubei Province, and 0.9% in the rest of China.[15]

Thus, even if some over-reaction did occur by the police, the authorities were scientifically justified in moving to close borders and implement policies of isolationism and quarantine, as the Invisible Enemy is more infectious than the seasonal flu (R0 number, the average number of people infected by an individual is 2-2.5, and the flu is 1.30), and is more deadly for older people and those with health issues such as cardiovascular conditions, and even those obese, and thus had the potential to overwhelm and collapse the healthcare system.

However, that being said, there are profound ramifications of the present pandemic, and beyond, which need to urgently be addressed, especially the economic consequences. This does not justify the do-nothing approach, because the harms discussed above are real whatever the economic consequences. What we see with such pandemic is a "social trap," where policies based upon neo-liberalism, such as open borders, may have had a short-term benefit for some, namely the one-percenters, the global super-capitalist elite, but have long-term adverse consequences, perhaps of a civilizational threatening level.[16]

What is to Come: Economic Collapse?

William McNeil in *Plagues and People*[17] has outlined in detail the relationship between epidemic disease and population movements. Diseases often arise through "horizontal" transmission from animals to humans, as hypothesized with disease. Smallpox and measles are likely to have arisen in this way. However, these diseases were transferred from Africa or Asia to the Mediterranean by the movement of peoples. Epidemics of leprosy did not occur in Europe before the expansion of the Roman Empire. The Justinian plague of the sixth century was thought to have begun in Egypt, and the black death of fourteenth-century Europe to come from China.[18] European sailors brought smallpox, measles, and swine flu to the "New World," which decimated the native populations of America. In turn, the sailors contracted syphilis from the native American populations and introduced it to Europe. Even the common cold proved lethal to populations who had no resistance to the disease, as the Australian Aborigines learned. In the early nineteenth century, cholera moved into Europe from India, transferred by merchants and armies. The first epidemic of *Encephalitis lethargica* was in China in 1928. The pathogen is thought to have arisen from a mutation of the influenza virus. From China, the disease spread globally, killing half a million people before disappearing.

The movement of humans around the Earth has been a key factor in the spread of epidemics. Immigration, through the spread of disease, has been responsible for the collapse of entire civilizations. Diseases brought by the Conquistadors killed a third to a half of the Aztecs and Incas. Today humanity is even more vulnerable given the rapid globalization of the world and mass movement of people, and virtually open borders, that prevailed until the present pandemic. As Ornstein and Ehrlich observed in 1989:

> For decades now, humanity has been setting itself up as the progressively ideal target for a worldwide epidemic. The combination of rapidly increasing numbers of malnourished people, who live in conditions of poor sanitation and with impure water, with evermore-rapid transportation systems has been making the human epidemiological environment ever more precarious. We have created a giant, crowded, "monoculture" of human beings, millions of whom are especially vulnerable to disease and among whom carriers can move with unprecedented speed.[19]

In the 14th century, the Black Death (the bubonic plague) killed between one third and two-thirds of Europe's population. The Spanish flu, between September and November 1918, killed over 20 million people, almost twice as many as died in World War I.[20] This flu affected about one-third of all people on the planet, and as a scientific philosopher, Quentin Smith has noted, if the infection/death ratio of the Spanish flu (actually from China) was higher (e.g., the Ebola virus kills around 90 percent of those affected, the bubonic plague, 50 percent) "the human race would have become extinct in late 1918 or 1919."[21] This, however, is probably incorrect, as it presupposes an unrealistic infection/death ratio of 100 percent. Nevertheless, human death rates would have been high enough to collapse civilization.

There is some evidence that new variants of avian influenza have, and are incorporating genetic material from other avian influenza strains, so that the viruses may be evolving to become better adapted to infecting humans with a potential pandemic. Ian MacKay, a virologist at the University of Queensland, has said: "Each new strain could be one that is better genetically equipped to transmit from person to person. Without contemporary sequence analysis, such a strain could emerge from among the 'noise' of human infection by less efficient strains, to begin spreading rapidly and with pandemic potential."[22] It was only a matter of time, then that the world would face a pandemic.

A pandemic flu may not naturally arise from viruses with an infection/death ratio approaching or exceeding that of Ebola's, but a genetically engineered viral bioterrorist weapon perhaps could. In December 2011, there were concerns about the journals *Science* and *Nature* publishing details of a genetically altered H5 N1 bird flu virus that was likely to be highly contagious among humans. The US National Science Advisory Board for Biosecurity was concerned that terrorists could replicate the experiments and unleash the virus, leading to a pandemic killer flu.[23] There are have issues about whether or not it escaped from a biological research facility in Wuhan, perhaps making it an unintentional "bioweapon."[24]

However, Andersen (et al.) examined the genetic features of the causative virus, and concluded that it was unlikely to have been cooked up in a lab, and accidentally released.[25] The idea that natural selection occurred in an animal host (e.g., bats) in the Huanan market in Wuhan, before zoonotic transfer occurred, faces the problem that "no animal [...] has been identified that is sufficiently similar to have served as the direct progenitor [...]." But further studies could support this hypothesis. The idea that natural selection of the virus occurred in humans after zoonotic transfer is also an explanation, but at present, evidence for this hypothesis is lacking. Scientific opinion thus seems to be that we do not know how this pandemic actually arose, but the idea of it being a laboratory construct, and a bioweapon seems unlikely. Even though infection can lead to a terrible disease and death for many people, it is still a long way away from what a military weapon of mass bio-destruction would be by genetic engineering. There are no doubt vastly more horrors in the labs of the super-powers that could be released. And, nature via the bio-magic of natural selection, may also unleash such future horrors.

A pandemic with high mortality globally would be capable of producing civilizational collapse.[26] Some indications that a high mortality pandemic could do this are the loss of personnel in key industries and the death of technicians. A severe pandemic could hypothetically threaten the nuclear industry. The death of key service personnel in the transport, fuel, and energy industries could have a knock-on effect leading to some of the nightmare scenarios discussed below. However, even if the nuclear industry is protected, shops and supermarkets will run out of food due to "just-in-time" delivery methods, which do not involve having stockpiles of goods beyond a few day's use on hand, something we have already had a taste of with the pandemic. As Mitchell Feierstein explains, and as will be discussed further, globalism and the just in time supply chains can be a dangerous mixture, something seen today with the shortage of essential medical supplies such as masks:

> Globalism's open borders and just-in-time supply chains have been providing cheap labor and products – but the [...] pandemic has shown us the huge cost of neglected independence.

> [...] has opened the kimono of globalism, and what's underneath is ugly. The virus has illustrated the importance of, and our reliance on, just-in-time supply chains. Supply chains are only as strong as their weakest link. If any ingredient is missing from that supply chain, the nation controlling that commodity can break it, causing devastating economic, geopolitical, and social consequences.

> For example, take emergency medical supplies and critical drugs. Most antibiotics, as well as the main ingredients to produce them, are made in China. India has prohibited the export of hydroxychloroquine, the malaria drug that President Trump touted as a "game changer" in the treatment of [...]. Even basic over-the-counter drugs like paracetamol are "out-of-stock." Hen's teeth and capable Central Bankers seem easier to find than N95 face masks, gloves, thermometers, pulse oximeters, hand sanitizer, and isopropyl alcohol.

We also rely on other nation's electrical parts to run critical infrastructure, trucks, trains, planes, and automobiles.

The imposition of national export bans on medical supply chain ingredients is a wakeup call for every nation state that has become reliant upon other nations for products they no longer produce domestically. Scarcity of critical commodities and medical supplies needs to be part of every National Security dialogue. People's lives depend upon the unrestricted access to and supply of these drugs, medical products, and equipment, which today, thanks to 30 years of neoliberal globalism, are now beyond our control. We need to rebuild this infrastructure and become self-sufficient in providing necessities. Right now, we don't have the ventilators or drugs required to combat and treat [...]—who decides who lives or dies? We should NEVER have been in this position—we must never be in it again.

Any disruption to our supply chain will result in a surge in unemployment and mortgage defaults, and people won't be able to feed their families. Civil unrest has already begun in Italy, and it will go viral globally.

Countries need to urgently review and categorize which industries are a matter of national security or, more simply put, are a matter of life or death to their citizens.[27]

The pandemic is very much a product of today's hyper-globalism and open borders, and—as even supporters of globalism are recognizing—the foundations of the cosmopolitan world view are crumbling.[28] As one leading Australian journalist states:

[it] has brought a world recession and has every chance of bringing a global depression. Don't think it's a short-term phenomenon or similar to anything we have seen before in our modern experience. It is chewing up and spitting out every tenet of globalization [...] As many commentators (including me) have argued, [...] is the killer of globalization or at least globalization as we have known it. One thing it is going to kill for sure is the idea of the free movement of people across open borders. [...] In recent decades, a positive ideology of globalization has been to wipe out borders. The EU has tried to do this internally, and for a time, tried to do it externally as well. It was a colossal disaster, and one most European people hated. It led directly to Brexit and its slogan: Take back control [...] may be with us for a long time. Even when it is suppressed in any nation, that nation remains vulnerable to infected international travelers. Until there is a vaccine, the international movement of people is likely to be restricted. After that, open borders will never again have the same appeal, and globalization will itself be fundamentally transformed.[29]

As Rich Lowry puts it in summary, we are all restrictionists now.[30] "The lyrics of the treacly John Lennon classic "Imagine"—recently performed by celebrities organized by actress Gal Gadot as a balm in this time of distress—have never been so absurdly inappropriate. If there were no countries and the world were as one, we'd be even more vulnerable to whatever threat arises across the globe in a city in central China."[31]

Nevertheless, when the disease was ravaging China, 500,000 Chinese people entered America, with 3.4 million travelers, and a large number may have already been infected, indicating the inertia present in the open borders system.[32] The US intelligence community may have known about the infection in China had the potential to be catastrophic in late November 2019, but the Trump administration did not act because it meant creating economic disruption, and they gambled that the problem would be contained by China, which it could not be in an open-borders world.[33] If this is so, it changes the argument, no doubt also correct, that China was less than transparent at the beginning of the crisis. Yes, no doubt, but grown-up nations get their own information, as noted by Ken Klippenstein, in an exclusive report in *The Nation*:

> [...] the Pentagon was not just well aware of the threat of a novel influenza but even anticipated the consequent scarcity of ventilators, face masks, and hospital beds, according to a 2017 Pentagon plan obtained by *The Nation*.

> "The most likely and significant threat is a novel respiratory disease, particularly a novel influenza disease," the military plan states. [...] is a respiratory disease caused by the novel (meaning new to humans) [...]. The document specifically refers to [...] on several occasions, in one instance saying, "[...] infections [are] common around the world." Titled "USNORTHCOM Branch Plan 3560: Pandemic Influenza and Infectious Disease Response," the draft plan is marked for official use only and dated January 6, 2017. The plan was provided to *The Nation* by a Pentagon official who requested anonymity to avoid professional reprisal.

> Denis Kaufman, who served as head of the Infectious Diseases and Countermeasures Division at the Defense Intelligence Agency from 2014 to 2017, stressed that US intelligence had been well aware of the dangers of

[...] for years. (He retired from his decades-long career in the military in December 2017.)

"The intelligence community has warned about the threat from highly pathogenic influenza viruses for two decades, at least. They have warned about [...] for at least five years," Kaufman said in an interview.

"There have been recent pronouncements that the [...] pandemic represents an intelligence failure. [...] It's letting people who ignored intelligence warnings off the hook." In addition to anticipating the [...] pandemic, the military plan predicted with uncanny accuracy many of the medical supply shortages that will now apparently soon cause untold deaths. The plan states, "Competition for, and scarcity of resources will include [...] non-pharmaceutical MCM [medical countermeasures] (e.g., ventilators, devices, personal protective equipment such as face masks and gloves), medical equipment, and logistical support. This will have a significant impact on the availability of the global workforce."[34]

Mongolia, a nation that shares a border with China, and centuries ago under warlord leader Genghis Khan (1162-1227), and was once one of the most aggressive globalist nations in history, moved quickly to shut its borders, and suspend all international flights.[35] Mongolia brought the current pandemic under control, better than all Western nations, who could not let go of their obsessive-compulsive commitment to open borders, the fanatic economic cult of the West. The untenability of the globalist philosophy has been shown by this confrontation with biological and ecological realities; human beings are a part of nature and subject to natural forces and are not removed by economics and money from biological interactions. This is not to say that we are experiencing a type of revenge of nature as the Pope seems to think,[36] a position which anthropomorphizes natural forces, but rather this crisis arises from a failure to see that the political system and its associated philosophical ideologies of open borders, which the Pope in fact also champions, has produced the conditions for this crisis. The truth of this proposition is seen by the solution of closing borders, even between states in nations.

Matters, though, are potentially much worse than merely the eclipse of globalism, free trade, and the mass movement of migrants being temporarily restricted, for this also concerns the ultimate failure of crucial supply chains. If coal-fired power plants cannot get supplies of coal because of chaos in the transport sector, there could be a destructive ripple effect throughout society, causing breakdown. With a breakdown in sewage systems, diseases would spread. The crippling of the financial system will make it difficult to re-establish social order, and there could be a downward spiral into chaos, what can be called "the great spiral down." This is what may be experienced to a degree with the 2020 pandemic, not so much from the death rate and severity of the disease, as with the measures of social wind-down and distancing needed to control the disease, if these measures go on for months, or much longer.

First, is the personal aspect, as millions of people across the world face unemployment, and hunger, as food banks supplying emergency food, fail to cope. As Michael Snyder of the Economic Collapse blog puts it:

> What are hungry Americans going to do when the food banks don't have any more food for them? Over the past couple of weeks, we have witnessed the largest spike in unemployment in all of US history. Since most of those workers did not have any sort of a cushion to fall back on, a lot of them have been forced to seek out emergency assistance for themselves and their families almost immediately. Of course, our national network of food banks was not built to handle this sort of scenario, and as you will see below, many of them are already starting to run out of food. But if things are this bad at the very beginning of this new economic downturn, what are things going to look like a few months from now? It is imperative for people to understand that we are now in uncharted territory. At this point, even the head of the IMF is warning that this new economic crisis will be "way worse" than the last recession […] The […] pandemic has created an economic crisis "like no other" – one that is "way worse" than the 2008 global financial crisis, the International Monetary Fund's top official said Friday. "Never in the history of the IMF have we witnessed the world economy come to a standstill," Kristalina Georgieva, managing director of the IMF, said at a news conference. And, of course, we already see economic numbers in the United States that absolutely blow away anything that we witnessed back in 2008 and 2009. I don't know that any of us ever anticipated seeing a single week when 6.6. million Americans [now 26.4 million and rising] would file new claims for unemployment benefits.[37]

Add to this that almost 60 percent of American workers will not be able to meet basic financial needs with a one month or less quarantine, according to a survey from the Society for Human Research Management.[38] The survey was conducted before Congress passed a $2 trillion stimulus package. Even so, this is a large band-aid short-term "solution," since at present about one in four small US businesses have shut down temporarily, and in a survey, 43 percent of small businesses said that they would be forced to close down permanently if the normal business could not resume soon, with 11 percent only one month from permanently going out of business.[39]

The macroeconomic effects of the current pandemic are nothing short of deadly, and already the IMF has said that the present economic situation, which has brought the world economy to a grinding halt, is worse than the 2008 global financial crisis. If the shutdown continues, a Great Depression 2.0 scenario will arise.[40] Some commentators see that the situation is already potentially worse than the Great Depression 1.0: "As stay-at-home orders to battle the [...] are effective in most states, the virus-related restrictions have already shed 29 percent of US daily output," Moody's Analytics warns as cited by the *Wall Street Journal*.

The full scale of economic disaster stemming from almost countrywide closures of businesses in various industries—from entertainment to retail—will not be seen for years. However, the first estimates have already started to emerge, and the picture is quite gloomy. According to Moody's study, which was carried when 41 states shut down non-essential businesses, California alone lost $2.8 billion a day, the equivalent of more than 31.5 percent of the state's daily gross domestic product (GDP). The drop of output in 15 other states, responsible for almost 70 percent of all the US daily GDP, is $12.5 billion, while 30 other states, together with Washington DC, are losing a total of $4.9 billion of GDP per day. The economic fallout (in terms of output drop) of the pandemic crisis has already turned worse that the consequences of the 9/11 terrorist attacks, according to the agency's data. As a result of three weeks of government-imposed closures, US output tumbled by around $350 billion, while the attacks had cut it by an estimated $111 billion in current dollars. "It's like if Indiana disappeared for an entire year," the chief economist of Moody's Analytics, Mark Zandi, told the WSJ. "This is a natural disaster. There's nothing in the Great Depression that is analogous to what we're experiencing now."[41]

Depending upon how long the shutdowns continued, the economic damage could be immense, if not leading to economic crashes of some economies, as some hypothesize.[42] The French Ministry of Foreign Affairs diplomatic note, obtained by the Agence Ecofin news agency, stated that some African states health systems would be "saturated automatically" and crash. The death of elderly African leaders could lead to further instabilities.[43] South American countries such as Ecuador, are well on the road to this hell.[44]

The end game of the this crisis is likely to be widespread social disruption, if not chaos, if not social collapse, depending upon what happens next. The opinion of Professor Ali Nouri, President of the Federation of American Scientists, is that the public will not be going back to normal life until a vaccine for is available, which may take up to a year (although Israeli scientists have said, possibly months).[45] A second rebound wave of the virus,[46] a wave of re-infections,[47] or a new even more potent mutated version (if it spreads readily through merely breathing[48]), or even a new pandemic altogether, would bring the world to its knees. The disease could also become a seasonal illness, if not controlled now, according to Dr. Anthony Fauci, Director of the National Institute of Allergy and Infectious Diseases.[49] That optimistically assumes that a vaccine will actually work, and there is no guarantee of that since failures regularly occur with various flu vaccines.[50] Already, Trump has activated one million military reservists, not necessarily for war with China, yet, or to fight a *Red Dawn*-style invasion, but most likely to keep civilian populations under control.[51] Possible scenarios could involve local law enforcement officers falling victims to death's embrace, leading to a "the cats are away, the rats will play," situation.[52] Food riots and looting are fears of the Italian authorities.[53]

J. D Tuccille at Reason.com puts the case for why social unrest is likely:

Could the stalled economy we've inflicted on ourselves in our frantic efforts to battle the [...] pandemic lead to civil disorder? History suggests that's a real danger.

Around the world, high unemployment and stagnant economic activity tend to lead to social unrest, including demonstrations, strikes, and other forms of potentially violent disruptions. That's a huge concern as forecasters expect the US unemployment rate in the months to come to surpass that seen during the depths of the Great Depression.

"We're putting this initial number at 30 percent; that's a 30 percent unemployment rate" in the second quarter of this year as a result of the planned economic shutdowns, Federal Reserve Bank of St. Louis President James Bullard told Bloomberg News on March 22. Gross Domestic Product, he adds, is expected to drop by 50 percent.

Unlike most bouts of economic malaise, this is a self-inflicted wound meant to counter a serious public health crisis. But, whatever the reasons, it means businesses shuttered and people without jobs and incomes. That's risky.

"Results from the empirical analysis indicate that economic growth and the unemployment rate are the two most important determinants of social unrest," notes the International Labour Organisation (ILO), a United Nations agency that maintains a Social Unrest Index in an attempt to predict civil disorder based, in part, on economic trends. For example, a one standard deviation increase in unemployment raises social unrest by 0.39 standard deviations, while a one standard deviation increase in GDP growth reduces social unrest by 0.19 standard deviations.

Why would economic shutdowns lead to social unrest? Because, contrary to the airy dismissals of some members of the political class and many ivory-tower types, commerce isn't a grubby embarrassment to be tolerated and avoided—it's the life's blood of a society. Jobs and businesses keep people alive. They represent the activities that meet demand for food, clothing, shelter—and that develop and distribute the medicine and medical supplies we need to battle [...].[54]

Another take on this impending social breakdown is given by Daisy Luther, who notes that US police in a number of jurisdictions are already limiting in-person police responses to crime, to limit contact, for a wide range of offenses, including assaults, unless the suspect is present, or someone requires medical attention. The end result of this trend will be police not turning up for work at all but staying home to protect their families. Add to this, numbers of criminals that state authorities are, or intend to release from jail. Those seeking prison release include mobsters, gang bangers, killers, rapists, and other fine outstanding citizens,[55] all supported by politically correct lobby groups.[56] Already, during this present lockdown, burglaries and thefts in many major US cities are up 75 percent.[57] Daisy Luther explains:

> Expect as the rules and enforcement efforts become more stringent for people to balk. As the money being dished out by the government dwindles to a trickle and as promises made by the government get broken, people will become more and more desperate. Imagine. Your ability to make a living was suddenly taken away through no fault of your own. You're all but under house arrest. Your government is threatening you with fines, incarceration, and even possible violence. Your family is hungry, and you have nothing to feed them. What would you do in that situation? There's virtually no way this continues without violence ensuing, either out of rebellion or hunger or possibly both. Fewer and fewer police officers are available to respond as more of them get diagnosed […]. In New York City, nearly ten thousand first responders are ill. When you put all this together, it's a recipe for violent crime. […] We're already watching our economy get destroyed right in front of our eyes. Never in history—including the Great Depression—have so many Americans been unemployed. And the fact that they all became unemployed at once is even worse. By the end of March, 7.1 million people had filed for unemployment […] We're just at the beginning of this bumpy ride, and there's really no place that it leads except to an economic depression even worse than the one that took place in the 1920s.[58]

The idea that the coming era of economic hardship, if not collapse, will lead to a dangerous world where ordinary people will face those who will want what they have stored, or otherwise have, is a common theme in numerous YouTube videos by preppers and survivalists, including in my opinion two of the most articulate: Canadian Prepper[59] (with recent titles such as: "When Food Runs Out," "Warning: the Bad News Hasn't Even Started," "Warning: Looting,

Protests, Riots, Hard Times are Coming," "Home Security During Lockdown: Prepare for the Purge," "Governments and Police are Terrified," "Empty Shelves, Panic, Hoarding") and Fernando "Ferfal" Aguirre.[60] Websites to examine daily, include Natural News.com,[61] Daisy Luther's The Organic Prepper,[62] and those with something of a survivalist flavor, mixed with sober economics, such as Peak Prosperity.com[63] and Zerohedge.com,[64] the latter with its own version of John Maynard Keynes's maxim: "In the long run we are all dead."[65] "On a long enough timeline the survival rate for everyone drops to zero." This could well be an apt phrase to characterize the new dawn of hyper-violence, rapidly approaching.

However, even mainstream sources are no longer regarding preppers as lunatics who think that some disaster may happen and prepare to survive it by accumulating things and skills because one such disaster is, in fact, now unfolding, obviously enough.[66] In fact, the ordinary people who began first buying hand sanitizer, then toilet paper, and as the epidemic became a pandemic, foodstuffs, leading to supermarket shelves emptying, were acting on natural survival instincts. Naturally, the true blood prepper community has prepared for the Event for years, if not decades. Even in the last few years, the super-capitalists had become preppers, securing bug-out locations in more remote places like New Zealand, having apocalypse on their mind, feeling that the modern world could collapse.[67] Thus, both camps, politically and culturally so different, were ready for the excrement hitting the fan, or is it now a giant industrial blower?[68] Both camps believed that society was fragile and always sitting, but nine or so lost meals away from a Hobbesian state of nature, of all against all.[69]

The aim of this book is to offer a general guide to prepping—or as I prefer, survivalism, survivalism being more hardcore, concerned with all that preppers concerned with, but with guns and other weapons—for what comes after the pandemic. This is thus a "Beyond the Plague" book. The primary orientation of this book is for people who are scared or terrified, but in an intelligent way, who can benefit from a sober academic discussion of issues and sources, dealing with the civilization-destroying threats to come. The discussion from this point thus goes beyond the present pandemic, as this is only one of many existential threats facing humanity in the 21st century. Not only are there likely to be other pandemics, some perhaps much more severe, but there are impending, converging and compounding catastrophes that will destroy techno-industrial civilization and produce a New Dark Age, one much darker than what Europe experienced after the fall of the Roman Empire, and almost certainly, our civilization will become rubble and dust like all others have before us.[70] The reason for this is that in our globalized monoculture, there is no longer any space for alternative civilizations to arise and replace the fallen, for China and East Asian are still part of the modern global market system, operating on the same, unsustainable principles as the West. And, as we will see with the economic fallout from the pandemic, the crash of the West, will also pull down an external market-driven economy like China's.

By way of summary, here is what will be discussed in the rest of this book, if we grant that from this point on, we face the serious threat of epic social breakdown, not only from the after-shocks of the pandemic, but other pandemics to come, and a mass of converging and compounding ecological and socio-political crises, each one of which is severe enough to pound modern techno-industrial society into the dust of history.

Chapter 2 will give a theoretical outline of the meaning of collapse, and what a new Dark Age would look like. Such a world will indeed be much like that depicted in fiction; only it will be non-fiction, real, painful, terrifying, and much more brutal. The reason why this is expected, rather than people bonding together in ecologically sustainable love-ins, as many Greens hope, is outlined in chapter 3, discussing the coming barbarism, and in fact, it will be shown that this savagery is already to be seen in the West, especially in the culture of mass rape, which resembles a war zone, and butchery by knives, seen in places like London, with its explosion of knife crime. The contemporary and historical evidence indicates that humans are extremely brutal, as part of our animal past. While

Steven Pinker is right to see a decline of personal and institutional violence in the modern era, because of the dampening factors of modern techno-industrial civilization, consumerism, and liberal values, the backside of this is that once these dam walls are broken, human viciousness, produced by resource deprivation, will create an utterly destructive flash flood. Think of your children starving and then think of what you might do, reasonably enough from a purely utilitarian perspective. Then imagine what those who commit brutal crimes now, and get away with them, often with the state turning a blind eye, will do.

Chapter 4 gives a technical discussion of the sorts of existential threats that comprise the said converging and compounding catastrophes. The world faces geophysical threats from the Earth below (super-volcanoes), the skies above, from small asteroids, that impact more than previously thought, and more seriously from the cosmos, by severe space weather events, such as EMP events, that if at the level of a new Carrington Event, could grind techno-industrial civilization into the dust. However, the immediate cancer-like threats come from the unsustainable use of resources, with impending resource shortages, even of oil, regardless of the present political adventures artificially lowering world oil prices.[71] Climate change is also shown to be another threat, something that conservatives are loath to consider given the way others have dominated the debate. But, that should not interfere with the cold logic of rational assessment, since the power elites would use global cooling to suit their ends, if that was what was occurring, just as they now twist and turn the pandemic to try and save their cosmopolitan world view from crashing and burning.

Chapter 5 argues that unless one prefers suicide, surely the coward's way out, and less dramatic and interesting than slugging it out to the bitter end, one needs to embrace the philosophy of survivalism, not merely prepping. This, it is shown, is a total philosophy of self-reliance and strength, that may begin with the storage of food and resources, even guns, ammunition, and other weapons, but ultimately involves developing inner strength,

23

toughness, and resilience, the will to survive, to struggle on perhaps in pain against the odds, and even if one perishes. The chapter covers the most important nuts and bolts aspects of survivalism, bugging out, bugging in, essential survival items, wilderness survival, medical and health issues, food storage, self-reliance, and homesteading, tools, and most important of all regaining manhood, raising testosterone levels for men, and attaining strength.

This leads naturally to issues of physical training, addressed in Chapter 6, including the principles of strength training, training without a gym, as we are experiencing now with gym closures across the West. Unarmed combat is integrated into physical training, and rather than recommend devoting valuable time to some martial system, which will be difficult to do with the schools now closed, and likely to be closed in the future, basics, such as fundamental strikes, and dealing with realistic unarmed self-defense situations, in the spirit of military kill of be killed systems like that of World War II unarmed combat instructors, William Fairbairn and Rex Applegate, should be adopted.

However, in the collapse situation of WROL, weapons are going to the primary equalizers, beginning with firearms, and this book has the standard survival firearm material in chapter 7. But unlike most other books, the focus is upon jurisdictions with severe gun controls, even now crossbow and archery control, so the focus needs to be upon melee weapons for people facing the scourge of gun control. Blades, knives, swords, and machetes will be of central concern, and it would be well for would-be survivors to acquire these weapons and begin training, with safety always in mind. Thus, the beginners should start with wooden weapons and train until one can safely use steel, and even then, it is best to train with dull blades, as accidents can happen, but should not; re-read the disclaimer to this book, if necessary. And, once guns and bows have been banned, those who never rest will start on swords, and in the Australian state of Victoria, swords and many other martial art weapons are severely restricted. At the end of the world, some people will be left with only chunks of wood to defend themselves, and I address that too. You will need the right chunk of wood, and know how to use it also if we are reduced to the Stone Age.

Thus, the present book is a beyond "the Plague" book, because there are coming threats that will dwarf what we are seeing now, and will come shortly. Hence, there is no need to repeat excellent work done on pandemic survival, such as Joseph Alton and Amy Alton, *Alton's Pandemic Preparedness Guide: Dealing with Emerging and Current Viral Threats* (2020),[72] and Cat Ellis' *Survival Manual: How to Prepare for Pandemics and Quarantines* (2020),[73] as there is little more to add. But, thinking beyond the health aspects is a task which now needs to be undertaken, and this book aims to make a small contribution to that labor.

2. THE COMING COLLAPSE

Nature is a vast field of carnage. Between living creatures conflict takes place every second, every minute, without truth and without respite. It takes place first between separate individuals, then between collective organisms, tribe against tribe, state against state, nationality against nationality. No cessation is possible.

- J. Novicow (1886)[74]

...and the life of man, solitary, poor, nasty, brutish, and short.

-Thomas Hobbes (1588-1679)[75]

It has been argued by those who have examined the evidence of the array of converging and compounding catastrophes,[76] that due to the interplay of a multitude of interacting and compounding factors and forces—such as natural human aggressiveness and violence; the lack of survival adaptability of modern humanity to life without advanced technology and infrastructure (which has made people into domestic human battery hens) and the immense destructive impact of the contemporary world upon ecological services and resources—that there will be no soft landing or green, tree-hugging transition to "sustainability." Instead, there will be a "rapid descent" into a Dark Age of barbarism and savagery. Civilization—represented by life in concentrated nucleated settlements, cities—is a product of the abundance of resources, especially energy resources, and an impending collision with the mountain of ecological scarcity will lead to civilization's destruction.[77] Civilization involves "political consolidation, economic specialization, social stratification, some sort of monumental architecture, and a flowering of artistic and intellectual endeavor."[78] Logically, a collapse of civilization involves a breakdown of these factors, and a Dark Age.[79]

A Dark Age, as Widdowson defines it, is a "time without government, without trade, and without any sense of community. It is a time of everyone for himself or herself. During the Dark Age, mere survival is the only concern. No one has the leisure for a higher activity, including keeping records. That is why a Dark Age is dark. Its principal feature is that we know little of what took place in it. The collapse that precipitates the Dark Age is abrupt and unexpected."[80] Shorter and sweeter (depending on your point of view) is James Ballou's definition in his *Long-Term Survival in the Coming Dark Age*, of a period of time "marked by frequent warfare and a virtual disappearance of urban life," as civilization, involving organized political power, the rule of law and some form of sociocultural and economic structure and organization, collapses.[81] Thus, it will be *Mad Max/Road Warrior*, sans the hot cars (fuel depletion), sans the leather-clad homoeroticism, and after a time, no ammunition. Moreover, given *Fury Road* (2015), it will also be sans feminism. The vision depicted in the movie and book *The Road* (2009),[82] with some qualifications, is essentially correct.

The collapse of civilization needs to be distinguished from the extinction of the human species itself from existential threats such as comet strikes, black hole collisions, runaway high energy experiments, or even if the human race has a use-by-date because of a species-genetic biological clock.[83] The human race seems to have survived a climate-change-induced drought that almost extinguished our species 70,000 years ago, reducing human numbers to as little as 2,000, but here we are, for the time being.[84] Civilization, though, is not as resilient and inevitably crashes.

The thesis of collapse is widely accepted by environmentalists, but most see a silver lining to a very dark cloud. Thus, W. H. Kötke in *The Final Empire: The Collapse of Civilization and the Seed of the Future*,[85] believes that the collapse of civilization is inevitable because economic growth has reached ecological limits and there are no more frontiers on Earth. Thus, our generation "is on the verge of the most profound catastrophe the human species has ever faced." Our present world is a "culture of suicide," and the only hope for humanity is "to regain balance with the earth" by creating "a utopian paradise, a new Garden of Eden." Dream on; based on the initial assumptions, we are doomed, doomed, doomed, and maybe doomed a wee bit more.[86]

Carolyn Baker, in *Sacred Demise: Walking the Spiritual Path of Industrial Civilization's Collapse* (2009),[87] expresses collapse optimism, a "sacred demise." For Baker, collapse is "more stable" than a "zombie apocalypse" and involves "subtle patterns of abandonment and decay that unfold over long periods of time."[88] Even so, the breakdown of techno-industrial civilization "is likely to be the most devastating holocaust in the recorded history, and will be the end of the world as any of us has known it." There will be "unprecedented escalations of violence."[89] The claims appear to be self-refuting.

Not as sweet, the "Health Ranger" Mike Adams sees the collapse of techno-industrial society occurring relatively soon.[90] There will be "untold human suffering and death," but a rebirth of human civilization will occur along with "human spiritual awakening." He says, "[i]t is my belief that the majority of today's living population will not survive the inevitable sequence." Nevertheless, after about a century, a rebirth will occur. That is nonsense, in my opinion, for once the great spiral down has happened, it will be virtually impossible for humanity to rise out of the primeval mud. However, Adams wisely recommends that people strive to achieve physical, mental, and spiritual toughness and the cultivation of all-round survival skills.

Clive Hamilton in *Requiem for a Species*,[91] focusing on climate change and humanity's inability to deal with the climate crisis, sees the end of modern civilization, if not the human species: "[t]he prospect of runaway climate change challenges our technological hubris, our Enlightenment faith in reason and the whole modernist project."[92] The evidence of global climate change shows that "the world is now on a path to a very unpleasant future, and it is too late to stop it."[93]

More controversially, Guy R. McPherson in *Going Dark*[94] argues that the Earth may no longer be a habitat for humans beyond the 2030s and that near-term human extinction will occur because of self-reinforcing feedback loops in the global climate system. The collapse will include the catastrophic meltdown of around 440 nuclear power plants destroying most organisms, as shutting down nuclear power plants requires 1-2 decades of "careful planning."

McPherson is an "extreme" example of an eco-collapse theorist, but he has made a plausible cause for human extinction, as I argue below. However, many other scientists and theorists have expressed alarm that the "compounding crises,"[95] "shock of history,"[96] and "converging catastrophes"[97] including the climate change crisis, energy scarcity, food and water insecurity, biodiversity destruction, economic insecurity, international terrorism, and militarization, threaten us with civilization collapse if present trends continue.

3. THE COMING BARBARISM

Civilization is a thin varnish, built up painfully over centuries; when it is removed, you discover egotistical, violent, and cruel human beings. Take a normal person and put him out in the cold, the rain, amid hunger and thirst, take away his comfort and habits, his television, beer, booze, cigarettes, and other drugs, and you will soon see the savage within. First, he will show irritation, then (very quickly) violence or a degree of degradation unthinkable a few days before. And if you think fraternity and social bond are still there after decades of consumerist, hedonist, narcissist, egocentric culture, you are in for a big surprise. A society that encourages immediate satisfaction of our basest desires and whims can only, in a crisis situation, transform itself into a horde of violent psychopaths.

-Piero San Giorgio[98]

We have already seen examples of some of the violent behavior people have exhibited in the earlier stages of the pandemic, but the worst will be yet to come. The savagery that has already been in Western societies from jihad attacks, such as knife attacks in London, and other places in Europe, as well as the rape culture, especially the rapes of up to one million British children by the grooming gangs, illustrates the level of sheer barbarism already existing in Western societies.[99] We need to ask what happens when social breakdown and decay worsens.

If people can act like that in the "springtime," the relatively good times, then how do they fare during times of disaster? Sociologists generally dispute that widespread looting and violence occur after *natural* disasters, seeing, in general, that people band together to help each other.[100] For example, in the case of Hurricane Katrina, the media came to retract earlier-made reports about widespread

31

violence, looting, and raping, such as claims that babies were raped. Sociologists claim that during natural disasters people exhibit prosocial helping behaviors. Looting is said to be common in civil disturbances, but rare in the aftermath of natural disasters. Thus, earlier media reports, such as that a seven-year-old child in the Superdome had her throat cut, of 30-40 bodies being stored in a freezer in the Superdome and of 300 bodies piled high at Marion Abramson High School in Eastern New Orleans, were *false*. The claims were soon retracted by the media, to be replaced by the other extreme, that there was not one official report of rape or sexual assault, and that likewise, looting was minimal.

Against this, there are many sources, while accepting that the savage, zombie-like murders and rampaging did not occur, do affirm from personal observations and reliable witnesses and photographs, that widespread violence, looting, and raping did occur. Brian Thevenot says that widespread looting was "definitely not a myth, I can confirm as an eyewitness."[101] Photographs of looters stealing not just food and essential items, but expensive electronic goods, can be viewed at various websites.[102] In fact, after Hurricane Katrina hit, the police arrested so many people for robbery that the New Orleans jails were soon full and temporary jails were set up. In early September 2005, 8,000 prisoners were moved out of New Orleans jails and transported to state prisons.[103]

Rape is an under-reported crime; the US Department of Justice estimates that in the US, over 300,000 women are raped every year, but less than one in three women report the rape to the police.[104] A number of sources have claimed that the incidence of rape was greater in the aftermath of Hurricane Katrina than the "normal" incidence of rape and that most rape victims did not report it.[105]

A study of Hurricane Katrina crimes, as a Master of Public Administration thesis by Kevin Bailey,[106] concluded that some types of crime increased after the disaster, but others decreased. In New Orleans, *most* crime rates increased significantly in January 2006 but returned to pre-Hurricane Katrina levels by December 2007. The annual murder rate increased in the years 2006 and 2007.

It has been claimed that there was no crime wave among Hurricane Katrina evacuees.[107] Others dispute this; one report states: "[w]hen New Orleans residents streamed into Houston six months ago to escape the floodwaters caused by Hurricane Katrina, they brought in gangs and the violence that goes with them. The city had 170 homicides from September through February 22, 28 percent more than in the same period a year earlier, according to the Police Department. In 29 cases, displaced Louisianans were the victims, the suspects, or both."[108] At the time, police said that once gangs had moved in and drug and prostitution rings were re-established, old scores were settled. To combat this, the police formed the Gang Murder Squad to help prevent a further increase in the murder rate.

L.G. Sun has said that prior research on looting in disaster situations may be skewed, being based on "small western populations experiencing more limited disasters in scale and scope."[109] Most research on the alleged absence of looting after disasters has been in developed countries, and in fact, "studies have occasionally observed large-scale looting after natural disasters in the developing world." For example, in the wake of Super Typhoon Haiyan in November 2013 in the Philippines, soldiers and police were deployed to halt large-scale looting; even a Red Cross convoy was attacked. Survivors were suffering from a lack of food, water, and shelter in a landscape littered with rotting corpses. However, the prevalence of *illegal* guns carried by insurgents and criminal gangs challenged security.

One alleged counter-example to this claim of increased crime in the wake of disasters is Superstorm Sandy during October/November 2012 in the US. Crime dropped by a third during the storm – e.g., murder dropped by 86 percent, rape by 44 percent, assault by 31 percent, but burglaries rose by 3 percent. Although this seems to support, *prima facie*, the position of Rebecca Solnit in *A Paradise Built in Hell*,[110] that people tend to work together in disasters, there is contrary evidence. First, crime was down because the goblins and ghouls were off the street; they did not want to be injured. Second, there were some nasty, collapse-style forms of looting, such as people pretending to be Con Ed workers, holding people up, and looting.

There were also tweets from Twitter accounts by twits intending to loot when the storm hit, mainly to secure electronic goods. This is hardly an example of the milk of human kindness. Reflecting on the issue of violence and disaster, environmentalist/peak oil theorist Richard Heinberg has concluded that for "every heart-warming anecdote about the convergence of rescuers and caregivers on a disaster site, there is a grim historic tale of resource completion turning normal people into monsters."[111]

So much then for disasters unleashing the "inner monster," what then about your garden vanity social breakdown? Consider flash mob crime involving "polar bear hunting," where people, using social media for organization, converge to a certain spot, destroy private property, riot, commit acts of violence and then disperse – quickly. After the crime wave in Europe, we do not hear much about this, but the activity continues. This may be a hit-and-run *group* crime against a *group* of people of another particular race. It may also involve a *group* or an *individual* targeting another small *group* or *individual*, who are the "polar bears" and knocking them down, i.e., bashing them into unconsciousness or death – hence its name, "the knockout game." The distinguished black scholar Thomas Sowell sees this as "early skirmishes in a race war."[112]

Fernando "Ferfal" Aguirre, a collapse-survivalist, believes that life after economic collapse will be much the same as it is now – but worse. That is, it will not be a zombie apocalypse.[113] Aguirre lived through the economic collapse of Argentina in (1998-2002), and reports on lessons learned from that experience. As we will see below, even though Ferfal rejects the idea that *economic* collapse will lead to a type of world like *The Walking Dead*, the world of *economic* collapse, even with a limited and dysfunctional government, will be a violent and dangerous place, as he has detailed in his excellent videos, and his most recent book, *Street Survival Skills*.[114]

Likewise, Dmitry Orlov, author of *The Five Stages of Collapse*,[115] who lived through the collapse of the Soviet Union (USSR), predicts the coming crash of the United States, and ultimately of techno-industrial civilization. This will be through resource shortages, passing through five stages of collapse (financial; commercial/ economic; political; social and cultural), leading to a more primitive Hobbesian existence where life is "nasty, brutish, and short." This is more to my taste.

British philosopher John Gray in *Straw Dogs* observes that even with the present growth of knowledge, "[t]he human animal will remain the same: a highly inventive species that is one of the most predatory and destructive."[116] Harold Bloom, in *The Lucifer Principle* argued that "evil" is a part of nature and moves the human world "to greater heights of organization, intricacy, and power."[117] The explanatory assumption of "inborn evil" makes sense of the blood bath of human history. Bloom's "barbarian principle" is also relevant to this book. Civilized societies ultimately become over-civilized and weak and are overcome by barbarians: the ancient Egyptians conquered by the Hyksos; the Babylonian Empire conquered by the Persians; the Persians conquered by the Greeks, even defeating Emperor Xerxes army of 1,700,000 men (according to Herodotus), with Alexander the Great later conquering the entire Persian empire. Today, they are all but a historical memory, and we of the West will be lucky to be even that.[118]

Supporting empirical material for this pessimistic view of human nature is given by Le Blanc and Register in *Constant Battles*,[119] who show that the idea of the peaceful noble "savage" is a myth and that warfare and violence, primarily for resources, including females, has been present throughout human history and in our evolutionary past. Lawrence Keeley in *War Before Civilization* says that primitive warfare was much deadlier than that conducted between civilized states because of the greater frequency of combat and the more merciless way it was conducted. "Primitive war was very efficient at inflicting damage through the destruction of property, especially the means of production and shelter, and inflicting terror by frequently visiting sudden death and mutilating its victims."[120] Prisoners, for example, were generally not taken, and if not killed on the spot, were stored, to be tortured and/or fattened and eaten.[121] Primitive societies were constantly at war, and if modern societies had the same casualty rate in the 20th century, wars would have yielded two billion deaths. On average, tribal societies lost 0.5 percent per annum of their populations due to war.[122] Sixty-five percent of primitive societies were at war continuously, and 87 percent fought more than one war annually.[123] According to Wade: "Warfare between pre-state societies was incessant, merciless, and conducted with the general purpose, often achieved, of annihilating the opponent. As far as human nature is concerned, people of early societies seem to have been considerably more war-like than people today."[124] That includes the Australian Aborigines: "The Australian Aboriginal tribes seemed to have lived in a state of constant warfare, with defended territories and neutral zones marked for trading. Their tool kit, designed for easy transport over long distances, included weapons like heavy war clubs, a special hooked boomerang, and spear-throwers."[125]

It is a myth to suppose that humans have lived in a harmonious ecological balance with their natural environment; rather, technological limits have limited human destructiveness.[126] Pre-civilization was no peaceful Garden of Eden. The violence of pre-civilization is well illustrated by the discovery of Neolithic mass graves in Europe of 6,000 to 7,000 years old, containing human skeletons and hacked off body parts.[127] One circular pit, uncovered in Bergheim, France, had seven human skeletons as well as an infant skull section laying on the remains of seven human left arms that had been hacked off, probably by axes, perhaps done for war trophies. Other mass graves in Europe have incomplete skeletons, indicating mutilation, and maybe cannibalism and the shinbones of victims are frequently broken, so it is likely torture occurred.[128]

Steven Pinker in his study of human violence, *The Better Angels of our Nature*,[129] concludes that the growth of cities, states, technology, commerce, and cosmopolitan morality and culture—in short, modern civilization—has dulled to a significant degree the edge of the normally sharp sword of human violence. He accepts that humans, like chimpanzees, have a genetic trait for violence (i.e., are hardwired for violence), but modern civilization has constrained violence and kept it on a tight leash. Given the extent of violence in the past, Pinker, I believe, has made a strong case for his thesis. Nevertheless, if this is so, consider the logical consequence of Pinker's position. If modern civilization collapses, then the restraints holding back the pit bull of human aggressiveness and violence will be removed, and Hobbesian humans in a war of all against all (or tribe against tribe) will stalk the earth once more. Given the principle "the bigger they are (or higher they fly), the harder they fall," the collapse could very well lead to levels of violence not yet experienced as "collapse shock" leads to many losing their "heads."[130]

But Won't We Be Able to Rebuild?

Annalee Newitz in *Scatter, Adapt, and Remember*,[131] accepts that humanity is heading towards disaster: "whether the disaster is caused by humans or by nature, it is inevitable."[132] Humanity has experienced population crashes in the past but bounced back over thousands of years. The fundamental survival strategies are to scatter/bug out, adapt to the new environment, and seek to preserve as much accumulated knowledge as possible.

Lewis Dartnell in *The Knowledge: How to Rebuild our World from Scratch*,[133] goes further and shows how, using the basic scientific method—empirical observation, experimentation and testing, instrument construction, and theorization—civilization can allegedly be rebuilt after The Great Collapse.

Dartnell argues that the preservation of the scientific method would enable many basic technologies to be rediscovered if lost from an apocalyptic disaster. The core scientific beliefs include the fundamental ideas of physics and chemistry, such as the atomic hypothesis (i.e., matter is composed of particles such as atoms), and the postulate of methodological materialism (explaining the physical world using physical rather than spiritual entities). On this basis, for example, the germ theory of disease would be preferred over say, the evil spirit theory. Sound principles of public health would be adopted, such as don't empty your bowels within 100 meters of your water source, and cover your poo-poo with dirt to prevent flies spreading your dung around when they feed on it and then land on your ham and cheese sandwich, and so on.

Dartnell also accepts another fundamental assumption of this book: that modern humans are weak, especially those in developed societies. In former times "everyone was a survivalist, with a far more intimate connection to the land and the methods of production," but today people in the developed world "are astoundingly ignorant of even the basics of the production of food, shelter, clothes, medicine, materials or vital substances. Our survival skills have atrophied to the point that much of humanity would be incapable of sustaining itself if the life-support system of modern civilization failed, if food no longer magically appeared on the shop shelves, or clothes on hangers." Core skills need to be relearned if post-apocalyptic survivors are to continue living.

Even a humble pencil, because of the sourcing of raw materials and dispersion of production methods, could not be made from scratch. Dartnell's proposal for rebuilding civilization is based on the proposition that there would be vast quantities of resources left for survivors after certain global disasters, thus giving a safety margin for the reboot of civilization.

Most knowledge, especially on the internet, would be lost, and many textbooks would only be accessible to specialists. Most books contain no relevant practical knowledge at all. Dartnell also accepts another core proposition of this book, that after The Collapse, violence and looting will be a way of life, and even once law-abiding citizens will now do what is necessary to survive. This will require having a gun (or many), as well as gangs/tribes of people uniting into a protective force to protect perimeters.

Darnell's proposal is based on a "sudden and extreme depopulation that leaves the material infrastructure of our technological civilization untouched."[134] The "best" way for the world to end, in this scenario, would be a nuclear holocaust or massive coronal mass ejection. However, Dartnell strangely does not consider the health impacts of ionizing radiation produced from the meltdown of nuclear power plants. He says that if there is a collapse without immediate depopulation: "[t]his wastes the grace period, and society promptly descends into *Mad Max*-style barbarism and subsequent mass depopulation, with little hope of rapidly bouncing back."[135] As Fred Hoyle put it:

> It has been often said that, if human species fails to make a go of it here on Earth, some other species will take over the running. In the sense of developing intelligence this is not correct. We have, or soon will have, exhausted the necessary physical prerequisites so far as this planet is concerned. With coal gone, oil gone, high-grade metallic ore gone, no species, however competent can make the long climb from primitive conditions to high-level technology. This is a one-shot affair. If we fail, this planetary system fails so far as intelligence is concerned. The same will be true of other planetary systems. On each of them there will be one chance, and one chance only.[136]

Apart from this problem, Dartnell says in an internet post that survivors will face a problem of learning practical skills, such as metalwork from guide books, as to obtain such skill takes years of an apprenticeship under a master.[137] There is also the problem of maintaining basic intellectual skills such as reading and mathematical knowledge and passing it on to the next generation. I believe that it should be possible to pass on basic reading and writing skills, even in a small group of survivors. Elementary mathematics—arithmetic, geometry, trigonometry, and basic algebra at a high school level— should also be possible in a survival group having a mathematically educated person. However, there may not be the time and resources to preserve much of higher mathematics (symbolic logic, metamathematics, transfinite set theory, projective and differential geometry, etc.). The joy of solving complex mathematical problems, such as nonlinear partial differential equations—perhaps a higher pleasure than an orgasm —will be sadly lost to humankind. Well, this is the apocalypse, and sacrifices will have to be made.

People may be interested in the remarks by Ashley Barkman, in her paper "Women in a Zombie Apocalypse."[138] She said: "[i]n a zombie apocalypse feminism is pretty much dead in the water" and Barkman rejects the trendy idea that sex and gender are social constructions: "men and women are not just biologically different (male and female), but also spiritually different: differences between masculine and feminine exist at conception." This proposition is known to be true "naturally," as a matter of empirical observation. Men are, in general, naturally stronger and more aggressive than women due to higher testosterone levels, and women of a childbearing age (if fertile) are vulnerable to pregnancy if consuming penis. Here is the kicker: "masculinity has qualities that lend itself to leadership, whereas femininity leads itself to being led." Hence, in a zombie apocalypse, feminism "which argues that gender is a social construct and thus woman should be given the same roles and duties as men is not only unrealistic but also ineffective and inefficient."

The scenario depicted in *Mad Max: Fury Road* (2015), which has a female warrior, Imperator Furiosa (played by Chalize Theron), who can out-shoot and out-fight a hardened warrior like Max, is possible, but improbable. It remains a liberal fantasy, much like *Kill Bill* (volume 1, 2003; volume 2, 2004). The situation is more likely to be as Barkman has depicted. This observation follows from a lifetime of street awareness, being in and witnessing fights, as well as from the theoretical considerations that Barkman references.

Another, more likely scenario for women has been given by Megan Hurwitt, an intelligent, attractive, young lady featured in an episode of season one of *Doomsday Preppers* (2012). When the crash comes she sees people killing each other for food. Moreover, for women who do not prep she said: "you don't want to have to resort to whoring yourself out; that's what a lot of women would face." Tragically, a large number of men are likely to become, as seen in war zones across history, sexual predators, making rape both a sport and political weapon. It is already happening. Hence, the need for women to take self-defense training very seriously.

A contemporary example of this return to savagery is supplied by the capture of Yazidi women by Islamic State fighters beginning in 2014. The Yazidi is, or was, a Kurdish ethno-racial community with significant Nordic genes, many women having blond hair and blue or green eyes. Why mention this in our age where race has been shown to be a social construct? Well, for one thing, as a *Daily Mail* article states, this "socially constructed" fact is of significance to both the persecuted minority and those doing the persecuting: "[t]he minority group is originally Aryan and has retained a fairer complexion, blond hair, and blue eyes by only marrying within the community."[139]

The Islamic State issued a document by its research and fatwa department, which "justified" using the captured woman as *sabaya* (sex slaves) and permitted the raping of pre-pubescent girls who are "fit." According to the October 2014 edition of the Islamic state's digital Magazine *Dabiq*, the revival of slavery is part of their belief that the end of the world was coming.[140] The "rape manual" states that women can also be beaten. Thousands of captured Yazidis women have been sold as sex slaves in slave markets, with blue-and green-eyed young girls bringing "top price." Some Yazidi were dragged into sexual slavery by their hair.[141] Price tags were apparently placed on the women.[142] Teenage girls abducted by Islamic State fighters were sold in slave markets for as little as the price of a packet of cigarettes. Girls that did not convert to Islam were tortured, raped, and murdered. Many raped Yazidi girls committed suicide, and in June 2016, ISIS burnt 19 Yazidi girls to death in iron cages after refusing to have sex with jihadists.[143] In "brothels" run by British female jihadis,[144] women were raped at a rate of up to 30 times in just a few hours; as one headline put it: "I've been raped 30 times, and it's not even lunchtime."[145]

While the rape and genocide of the Yazidis were proceeding, on December 16, 2014, the Al-Qaeda affiliated terrorist group Tekreek-e-Taliban Pakistan, conducted a school slaughter of unmitigated depravity. Seven jihadists, who wore suicide bomb vests, attacked the Army Public School in the Pakistani city of Peshawar ("City of Flowers"). The massacre of 132 teenage children and nine teachers (121 children and three staff were wounded), involved shooting them at point-blank range, throat-slitting, head severing and burning them alive. The jihadists, cornered by Pakistan's Special Service Group, detonated their suicide bomb vests, all seven dying.

In general, these attacks have been seen as a product of Islamic extremism, shaped by their medieval outlook and philosophy. While this is undoubtedly true, these acts of brutality arise from those who have put themselves beyond the pale of civilization and who see the end as nigh. We would expect similar, if not more extreme acts of savagery during the collapse of civilization, and in Post Apocalyptica. So, the phenomenon is not just a product of radical Islam. All of this and more will be coming to your street if you survive and remain in the cities.

So, why then is a collapse of civilization inevitable?

4. EXISTENTIAL THREATS

We are in for a period of sustained chaos whose magnitude we are unable to foresee.

- Dennis Meadows[146]

[T]he coming years will prove increasingly cynical and cruel. People will definitely not slip into oblivion while hugging each other. The final stages in the life of humanity will be marked by the monstrous war of all against all: the amount of suffering will be maximal.

- Pentti Linkola[147]

Collapseology: Is Earth Already Doomed?

Leading British scientist Sir Martin Rees, in his book *Our Final Century?* (2003)States that "humanity is more at risk than at any earlier phase in its history," and he believes that "the odds are no better than fifty-fifty that our present civilization on Earth will survive to the end of the present century." There is a considerable amount of literature which indicates that Rees is too optimistic in his Bayesian probability (personal probability estimate) and that the probability of the destruction of modern civilization, if not the human species and perhaps life on Earth itself, is greater than fifty-fifty.[148] The late Stephen Hawking (1942-2018), a physicist, believed that the fate of humans on Earth is sealed already by the socio-political and environmental problems which we face and that the probability of survival will be increased by abandoning Earth and seeking other planets and space colonies.[149]

Brad Werner, in his paper "Is Earth Fucked?" (his actual title), delivered to the American Geophysical Union in 2012, used a numerical computer model of human-environment interactions, and concluded: "the dynamics of the global coupled human-environmental system within the dominant culture precludes management for stable, sustainable pathways and promotes instability."

Along similar lines, Motesharrei (et al.) used a mathematical model (Human and Nature Dynamic Model, (HANDY), based on predator-prey models, to model the human population as a "predator" and nature as "prey."[150] With economic stratification, collapse "within decades" was difficult to avoid because the elites/the rich consume resources until collapse occurred. Similar conclusions have been reached by a limits to growth study by Graham Turner, who concludes from a survey of the scientific literature on resource depletion that on a business as usual scenario the world is already on the cusp of collapse with the first stage of collapse already beginning, and with death rates rising from 2020 onwards.[151]

What is "collapse"? Jared Diamond has defined collapse as "a local drastic decrease in human population numbers and/or in political, economic, or social complexity."[152] Butzer and Endfield give a "broader, integrative" definition of "social collapse" as representing a "transformation at a large social or spatial scale, with long-term impact on combinations of independent variables: (i) environmental change and resilience; (ii) demography or settlement; (iii) socio-economic patterns; (iv) political or social structures; and (v) ideology or cultural memory."[153] Collapse really is the end of the world as we know it. However, we won't "feel fine," contrary to the band R.E.M.[154]

Media commentators and journalists ridicule those who propose that there are ecological limits to economic growth and that the world may be rapidly approaching such limits with respect to environmental sustainability[155] from water,[156] soil,[157] food resources,[158] and other variables such as biodiversity[159] and human population growth. In June 2019, the UN Population Division had a further revision of its demographic statistics: UN Department of Economic and Social Affairs, *2019 Revision of World Population Prospects.* The populations of some African countries were thought to be certain to at least more than double, with Africa's population of an estimated 1.3 billion in 2020, exploding to 4.3 billion in 2100.[160] With the replacement of jobs by AI throughout the West, expect the forthcoming billions of migrants to the West to be rocket scientists, paying for boomer pensions.[161]

However, Anglia Ruskin University's Global Sustainability Institute, using computer modeling, predicted a collapse of society on a business-as-usual scenario.[162] A catastrophic collapse of the global food supply would occur due to human population expansion and ecological destruction. Commenters on this study took comfort that its predictions were based on "things" continuing as they are, but they chirped, people will change their behavior. It is argued in this book that they will not, and people will consume more, not less, and economic globalization will accelerate resource depletion, producing increasing environmental degradation and catastrophic shifts in the planet's ecosystems.[163]

Further, Lloyd's Emerging Risk Report, *Food System Shock* (2015), points out that global agricultural production needs to more than double by 2050 to meet food demands by expanding populations and rising affluence, but this makes food systems vulnerable to food shocks such as water stress, climate change, globalization, and political instability. Climate change and related impacts could lead, they say, to wide-spread economic chaos, food riots, civil unrest, and terrorist-style attacks.[164]

Intellectuals from the optimist camp also attack the very idea of such pessimism, which calls into question the fundamental basis of our present techno-industrial society: there are no limits to growth, technology and economics will ultimately solve all problems and humans are "special," not just another vicious animal species. Thus, French philosopher Pascal Bruckner sees the Western world as flirting with the trendy idea of apocalyptic angst, which is chic and "cool" for the chattering class.[165] According to Bruckner, non-European people "are likely to receive our professionals of environmental faith with polite indifference. Billions of people look at economic growth, with all the pollution that accompanies it, to improve their condition. Who are we to refuse it to them?" According to other intellectuals, the West would not, in the future, be able to stop the Asian dragons, even if it wished to, for societies such as China, are set to eclipse the declining West and consume like there is no tomorrow – because there will not be.

Environmental angst may well be a potent symbol of the alleged decline, decay, and fall of the West – or a reflection of the decadence and "treason" of Western intellectuals and universities, not naming anyone in particular. However, such angst, whatever its social cause, does not merely by its alleged existence demonstrate that there is no rational, scientific basis for believing that modern techno-industrial civilization is immune to collapse. Indeed, pursuing this idea to its logical conclusion, we should conclude that the cultural decadence of the West thesis presents a piece of evidence for the collapse thesis explored in this book. I explain further.

Mark Steyn in *American Alone* (2006)[166] said that "much of what we loosely call the Western world will not survive the twenty-first century and much of it will effectively disappear within our lifetimes, including many if not most European countries." America stands alone to preserve civilization (and neo-liberal capitalism, of course), and if America fails, then "much of the map is reprimitivized" and a New "Dark Age" will occur. But, in Steyn's later book, *After America: Get Ready for Armageddon*,[167] he is pessimistic about America's future, seeing America as facing the same fate as Europe unless a radical 11th-hour movement away from Big Government and the oppressive ideologies of centralist control occur. This form of cultural pessimism arises essentially from seeing neo-liberal market forces being frustrated by centralist control, and the pessimism about civilizational collapse is contingent on that assumption. As ecological limits are approached, financial collapse becomes likely without cheap fossil fuels to maintain the system. Rising energy costs and availability ultimately leads to financial collapse. Tim Morgan, in a Tullett Prebon Strategy Insights publication, sees the coming economic crisis as due to a "perfect storm" of economic mismanagement, resource depletion, and rising costs.[168] Thus, matters are much worse than even in Mark Steyn's worst neoliberal nightmare.

Apart from economic liberty considerations, Steyn's pessimism about Europe's survival is based on the development of Samuel Huntington's "clash of civilizations" thesis,[169] which sees fundamental incompatibilities and tensions between Western liberalism and Islamic fundamentalism. Steyn and others[170] predict a transformation of Europe due to massive Islamic immigration (e.g., Germany's 2015-2019, Syrian refugee intake), high Islamic migrant birth rates, and Europeans having below replacement level fertility rates.

As mentioned previously here, but it is important enough to state again, the grooming rapes of British children in Rotherham, right through the UK and Northern Europe, the sexual assaults, rapes, and bashings (*taharrush gamea* and *taharrush el-ginsy*: collective harassment and sexual assault) on New Year's Eve at Cologne, Hamburg, Stuttgart, Dusseldorf, Frankfurt, Bielefeld, Vienna, Salzburg, and also in Sweden and Finland, and many other assaults, rapes, murders, and tortures, are an indication of how well society is performing. Some see this as a "colonization of Europe," if not the end, or collapse of Europe, by demographic swamping.[171]

Along similar cultural conservative lines are the works of Lee Harris,[172] Patrick J Buchanan,[173] John Derbyshire,[174] Thomas W. Chittum,[175] and Morris Berman.[176] The critique of most of these writers would be rejected by many, who see a world of love, joy, and streams of chocolate, where these conservative critics see decay, disintegration, despair, and raging rivers of blood. But, the critique of Morris Berman is not as easily dismissed. Berman sees a Dark Age, a time of cultural and moral decay, "cultural disintegration," and "spiritual death" occurring. He believes that collapse is inevitable, being built into "the process of civilization itself."

Collapse is especially evident in America, Berman argues, because of: (1) accelerating social and economic inequality; (2)

declining marginal returns with respect to the investment of effort in organized solutions to socioeconomic problems; (3) declining levels of literacy and general intellectual awareness in the population and (4) spiritual death, i.e., the dumbing down of culture. Thus, in America the top one percent of the nation owns more than the bottom 90 percent; 11 percent of young adults cannot locate the United States on a world map; 45 percent of the US population believe that space aliens visited the Earth[177]; 69 percent of under 30 years olds do not know basic facts of US history such as America declaring its independence in 1776 and almost 30 percent of the US population believes that the sun revolves around the Earth or is unsure of which revolves around which.

Berman's specific critique of the United States is that the "American dream" is based on a hustling paradigm that is not about working hard and playing fair so that one can have a better lifestyle than one's parents in a wholesome community, but rather about hustling, cheating, swindling, conning and manipulating the system. One aims to get more than one's fair slice of the "pie" and to hell with ethics, compassion, and the community. Self-interest and greed have replaced the idea of the common good because there is little "common" now which is good. Consequently, Berman sees America as doomed because the social capital necessary to sustain society has been eroded. By implication, other nations, including much of the West, based upon the same values of economic selfishness and crude utilitarianism, also face implosion or rot and decay.

Journalist Robert D. Kaplan in his "coming anarchy" thesis, gave a perhaps bleaker vision of humanity's future.[178] Here the interplay of environmental disintegration and social unrest could lead to a breakdown of societies as has occurred in West Africa in failed states such as Somalia. The United States may not survive the 21st century in its present form Kaplan says, perhaps alluding to demographical changes caused by present mass migration to America, which is leading to Europeans ceasing to be a majority in the country, perhaps earlier than 2040.[179] Kaplan says that although "the distant future will probably see the emergence of a racially hybrid globalized man, the coming decades will see us more aware of our differences than of our similarities."[180] He does not explain how "globoperson" will arise, especially as ethnic conflict, polarization, and segregation may increase if economic decline and ultimate economic collapse occurs.

Robert Harvey,[181] for example, sees the possibility of "doomsday-global anarchy" occurring unless America and the West prevent it. However, if the conservative pessimists such as John Derbyshire, Thomas Chittum, Morris Berman, and Mark Steyn are correct about the decline and fall of America, and by a domino effect, the rest of the West, Harvey's "doomsday-global anarchy" is essentially "in the bag."

Niall Ferguson, in *The Great Degeneration*,[182] argues that Western institutions are already exhibiting evidence of decay. French New Right intellectual Alain de Benoist in his article "La fin du monde a bien en lieu,"[183] puts the case that the world has already "ended"—that is, a Traditional world based on communities of meaning—to be replaced by a culturally fluid world where the only fixed meaning is the religion of self-gratification and consumption in the global supermarket and where profit and greed trumps all values. Such a world, which seems overwhelming and invincible to Traditionalist Right thinkers, will I argue, itself be smashed by the stronger forces of ecological scarcity.

In his book *Immoderate Greatness Why Civilizations Fail*,[184] William Ophuls puts the case that civilizations inevitably breakdown and collapse because of human hubris or what Edward Gibbon (1737-1794) in his *The History of the Decline and Fall of the Roman Empire* described as follows: "[t]he decline of Rome was the natural and inevitable effect of immoderate greatness. Prosperity ripened the principle of decay; the causes of destruction multiplied with the extent of conquest; as soon as time or accident had removed the artificial supports, the stupendous fabric yielded to the pressure of its own weight."[185] The collapse was thus inevitable after a certain point of decay; instead of asking *why* Rome fell, Gibbon wrote, "we should rather be surprised that it had subsisted so long."[186] Civilizational destruction is thus often a form of suicide; as Will Durant has put it: "A great civilization is not conquered from without until it has destroyed itself from within."[187]

Ophuls gives a general theoretical argument for civilizational breakdown that I expand and develop in this chapter. First, there is the problem of ecological resource exhaustion and the limits to growth. Prosperity may be a short-term wonder, but in the long-term, it results in the destruction of a civilization's basis for its own sustainability, because economic systems mask environmental decline: the economy can grow and bloom while the ecology dies. Conventional economists, in particular, have an inability to understand exponential growth and how collapse can sneak up on a society. The human mind is still essentially Paleolithic, hardwired for a hunter-gatherer lifestyle, and is not well adapted to understand the concept of *entropy*, a trend towards increasing disorder and breakdown as available energy over time is transformed into less useful forms.[188] The "thermodynamic vicious circle" of civilization is that high civilization means high production and consumption, and the larger the entropy increase, the greater the "depletion, decay, degradation, and disorder" in the system. At some point, "a civilization exhausts its thermodynamic "credit" and begins to implode."

Second, civilizations are complex ("complexity" referring to both the quantitative size of the number of interrelationships as well as the qualitative dimension), and no past civilization is as complex as ours is. The growth in complexity leads to a compounding of problems, and even though more people does mean more problem-solvers, it also means more problem-creators, a situation of problem overload and an "ingenuity gap," a lack of ability to solve problems. Problems that were once seemingly separate "begin to coalesce into a "problematique," a nexus of problems that mutually aggravate each other."

Complex socio-ecological systems are also non-linear and exhibit "chaotic" behavior, making accurate predictions impossible. Such systems become unstable after a certain critical threshold is reached and are subject to catastrophic collapse. Ophuls gives a general theoretical argument is his book *Immoderate Greatness* in support of this proposition. Still, the evidence is presented in this chapter, which indicates that the Earth's ecosystems are fast approaching such critical thresholds.

Another human factor leading to the collapse of civilizations is that humans are not supremely rational problem-solvers, but typically "muddle through," making suboptimal decisions. The ruling elites of the society may know that the system is decaying and dying, but may not act because they do not want to endanger their share of the loot. They will have comfortable lives, for a time, while the great unwashed slowly suffer. Ultimately, the heads of the elite rest on the chopper. Moreover, beyond this, most people, especially "intellectuals," are blindly and unthinkably committed to the ruling ideologies of the day and move to punish free and critical thinkers. Chris Hedges in an article "The Treason of the Intellectuals," powerfully sums up this point: "[t]hose who doggedly challenge the orthodoxy of belief, who question the reigning political passions, who refuse to sacrifice their integrity to serve the cult of power, are pushed to the margins. They are denounced by the very people who, years later, will often claim these moral battles as their own. It is only the outcasts and the rebels who keep truth and intellectual inquiry alive. They alone name the crimes of the state. They alone give a voice to the victims of oppression. They alone ask the difficult questions. Most important, they expose the powerful, along with their liberal apologists, for what they are."[189]

Civilizations, as Oswald Spengler and Ophuls have proposed, are like organisms, going from birth, to adolescence, to the prime of their lives, and finally to twilight and ultimate death. Alternatively, civilizations go through a rise and fall from the age of pioneers and/ or conquest, to an age of commerce, affluence, and intellect, before suffering moral decay and disintegrating in an age of decadence. In the beginning, a people believes in itself and the virtues of sacrifice, courage, and determination, which eventually leads to success, riches, and luxury. But when the love of money replaces the love of honor, courage, and the in-group, greed and selfishness begin to kill off society as the exuberant growth of weeds might strangle a once ordered vegetable garden. The society begins to wither and decay from within. With a loss of identity, mass immigration is undertaken, with the influx of eager foreigners cashing in on the existing affluence. The result, as Ophuls puts it, "is an increasingly polyglot population that no longer shares the same values. This diversity overload alone poses a substantial challenge to social sustainability."[190]

Combine biophysical entropy and moral decay, and one has, Ophuls concludes, *over-determination*, more than enough factors for collapse. As our techno-industrial civilizations are now global, the collapse will be global, with a vast die-off of the human race. The loss of life will be so high because human hubris being what it is, most people even if they believed that a collapse of civilization was inevitable, and soon, would not *adequately* prepare, although the 2020 crisis did show that many people are at a base level of prepping.

Ophuls is not the only one who has said this; writing about the zombie apocalypse, Jonathan Maberry says that humanity is ill-prepared for a global catastrophe of this magnitude. The odds are against most of us surviving:

> We have become fatally soft, weakened by the technology that has allowed us to conquer the rest of the planet. The weaknesses come from being continually resource-rich in our daily lives. We have clothing, multiple forms of transportation, medicine, readily available food sources, deliveries of foods, affordable repairs or replaceable parts, and access to virtually endless information via cell phones and internet [...] The fact that we are surrounded by structure encourages us to believe in its effectiveness and permanence.[191]

When systems fail, people no longer know how to adapt because "the average person in a post-industrial society is not skilled in repairs, combat, farming, emergency medicine, outdoor survival, general mechanics, or other useful trades."

Ophuls, in an earlier book, *Plato's Revenge*, expressed hope that an ecological politics of consciousness will develop, ushering the world into a "smaller, simpler, humbler vessel"[192] from the doom-bound *Titanic* which humanity is presently on. He wants America to return to a Jeffersonian, limited republican government, basically what it was like in the beginning. America, as I stated earlier in this chapter, is more likely to spiral into "Civil War II," and ultimate destruction.

Complexity, Chaos and Collapse

One of the themes running through the collapseology literature is that complex systems are vulnerable to collapse because complexity itself means that there are more components that can break down.

Roberto Vacca in his *The Coming of the Dark Age* thought (so far, wrongly) that a collapse of modern civilization would occur in the early 21st century because technological systems are becoming so complicated that they are reaching "critical dimensions of instability"[193] and becoming uncontrollable. Thus, a "chance concomitance of stoppages in the same area could start a catastrophic process that could paralyze most developed societies and lead to the deaths of millions of people." The deaths of substantial numbers of the scientific and technological elite would contribute to this paralysis, and spiral down, and if enough of the elite died, the end of science would occur: "[a]lmost no one will be free from immediate burdens and able to think with detachment about abstract and general issues." This great die off will leave plenty of houses "once the corpses have been removed," but ultimately the world as we know it will crumble away due to lack of maintenance.

In this context, both the United States and India's infrastructure, to cite but two examples, are "on the brink" of collapse. In July 2012, the electricity grid supplying electricity to half of India collapsed in a cascading failure. The failure was due to the inadequate response of the government to have enough power capacity to meet India's demands from its rapid industrialization. India's power grid, like its road and railway infrastructure, is poorly constructed and constantly tottering on breakdown.[194] The United States' infrastructure received a "D" grade from the American Society of Civil Engineers, its drinking water infrastructure a "D-" aviation a "D," energy a "D+" and roads a "D-." Bridges have collapsed and the power infrastructure failed during the July 1-3, 2012 heatwave. Beneath the streets of most cities in the West, water and sewerage pipes continue to age, many being over a century or more.[195]

Ancient Rome's concrete structures lasted over 2,000 years but ours will be crumbling in under a century. High strength (Portland) concrete structures are falling apart twice as fast as pre-1930s concrete structures. The concrete cracks and erodes, leading to air, moisture and chemicals oxidizing the rebar, which then expands in diameter, wrecking the rest of the concrete. Infrastructure across the world is crumbling, including highway bridges, sewer pipes, plumbing stations and so on.[196] The West really is in an advanced state of decay.

Infrastructure deficiencies in the US already cost US $129 billion a year from decaying roads, railways, bridges, and transit systems and an investment of US $1.7 trillion is needed to stop costs growing exponentially. This infrastructure is unlikely to be repaired in the crisis times ahead, so watch America literally fall apart.[197]

Vacca, while seeing the cities as we know them ultimately crumbling away, predicted in the short term that dwellings would become fortified citadels, manned by armed inhibitors and security guards. Cities such as Johannesburg today confirm this prediction. Sieges, he also thought, will become common. There will be a return of man the warrior: "[t]hough modern firearms will be available, physical strength will also be important. It will be necessary in man-to-man combat, in trifling day-to-day emergencies once dealt with by machines, and also in handling obstacles caused by nature or the enemy."[198]

A number of scientists and thinkers have defended the idea that the complexity of modern civilization is a vulnerability that can lead to collapse. The cover story edition of *New Scientist*, April 5, 2008 "The Collapse of Civilization: It's More Precarious than We Realized," featured an article by Debora MacKenzie, "Are

We Doomed?"[199] summarizing the ideas of theorists who can see breakdown and collapse as inherent in societies once a certain point of complexity is reached. The work of Professor Joseph Tainter, an archaeologist at the University of Utah and author of *The Collapse of Complex Societies*,[200] is highly relevant. Tainter believes that complex societies can collapse because of the diminishing returns of increased complexity. His position is that: (1) human societies are problem-solving organizations; (2) socio-political systems require energy for their sustainability; (3) increased complexity results in increased costs per capita; (4) investment in social complexity as a problem-solving response to problems yields declining marginal return.[201] The cost of increased complexity results in societies becoming less capable of dealing with challenges and threats over time leaving societies vulnerable to social collapse.

The complexity of modern technological systems also has an inherent vulnerability as Robin Hanson has observed:

> [The] intricate coordination that makes a society more productive also makes it more vulnerable to disruptions. For example, productivity in our society requires continued inputs from a large number of specialized systems, such as electricity, water, food, heat, transportation, communication, medicine, defense, training, and sewage. Failure of any one of these systems for an extended period can destroy the entire system.[202]

Mike Adams has put it thus: "[t]he more complex a society becomes, the more the loss of efficiency in just one small area of service or manufacturing ripples across the entire economy, magnifying its negative effect."[203] Thus, the long-term disruption of the supply of even one resource, such as rubber, would grind modern transportation systems to a halt. Any number of events may cause supply-line disruptions, but they may also occur by what Sidney Dekker calls the "drift to failure."[204] The "drift into failure" occurs when an organization, by a "slow incremental process," "gradually borrows more and more from the margins that once buffered it from assumed boundaries of failure," so that over time, under conditions of competition and scarcity, the very pursuit of the organization's mandate "creates the conditions for its eventual collapse." Complex systems often have a sensitivity to small influences (chaos), so that system instabilities may arise once some "critical state" is reached, making systems catastrophically unstable.[205]

Self-organized criticality applies to the Earth's biosphere as well.[206] Barnosky (et. al) have argued that local ecological systems have been known to shift abruptly and irreversibly across critical thresholds once "tipping points" are reached, and that global ecosystems also exhibit state shift changes when human influence causes the planet to reach critical transition points: "[c]ritical transitions lead to state shifts, which abruptly, override trends and produce unanticipated biotic effects."[207] Global scale forcing mechanisms operating today— including human population growth, habitat transformation, energy production and consumption and climate change—exceed both the rate and magnitude of the last global-scale state shift. That was the last glacial-interglacial transition, 14,300-11,000 years ago. It involved a rapid warm-cold-warm fluctuation, caused by Earth's orbital changes, that affected solar insolation, leading to the extinction of around half of the species of large mammals and several species of large birds and reptiles. Present global-scale shifts may have already been initiated, leading us to a new period of mass extinctions. Homo sapiens may be one more species that ultimately bites the dust.

The Mechanisms of Collapse

More will be said below about the environmental crisis as a major mechanism of collapse. Systems collapse can arise from a number of other trigger events and there is a considerable literature covering a number of disciplines from theoretical physics, cosmology, geology and biology. Scenarios include natural events, however unlikely or distant in time, such as time itself "leaking away," collisions of galaxies (e.g. the Milky Way colliding with the Andromeda galaxy); solar collisions (e.g. with a white dwarf), hostile extra-terrestrial alien invasion, the reversal of the Earth's magnetic field leaving the planet vulnerable to cosmic radiation influx, and Hollywood's favorite, asteroid impacts.[208] Other doomsday scenarios are linked to runaway physics and scientific experiments, such as nanotechnology and the "grey goo" problem, and physics catastrophes such as the formation of a small black hole in the lab that swallows the Earth, the formation of negatively charged stable strangelets which convert ordinary matter into strange matter, and the initiation of a phase transition of the vacuum state, destroying the universe. Bioterrorism, cyberwar/cyberterrorism, runaway artificial intelligence (e.g. *Terminator* scenarios of the revolt of the thinking, killing machine), biotechnology and genetic engineering disasters, also present doomsday scenarios. The probability of the occurrence of many of these events is low or unknown (e.g. extra-terrestrial invasion).

Disaster could come from geophysical threats such as the eruption of a super-volcano, which could end the problem of global warming, but confront humanity with the new threat of global "volcanic winter," as temperatures drop, world agriculture production crashes and famine becomes the principal horseman of the apocalypse, the great new Grim Reaper, culler of the human race.

Optimists generally believe that asteroid/comet impacts with the Earth are not a major threat since no large asteroids or comets are on a collision path with the Earth for at least two centuries. Think again. There has been a revision of the number of *smaller* asteroids believed to be capable of impacting with the Earth; there are up to 10 times as many *medium*-sized asteroids less than 50 meters in diameter capable of striking the Earth. The meteor is estimated to have been less than 20 meters across when it exploded in the atmosphere on February 15, 2013.[209] It had the energy equivalent of 500 (±100) tons of TNT. This rock was about 12,000-13,000 tonnes when it entered the atmosphere from an asteroid belt between Mars and Jupiter in a region of the sky inaccessible to ground-based telescopes. It would only have been visible during the daytime but the sky is too bright to see such small objects.

Bill McGuire, Benfield Professor of Geophysical Hazards at University College London and Director of the University's Benfield

Hazard Research Centre, in his book, *Surviving Armageddon*, has discussed another less known geophysical threat.[210] The Cumbre Vieja volcano is on the western Canary Island of La Palma. An eruption in 1949 led to large fractures in the volcano's flank. It is hypothesized by McGuire and others, that the entire flank could separate from the rest of the volcano and slide into the North Atlantic. Measurements by McGuire's research team from 1992-1997 found the landslide at La Palma to still be moving slowly, although the small recorded values are within the range of instrument error. The mass of rock is as large as the UK's Isle of Man and if and when it crashes into the North Atlantic, it will "trash half the planet" with "an enormously destructive mega-tsunami." Much of the modern civilized world is built on coastlines and is vulnerable to mega-tsunamis.

One of the physical scientific arguments advanced by those believing that a global catastrophe may occur is based on anticipated severe space weather events. Here is the problem: in 1859 the "Carrington Event" occurred which involved intense coronal mass ejections (CMEs) from the sun that produced auroras borealis visible at the equator and caused telegraph lines, towers and stations across the world to catch on fire. The red illumination of aurora borealis was so bright that people in Cuba could read their paper in the early morning by its lights. The energetic particles also altered the chemistry of polar ice.[211] As we will see, another Carrington Event could happen at any time.

Matters will be made worse because NASA's THEMIS satellites discovered a large hole in the magnetosphere, the Earth's magnetic field, which normally defends against such solar blasts.[212] The hole is about four times the size of the Earth and 10 times larger than previously thought. In the past, physicists have observed breaches in the Earth's magnetosphere in response to solar magnetic fields pointing *south*. The present breach occurred with a solar magnetic field aligned *north*. Normally a north-pointing magnetic field impacting with the Earth's magnetosphere directly above the equator, where the Earth's magnetic field points north, would intensify the field preventing solar winds entering – but the opposite has occurred. Such events load the magnetosphere with plasma and when a coronal mass ejection takes place, power outages and other destructive events can occur on Earth. This could result in stronger geomagnetic storms than previously seen, as Jimmy Raeder of the University of New Hampshire has said:

> We're entering Solar Cycle 24. For some reason not fully understood CMEs (coronal mass ejections) in even-numbered solar cycles (like 24) tend to hit Earth with a leading edge that is magnetized north. Such a CME should open a breach and load the magnetosphere with plasma just before the storm gets underway. It's the perfect sequence for a really big event.[213]

The sun is presently in a period of low activity, so low that some physicists such as Habibullo Abdussamotov, director of the Russian section of the International Space Station, believes that a mini-ice age could develop.[214] However, as will be argued below, this does not rule out the occurrence of a new Carrington Event, and as will be discussed, a coronal mass ejection on July 23, 2012, of near-Carrington Event proportions, narrowly missed the Earth. Lower solar activity only lowers the probability of such an event but does not eliminate it.[215]

A report by the National Academy of Sciences, *Severe Space Weather Events: Understanding Societal and Economic Inputs* (December, 2008), says that if a Carrington Event occurred today it would cause the US $1-2 trillion in damage to our high-tech society and take four to ten years to completely repair, they rather optimistically predict.[216]

Ex-CIA analyst, Peter Pry has said that an EMP, either natural or via a terrorist and/or military attack, could kill 9 out of 10 Americans.[217] Disaster preparation expert Matthew Stein noted another alarming consequence of geomagnetic disturbances.[218] He observed that all of the world's almost 450 nuclear reactors are critically dependent upon a functioning electric grid to keep their reactor cores cool to avoid meltdowns. In the case of a "grid-down" scenario because of a repeat Carrington Event, only back-up generators would prevent meltdown occurring. When these generators run out of fuel in a situation of widespread social chaos, or when the back-up generators breakdown, after a few days, the water covering the spent fuel rods in the spent fuel ponds will boil away, and a meltdown will occur. This, Stein says, "will end the industrialized world as we know it, incurring almost incalculable suffering, death and environmental destruction on a scale not seen since the extinction of the dinosaurs some 65 million years ago." How likely is this?

In February 2011 a class X (meaning the strongest type of solar flare, with >10^{-4} watts/square meter) flash from a solar flare disrupted short-wave radio communications in South China.[219] In March 1989, a geomagnetic storm knocked out the power over the bulk of Quebec for nine hours. In January 1994, Canada's US $290 million Anik F2 telecommunications satellite was hit by a solar storm; it required six months and US $50-70 million to get the satellite working again. In 1998, a coronal mass ejection hit a communications satellite, causing it to crash in the middle of the United States. Another geomagnetic storm in October 2003 caused blackouts in Sweden and damaged the South African power grid. Storms of greater intensity will severely damage power transformers and the grid. Stein points out that the Fukushima Daiichi nuclear reactor disaster arose not from direct damage from the Tohoku earthquake but because the facility's back-up diesel generators were destroyed by the tidal wave.

On July 23, 2012, the most powerful solar storm in 150 years narrowly missed the Earth but did hit the STEREO-A spacecraft. One week earlier and it would have struck the Earth, turning civilization back to the 18th century.[220] The emissions of X-rays and extreme UV radiation can produce radio blackouts, and errors in GPS navigation and electrons and protons can damage satellites, but the CME magnetized plasma, according to NASA, "could cause widespread power blackouts, disabling everything that plugs into a wall socket [...] Most people wouldn't even be able to flush their toilet because urban water supplies largely rely on electric pumps." The CME hit with the energy of a billion hydrogen bombs, but it would also create a southward-orientated magnetic field that could interact with the Earth's northward-orientated magnetic field (magnetic reconnection), rearranging the field and causing even more damage to electronics.

According to one research paper, the probability of another Carrington Event occurring in the next decade is a surprisingly high 12 percent.[221] Although humanity has the technical capability of preparing for such an event and largely mitigating its effects, the political will to do so, by spending money, is lacking.[222]

Another paper hypothesizes that our sun is capable of superflares. A study by researchers at the University of Warwick, using NASA's Kepler space telescope, was made of wave patterns of solar superflares emitted by the star KIC9655129, in the outer edges of the Milky Way galaxy. The flares seen on this star are similar to our own sun's solar flares, probably having the same basic physics, with the main difference being that KIC9655129's flares are more powerful, with the energy of 100 billion megaton bombs. Such a superflare occurring in our solar system would destroy the electronic society (question: what about neural electronics?), but the probability of this is thought to be low.[223] Others though, believe that a superflare more powerful than the Carrington event may occur sometime in the next 100 years.[224]

John Kappenman, CEO of electromagnetic damage company Metatech, believes that the prevention of geomagnetic collapse can be done relatively cheaply by adding resistors to the ground connections of transformers, as recommended by the US Electromagnetic Pulse Commission's report to US Congress.[225]

The White House in November 2015 recognized these problems, and took the first baby steps of dealing with the EMP threat, by undertaking to prepare a space weather action plan, with emergency management, education, and improved prediction technologies.[226] On March 26, 2019, President Trump issued "Executive Order on Coordinating National Resilience to Electromagnetic Pulses" to assess the risks of such an attack on critical US infrastructure, beginning the cycle over again.[227] This is all a good start that should have been undertaken at least a decade ago. My bet is that a geomagnetic apocalypse *does not* occur in the next few years and that humanity, because of sloth, will continue to fail to implement safeguards with the needed urgency, lulled into complacency and moving at a snail's pace – then, sometime in the near future, our phenomenal and undeserved luck runs out, and it's lights out, forever.[228]

It is also worth noting, relevant to our zombie theme, that there is considerable evidence of the negative effects of geomagnetic storms on human health, affecting sleep, depression levels, mood, and thus indirectly, aggression. However, the threat from nuclear disasters remains the gravest health risk.

In May 2012, there was considerable concern about the threat to the world posed by Fukushima reactor No. 4, which could have released 85 times the cesium -137 spewed forth at Chernobyl. Mitshuhei Murata, former Japanese Ambassador to Switzerland, said: "It is no exaggeration to say that the fate of Japan and the whole world depends on No. 4 reactor."[229] There are 10,893 spent fuel assemblies at the Fukushima Daiichi plant lying in pools that are vulnerable to destruction from future earthquakes. US Senator Ray Wyden (Democrats, Oregon) visited the Fukushima Daiichi nuclear plant on April 6, 2012, and issued a press release on April 16, expressing alarm at the catastrophic risk the plant posed to humanity, and he urged immediate US government intervention.[230] He also sent a letter to Japan's Ambassador to the United States, requesting Japan to accept international assistance to address the crisis. Senator Wyden said that the problem was "worse than reported" with "spent fuel rods currently being stored in unsound structures immediately adjacent to the ocean," and the area was highly susceptible to earthquakes with only a small makeshift seawall of bags of rocks offering protection from a future tsunami. This problem, over six years later, still exists, with radiation at "unimaginable levels."[231] It is worth reviewing the Fukushima disaster as it reveals important lessons about human error, carelessness, and corruption.

The worst-case scenario involving a fire at unit 4, igniting the irradiated fuel, could release what some regard as a doomsday dose of radiation that could destroy human civilization, although there is, as we will see, room for the irradiated to debate this issue.

At Chernobyl, after its nuclear disaster, the birds and animals—deer, wild boar, moose, lynx, and wolves—have returned, all radioactive. There is controversy about the radiation effects on humans from the Chernobyl disaster. Thus, the report by the UN Scientific Committee on the Effects of Atomic Radiation (2000)[232] found that 134 plant staff and emergency workers suffered acute radiation syndrome. The prevalence of birth defects and leukemia was allegedly no higher than experienced before the accident, with the exception of thyroid cancer in local children, the large cases due to authorities allowing contaminated milk to be used. By the year 2005, there were 6,000 cases of thyroid cancer in children, but thyroid cancer is treatable. Allegedly, only 15 children died by 2005.[233] Other sources see the Chernobyl disaster as having much greater effects, with losses of hundreds of thousands of lives and ill-health effects for generations.[234]

How much radiation was, and may still be released from the Fukushima site is unknown as plant workers were told to lie about radiation readings, being given lead boxes used as shields to block radiation and make readings appear lower than they were in reality. Radiation levels at Reactor 1 in the base water reached levels of 10,300 millisieverts per hour "the equivalent of receiving the maximum annual dose of radiation in just 20 seconds, or enough to become gravely ill in just a few minutes." Whatever the true Fukushima radiation levels, according to scientists from the National Oceanic and Atmospheric Administration's (NOAA) Pacific Marine Environmental Laboratory, computer models simulating ocean currents in the Pacific, indicate that radioactive ocean water will be breaking on the beaches of the US West Coast within five years – but the evidence presented at the October 2013 North Pacific Marine Science Organization (PICES) annual meeting indicated that a radioactive plume was detected reaching the shores of Canada and the US by July 2013 both in ocean surface waters and the atmosphere. It took until April 2016 for the Japanese to attempt to build a wall of ice around the reactors in an attempt to contain the massive outpouring of radioactive water into the Pacific Ocean, using underground pipes to freeze the ground. Time will tell if this strategy actually works.[235]

An article in *The Australian* reported that nuclear workers "had received massive undocumented exposures to radiation" and "the danger money supposed to flow to employees from working at Fukushima Daiichi was being creamed off by unscrupulous companies."[236] *The Australian* quoted a nuclear engineer at the plant who said: "What remained intact after the disaster is completely fragile and when the next one comes it's going to collapse," meaning that the Fukushima nuclear plant is vulnerable to a new quake or tsunami. The cooling system is makeshift, and the nuclear engineer believes that the next big earthquake will fracture it. He also had doubts about back-up power gear keeping the plant's six reactors cool, because only temporary gear "not proper equipment" is being used. The nuclear engineer also said that earthquake protection measures had not been made. A contractor had identified 20,000 points to be fixed for anti-seismic protection after the 2007 Niigata earthquake; none had been done due to shortages of money. Further, the engineer believes that the reactors were damaged in the 2011 earthquake.

The Australian article mentions the risk of spent fuel in a tank alongside Reactor No. 4, "which must be kept submerged at all times to avoid a catastrophic chain reaction that could render Tokyo uninhabitable." Workers paid to deal with this fuel had had their real wages slashed to as low as 8,000 yen (about US $80) a day when some workers earned as high as US $5,000 a day for this work in the days before the quake. It is not a proven way to maintain worker morale. Along with this is corruption; after the disaster, Japan's mafia (Yakuza) supplied workers who owed them money to work at the plant. These workers violated workplace safety regulations, such as not wearing dosimeters or shielding them inside clothing to minimize exposure recordings. After Yakuza workers left the plant, at least in 2013, these practices continued. *The Australian* article says: "One worker who was in charge of handing out dosimeters to staff in the bunker during the first few months after the disaster said many simply refused to take the devices, saying they would never be able to complete their work if their true readings were recorded."

Tokyo Electric Power Company had initially said that the radiation emitted by the leaking water was about 100 millisieverts an hour, but the equipment used could only record emissions at a maximum rate of up to 100 millisieverts an hour. When more sensitive equipment was used, the correct reading of 1,800 millisieverts an hour, readings 18 times higher than the previous readings, was recorded.[237]

Japanese informants reported that their government had experts on a speaking tour, one of whom told people that radiation wouldn't affect happy people and people smiling. Japanese TV news said that rising radiation levels were due to Chinese atmospheric pollution blowing to Japan!

Singapore-based news outlet AsiaOne reported in April 2013 that 120 tons of radioactively contaminated water, containing about 710 billion becquerels of radioactive materials, had leaked from an underground storage facility at the No. 1 power plant site. Japan's Ministry of Health, Labor and Welfare (MHLW) said in April 2013 that levels of cesium-137 (Cs-137) and cesium-134 (Cs-134), found in tangerines and rice crackers produced in the Shizuoka prefecture, about 225 miles from Fukushima, tested high for both Cs-137 and Cs-134, rice crackers = 3.7 becquerels per kilogram of Cs-137 and tangerines = 1.46 becquerels per kilogram of Cs-134 and 3.14 becquerels per kilogram of Cs-137. The average adult eating such foods at those radiation levels would exceed the safe maximum radiation level of 50 millisieverts of radiation per year in only a few weeks.

In August 2013, *The Australian* reported that the Japanese Nuclear Regulation Authority was concerned about an "emergency" at Fukushima with the release of tritium-laced groundwater into the sea beside the plant: TEPCO admitted that 20-40 trillion becquerels of radioactive tritium have leaked into the sea since the nuclear disaster.[238] Another report states that 300 tonnes of radioactive water a day has entered the sea since March 2011, also admitted in August 2013 by TEPCO. As well, radioactive ground-water beneath the reactors had breached an underground barrier and was rising towards the surface. High levels of strontium 90 had been detected in the groundwater.[239] The buildings of Reactors No. 1 and 4 receive 400 tonnes of groundwater each day.[240]

Michio Aoyama, the senior researcher of the geochemical research department of the Meteorological Research Institute, found 60 billion becquerels of cesium-137 and strontium-90 discharged into the Pacific Ocean every day from a ditch at the northern end of the reactor. Unsurprisingly, there have been rising radiation levels in Japan's seas and prefectures surrounding Fukushima. On January 10, 2014, the Japanese Fisheries Research Agency caught a fish contaminated with 12,400 becquerels per kilogram of radioactive cesium, 124 times higher than the safety standard. Fish catches around Fukushima are mostly destroyed because of dangerous radiation levels.

The Fukushima reactors have melted through the steel vessels into the ground and are continuing fission reactions. To prevent a nuclear explosion, it is necessary to cool this melted core; hence huge quantities of water must be pumped over the core, resulting in radionuclides dissolving in the water and other insoluble radioactive material such as plutonium being held in colloidal suspension. The radioactive water has not been controlled and pours into the Pacific Ocean. This will continue forever unless the radioactive material can be removed, but radiation levels are too high to do this. The present attempt to freeze the ground can only be a short-term solution.

David Webb, Chief Executive Officer at Origin Investments AB, is quoted at Voice of Russia.com as saying that the cooling pool of unit 4 at Fukushima is crucial as it contains 400,000 kilograms of hot plutonium: "There is a great danger of a thermo-nuclear reaction if these rods become exposed to the air and the cooling pool itself is just barely containing the temperature levels of the core as it is [..] [O]ne microgram of plutonium could theoretically kill a person. There are a billion micrograms in a kilogram, and there are 400,000 hot kilograms in this pool. So, if these rods combust, if the set of rods begins a thermonuclear reaction, it will vaporize the water in the pool, and the entire pool can become an uncontrolled nuclear reaction open to the air. These particles will be spread through the northern hemisphere. This is perhaps the greatest threat humanity has ever faced."[241] This is known as the "open-air super reactor spectacular." One fuel rod has the potential to kill 2.89 billion people, and the number of fuel roads at Fukushima, excluding those in the pressure vessel, is 11,421. Some fear a "series of cascading failures with an apocalyptic outcome."[242]

The nuclear risk of Fukushima is dwarfed by the spent fuel rod problem in the United States, the largest store of radioactivity on Earth.[243] The US has 65,000 tonnes of spent fuel, of which 75 percent is stored in pools, and there are 30 million rods in spent fuel pools. In the pools, the cesium-137 is over 20 times more than that released from all previous atomic explosions and 15-30 times more than released at the Chernobyl disaster.[244] All of this radioactive material is vulnerable to a 9/11 terrorist attack.[245] The US has 23 reactors the same as the General Electric ones in Fukushima No.1 and also has atomic plants built on fault lines (e.g., Diablo Canyon Nuclear Power Plant's units 1 and 2 near Santa Barbara and the San Onofre Nuclear Generating Station, outside of San Clemente, shut down in 2012, but continues in 2018 to leak radioactive material).[246] A quarter of the US's aging reactors have leaked radioactive tritium-polluted water.[247] There have been nuclear reactor partial meltdowns (Santa Susana Field Laboratory, July 13, 1959) that contaminated surrounding areas, with radiation 300 times the acceptable levels, complete with a cover-up that could have taught the Japanese a thing or two.

The US is also vulnerable to geomagnetic disturbances such as solar flares and EMP events caused by an enemy nuclear attack. Nuclear power plants are not likely, in the US, at least, to immediately go "boom," as modern nuclear reactors are designed to shut down if safety limits are reached or exceeded, such as if the electric power shuts down. The problem is in the longer term when diesel runs out, supplying fuel to back-up generators. If the water boils off of the cooling pools and the rods catch fire, massive quantities of radiation would be released, more than in a meltdown. The US Nuclear Regulatory Commission has said that US nuclear power plants affected by a blackout would be able to function without electricity for about eight hours and would be able to keep the reactor and spent-fuel pool cool for 72 hours. However, according to an article in the ibtimes.com:

> Nuclear plants depend on standby batteries and backup diesel generators. Most standby power systems would continue to function after a severe solar storm, but supplying the standby power systems with adequate fuel, when the main power grids are offline for years, could become a very critical problem.
>
> [...] If the spent fuel rod pools at the country's 104 nuclear power plants lose their connection to the power grid, the current regulations aren't sufficient to guarantee those pools won't boil over exposing the hot, zirconium-clad rods and sparking fires that would release deadly radiation.
>
> [...] A report by the Oak Ridge National Laboratory said that over the standard 40-year license term of nuclear power plants, solar flare activity enables a 33 percent chance of a long-term power loss, a risk that significantly outweighs that of major earthquakes and tsunamis.[248]

A solar flare is only one dramatic way for the US power grid to collapse. A study by the Federal Energy Regulatory Commission has concluded that a coordinated terrorist attack on three separate electric systems could collapse the entire US power network.[249] "The US could suffer a coast-to-coast blackout if saboteurs knock out just nine of the country's 55,000 electric-transmission substations on a scorching summer day." The US power grid has been compared to a big pile of sand, stable until a certain "height" is reached.[250]Iranian cyberattacks have already breached cybersecurity at dozens of US power plants, and in late January 2016, hackers caused a partial shutdown of the grid in Israel.

And then there is nuclear war. There is continuing debate about the effects of limited and all-out global nuclear war. The really bad news from one study is that nuclear war will "end civilization" with famine, perhaps similar to the movie *The Road* (2009). The study by International Physicians for the Prevention of Nuclear War and Physicians for Social Responsibility predicted that a limited nuclear war between India and Pakistan (itself hardly a remote probability[251]) could kill up to two billion people through nuclear winter, with black carbon aerosol particles reducing food production across the world.[252] An all-out nuclear exchange between the US and Russia, or even a threesome with China, could possibly lead to the extinction of the human race. "Let us eat and drink, for tomorrow we shall die": Isaiah 22:13.

Ecological Collapse and Looming Resource Shortages

So far, we have considered collapse/disorder scenarios that may or may not occur. However, there are other threats that are occurring right now. For example, environmental degradation and climate change may also drive social and civilizational collapse.[253] Professor John Beddington, a chief science advisor to the UK government, said in March 2009 that the world was facing a "perfect storm" of "food shortages, water scarcity, and costly oil by 2030. These developments, plus accelerating climate change and mass migration across national borders, could lead to major upheavals."[254] Jonathon Porritt, former chair of the UK Sustainable Development Commission, agreed with Beddington, but put the time of the crisis closer to 2020 than 2030, being a "perfect storm" of environmental and economic collapse.[255] Lester Brown of the Earth Policy Institute says in his preface to his book *World on the Edge*[256] that he does not know how much time civilization has left on a business-as-usual scenario, but "the time is more likely measured in years than in decades. We are now so close to the edge that it could come at any time."

Our civilization may already be approaching its demise, as the late theoretical physicist Professor Stephen Hawking has said: "We are entering an increasingly dangerous period in our history. Our population and our use of the finite resources of the planet earth are growing exponentially along with our technological ability to change the environment for good or ill [...] It will be difficult enough to avoid disaster in the next 100 years, let alone the next thousand or million."[257]

In the first section of this chapter, some of our interconnected environmental problems were mentioned, including the depletion and/or degradation of water, soil, and food resources. Many other such problems can be mentioned.

For example, the sustainability of world food production is threatened not only by global climate change (discussed below) but also by more, seemingly humble problems such as "peak phosphorus."[258] Phosphate supplies are becoming increasingly scarce. Phosphorus is a limiting nutrient in agricultural plant growth; it can be recycled (i.e., returned to the soil through the use of sewage sludge composted), but in modern agriculture, it is wasted and becomes too dissipated to recycle. Patrick Déry applied the linearization depletion analysis devised by M. King Hubbert (applied in Hubbert's case to oil[259]), to phosphorous. It was concluded that the peak of US phosphorous occurred in 1988, and for the world in 1989.[260]

Financial analyst Jeremy Grantham has said about the coming shortage of phosphorous (phosphate) and potassium (potash):

> These two elements cannot be made, cannot be substituted, are necessary to grow all life forms, and are mined and depleted. It's a scary set of statements. Former Soviet states and Canada have more than 70 percent of the potash. Morocco has 85 percent of all high-grade phosphates. It is the most important quasi-monopoly in economic history. What happens when these fertilizers run out is a question I can't get satisfactorily answered and, believe me, I have tried. There seems to be only one conclusion: their use must be drastically reduced in the next 20-40 years, or we will begin to starve.[261]

Peak fertilizer, along with other interacting and compounding problems such as water shortages, land degradation (peak soil), climate change, and peak fuel is producing a world food crisis Grantham argues, and this food crisis is unlikely to disappear until global population peaks and considerably declines.[262] Already grain productivity has fallen each decade since 1970 from 3.5 to 1.5 percent. Genetic engineering could result in more efficient genes being inserted in plants such as rice and wheat in 20-30 years' time, which could increase outputs by up to 50 percent. However, to feed 9+ billion people by 2050 will require an increase in food production by 60-100 percent of present-day levels. Grantham concludes: "If food pressures recur *and are reinforced by fuel price increases*, the risks of social collapse and global instability increase to a point where they probably become the major source of international confrontations."[263] Further: "[i]n the longer term [...] energy costs and absolute shortage in the case of oil form a serious problem second only to food shortages and will result in prices so high they will impact global growth and even the viability of modern, rather fragile, economies."[264] There will be "soaring commodity prices and impending shortages" because humanity is simply running out of raw materials.

In conclusion, Grantham believes, as do many environmentalists, that the world human population is now unsustainable and that the Earth can only sustainably support 1.5 billion people, not 7+ or 9+ billion – hence most people are, in the future, going to starve to death.

There are looming shortages of many metal stocks. Gordon (et al.) concluded that "virgin stocks of several metals appear inadequate to sustain the modern 'developed world' quality of life for all Earth's peoples under contemporary technology."[265] Global supplies of platinum are diminishing, and there is no synthetic alternative for this chemical element.[266] China produces 97 percent of the world's rare earth metal such as indium (used in making LCDs for flat-screen TVs) and gallium (used in indium gallium arsenide semiconductors), and these and other rare earths are used in a wide range of high tech devices, from giant electromagnets in wind turbines to satellite components. Shortages of these "alternative energy minerals" may trigger a trade war or even a shooting war, if military hardware still works.[267]

Alice Friedemann has observed that "computers are the top card in the house-of-cards complex civilization we built with coal and oil, and computers will be the first to go when supply chains fail."[268] Further: "[a]s global shipping, factories, and countries have a hard time keeping the lights on, computers will stop being made as supply chains breakdown. If even one of the dozens of types of single-sourced equipment or pure chemical supplies goes out of business, the assembly line stops."[269] Human knowledge is increasingly being preserved using computer technology, with libraries often getting only electronic versions of scientific journals and e-books. Computers are too vulnerable for the preservation of knowledge as they "are the top cards in the civilization house of cards. Knock out any below, and it all crumbles. Computers have too many complex, energy-intensive inputs and dependencies."[270] Some human knowledge could be preserved on archival paper, which at ideal temperatures can last up to 500 years and words can be etched into metallic substances to preserve knowledge for a coming Dark Age, but since the status quo is "comfortably numb," convinced that our present society is invulnerable, little will be done to save human knowledge. When the spiral down to chaos happens, much of the knowledge, which we now take for granted, will be lost. Welcome to the new Dark Age of barbarism.

Peak Energy

I view the entire American political and economic system as broken and corrupt, subservient to corporate/financial interests and an economic paradigm (based on fiat currency, fractional reserve banking, and debt-based expansion) which demands infinite growth. That economic pyramid scheme—that mandate for infinite growth— is the beast which has driven us headlong into the unyielding steel wall of Peak Oil and the edge of the cliff lying just beyond.[271]

Jeremy Leggett, a former faculty member of the Royal School of Mines, London, said in his 2005 book *The Empty Tank: Oil, Gas, Hot Air, and the Coming Global Financial Catastrophe*,[272] that he believed that a change to a renewable energy infrastructure was possible, given the political will, but "the shortfall between current expectation of oil supply and actual availability will be such that neither gas, nor renewables, nor liquids from gas and coal, nor nuclear, nor any combinations thereof, will be able to plug the gap in time to head off the economic trauma resulting from the oil tipping point."[273] Consequently, economic collapse looms:

> The price of houses will collapse. Stock markets will crash. Within a short period, human wealth—little more than a pile of paper at the best of times, even with confidence about the future high among traders—will shrivel. The inescapable consequences of the crisis will then roll out in slow motion. Companies will go bankrupt by the hundreds and then thousands. Workers will fall into unemployment by the hundreds of thousands and then millions. Once affluent cities with street cafes will have queues at soup kitchens and armies of beggars on the streets. The crime rate will soar. The Earth has always been a dangerous place, but now it will become a tinderbox.[274]

This position can be contrasted with that of Matt Ridley in *The Rational Optimist*,[275] who dismisses such fears and expresses (with little evidence and argument) a common optimistic view about humanity's energy future: "Oil, coal, and gas are finite. But between them they will last decades, perhaps centuries, and people will find alternatives long before they run out."[276] Such claims—that technology will save humanity just in time, and that substitutes for depleting resources will *always* be found—are not rationally justified claims – and are undermined by the unsolved problem of induction.[277] To explain: technology may have solved our problems in the *past,* but how can that supply a non-circular justification for believing that it will do so in the *future*? Substitutes have been found for many depleted resources *so far*, but that is no basis for believing that substitutes will *always* be found: our "luck" may run out. Further, it takes at least 30 years to change an energy infrastructure; society cannot be rebuilt overnight, especially our trucking infrastructure.[278]

The issue of peak oil has been debated for almost 20 years and has generated its own technical books, articles, and websites.[279] The argument for peak oil has been summarized as follows:

- "The peak of oil discoveries was reached in the 1960s [...]

- This peak in discoveries has to be followed by a peak in production since we can only produce what has been found before.

- The production peak of individual fields is a historical fact [and] almost all large oil fields have already passed their production maximum and are in decline.

- The aggregation of the production profiles of individual fields (with their individual peaks) sums up to a production peak of individual oil regions. Historically, peak production was reached in Austria in 1955, in Germany in 1968, and in the USA in 1971, and in Indonesia in 1977. Recent regions joining the club of countries with declining production rates are Gabon (1997), UK (1999), Australia (2000), Oman (2000), and Norway (2001).

- The aggregate decline of mature regions is getting steeper with every "new member of the club." In order to keep over-all production just flat, ever fewer regions have to increase their production.

- This pattern [has been observed for] more than thirty years."[280]

Owen (et al.), have said that they support "the contention held by many independent institutions that conventional oil production may soon go into decline [...] and it is likely that the era of plentiful, low cost petroleum is coming to an end."[281] Further: "[r]eserves that provide liquid fuels today will only have the capacity to service just over half of BAU (business as usual) demand by 2023."[282]

Although the International Energy Agency (IEA) sees the peak of world oil production as some time off, Aleklett (et al.) reanalyzed IEA data and concluded that peak oil occurred in 2008.[283] To repeat: this follows from IEA's own data. Indeed, the International Energy Agency in its *World Energy Outlook* (WEO) (2010) said that by 2035 global oil production "reaches 96 mb/d, the balance of 3 mb/d coming from processing gains." Crude oil output "reaches an undulating plateau of around 68-69 mb/d by 2020, but never regains its all-time peak of 70 mb/d reached in 2006, while production of natural gas liquids (NGLs) and unconventional oil grows strongly."[284]

Unconventional oil has been said to be generating what Alan Kohler enthusiastically describes as a "new global oil rush" and to have led to the "death of peak oil."[285] Matt Ridley has proclaimed that when the shale revolution goes "global," "oil and gas in tight rock formations will give the world ample supplies of hydrocarbons for decades, if not centuries." Ever the "rational optimist."[286] However, some establishment sources are not as optimistic. Brian Walsh, in his April 9, 2012, *Time* magazine article "The Truth about Oil,"[287] says that new technological breakthroughs are increasing global supplies, but "the era of cheap oil may be gone forever." Unconventional oil includes pre-salt and deep-water (50-100 billion barrels), oil shale (800 billion barrels), and oil sands (169 billion barrels). However, these sources "are often dirtier, with higher risks of accidents. The decline of major conventional oil fields and the rise in demand mean the spare production capacity that once cushioned prices could be gone, ushering in an era of volatile market swings. And burning all this leftover oil could lock the world into dangerous climate change."

Energy researcher Jean Laherrére believes that the deep-water oil reserve figures are too optimistic and that most discoveries will be made before 2025.[288] The US Legislative Peak Oil and Natural Gas Caucus concluded that "oil shale cannot compensate in a timely way for loss of conventional oil production and cannot meet sustainable productions at a rate that will offset high oil prices."[289] On the subject of shale oil, or organic marlstone, the Caucus concluded:

The US contains massive amounts of oil shale but it is a low grade material with about the equivalent energy proud for pound of a baked potato. Regardless of its low EROEI [Energy Returned on Energy Invested] oil shale production appears to be feasible at some scale. That scale, however, appears not to be significant enough to alter oil supply trends in coming years. It is clear that limiting factors such as water, safe deposits of spent process material, and other issues remain unanswered.[290]

The comprehensive assessment of the sustainability of unconventional oil given by Kjell Aleklett in *Peeking at Peak Oil*[291] agrees with the

Caucus conclusion cited above: "Oil production from oil shale is insignificant." And: "There is nothing to indicate that the United States will become self-sufficient in oil production or even become an oil exporter despite enthusiastic reportage in the news media." For example, the average Bakken well makes use of horizontal drilling to get to the layer of rock containing the oil that does not flow and then fracturing or "fracking," involving pumping down a chemical mixture at high pressure to allow the oil to be pumped out. There has been observed to be a rapid decline in oil output from shale oil drilling in Montana, part of the Bakken Field and at the Eagle Ford play in Texas; of the 16 wells completed between December 2005 and November 2009, only seven remain productive, and US officials have reduced by 96 percent the estimated recoverable oil from California's Monterey shale deposits.[292]

Michael Klare has pointed out that there are environmental limits to shale oil mining as well.[293] Hydraulic fracturing uses millions of liters of water and creates a problem of disposal of toxic water, which can contaminate other water resources. These vast quantities of water may not be available because of droughts, arguably due to climate change. In July 2012, in Pennsylvania, some drillers suspended operations after the Susquehanna River Basin Commission suspended permits for water withdrawals from the Susquehanna River. According to Chris Faulkner, the president and CEO of Breitling Oil and Gas: "Without water, drilling shale gas and oil wells is not possible. A continuing drought could cause our domestic production to decline and derail our road to energy independence in a hurry."

Deep-water drills are another example of "extreme oil," and dangers of large-scale mishaps are always present. The 2010 BP Deep-water Horizon disaster in the Gulf of Mexico is an example, but Shell Oil's drilling in the Alaskan Arctic was suspended until 2013 (and plans resumed in 2015), due to a series of accidents. In any case, total oil production from all existing deep-water wells by 2020 is thought to be 8.4 mb/d, and as Aleklett puts it, "not even 10% of the necessary increase can be provided by production from deep water."[294] Aleklett concludes: "[d]eep water is the last output of global oil production. The production journey that began in the United States and Russia in the 1850s has now reached the end of the road."[295]

Proponents of the peak oil hypothesis are allegedly in "disgrace," according to Steven F. Hayward, visiting professor at Pepperdine University's Graduate School of Public Policy, Los Angeles, as all "of the recent projections forecast that the age of hydrocarbon dominance (including coal) will last several decades longer than previously thought."[296] This in itself is an admittance that peak energy will eventually be reached, albeit "several decades longer than previously thought." However, as J. David Hughes points out, the Energy Information Administration (EIA) sees US domestic crude oil production, including "tight oil (shale oil), peaking at 7.5 million barrels per day in 2019/2020. By 2040, the percentage of US domestically produced crude oil of total US crude oil used will be only 32 percent, lower than today's share of 34 percent."[297] Thus, the idea of a century of US energy independence, based on *in situ* unconventional oil resources, is a myth. Hughes summarizes: "although resources such as oil shale, gas hydrates, and in situ coal gasification have very large in situ potential, they have been produced at only minuscule rates if at all, despite major expenditures over many years on pilot projects. Tar sands similarly have immense in situ resources, but more than four decades of very large capital inputs and collateral environmental impacts have yielded production of less than two percent of world oil requirements."[298] Shale gas wells, for example, have a high rate of production decline – conventional gas wells usually decline by 25-40 percent in the first year of production, whereas shale wells decline by 63-85 percent, and then require re-fracking, hence generating the need to drill faster and faster.

Richard Heinberg in *Snake Oil: How Fracking's False Promise of Plenty Imperils Our Future*, reaches this conclusion on unconventional oil: "Rather than a century of plenty, we face the likely recommencement of declines in US oil and gas production *before* 2020. We've purchased a few years of respite from the relentless and inevitable erosion of our nation's oil and gas production rates, but at what cost?"[299]

The US shale oil boom had also had a question mark placed over it by the recent instability of oil prices. The world oil market is artificial, not economically free, with supply regulated by the Organization of Petroleum Exporting Countries. The Saudis have not reduced supply, as they have done in 1977, 1985, 1991, and 2008. Some speculate that this is an attempt to slow down the US's unconventional oil industry; others, that it is a strategy to visit economic pain on regimes that the Saudis are in conflict with such as Iran and Russia (an ally of Syria's Bashar al-Assad), or maybe both. In any case, the instability of oil prices has nothing to do with any vast new oil reserves suddenly being discovered in Saudi Arabia and everything to do with geopolitics.

The frantic scramble to secure what is left of declining world oil resources, Michael Klare has argued, raises the likelihood of resource wars through the 21st century – if nation-states even survive the threat of peak energy.[300] China is already driving up global oil prices, with its consumption rising by 0.5 m/bpd each year – this being 9.2 m/bdp in a world market of 90 m/bpd. David Greely, "oil guru" of Goldman Sachs, has said: "It is only a matter of time before inventories and OPEC spare capacity become effectively exhausted, requiring higher oil prices to restrain demand."[301]

Other energy resources are fast approaching their peak. In 2006, the Energy Watch Group predicted that the peak of world uranium production would occur in 2040,[302] but there are more pessimistic predictions of peak uranium, such as 2016, that the peak has already been reached. Even coal reserves are depleting faster than previously thought, with one study concluding that the peak occurred in 2011,[303] and other studies putting peak coal in 2026.[304] Peak coal will lead to the "blackout" of industrial society as Richard Heinberg predicts: "Grid failure becomes the norm; lights are on only occasionally and electricity is strictly rationed. Communication networks are drastically reduced in scope and are continually strained. Industrial activity contracts and gradually disappears."[305]

Both Richard Heinberg[306] and Ted Trainer[307] have put the case that no combination of alternative energy options would enable the consumer society to continue on a business-as-usual basis, let alone grow exponentially. Further, many conventional economists, who reject the peak oil hypothesis, also believe that alternative energy resources will not fuel our bubbling global consumer society. For example, wind turbines face a "ballooning cost" compared to the cheapest fossil fuel.[308] Alternative energy sources such as solar have been cut back throughout the world because of economic conditions. There was a push in Spain for the nation to become the world leader in renewable energy. In 2008 Spain accounted for about half of the world's new solar power installation re wattage due to generous government subsidies. Now, however, due to poor economic conditions and the need to curb the public deficit, these subsidies have been temporarily suspended, and a dark cloud has passed over solar optimism.[309]

Safety concerns continue to be an issue with nuclear power, as we have seen from the discussion given previously in this chapter.[310] Claims by Lockheed Martin to have made a breakthrough in nuclear fusion, and to have a working nuclear fusion reactor by about 2017 (it does not seem to have happened by 2019, but some media reports say 2020), have been greeted with skepticism by the scientific community. The project lead at Lockheed Martin has said that a commercial application would take about a decade. However, others see this as optimistic, with domestic fusion unlikely before 2050.

Richard C. Duncan has seen peak energy leading to the end of industrial society by 2025-2030, with a Malthusian catastrophe and global population crash, culling the human population to two billion by 2050.[311] An "Olduvai" die-off will occur everywhere, and large cities will be very dangerous (and sources of disease from rotting corpses) when the lights of modernity go out. C. Stager, *Deep Future: The Next 100,000 Years of Life on Earth*, writes: "We're already near the limits of economically viable petroleum production, and the decline of cheap oil will have swift and severe consequences for those who will inherit the full measure of that problem. If and when the prices and availability of petroleum-based fuels, fertilizers, plastics, pharmaceuticals, cosmetics, synthetic fabrics, and even roadway pavement go haywire, the scale of human suffering could outstrip anything in the works for us from climate [change]."[312]

But, peak energy is not humanity's only existential problem.

Global Meltdown: The Climate Cataclysm

The best-known doomsday predictions arising from the issue of global climate change were made by James Lovelock, known for his Gaia hypothesis that the Earth ("Mother Earth") behaves like an organism, exhibiting systems-self-regulation. Lovelock, in his various books on the topic, used metaphors that transcended normal science and essentially involved philosophical speculation and metaphysics, in my opinion. Nevertheless, at a minimum, he saw the world as a non-linear system, subject to chaotic effects. In 2006, he said: "Before this century is over, billions of us will die, and the few breeding pairs of people that survive will be in the Arctic where the climate remains tolerable."[313] In his 2009 book, *The Vanishing Face of Gaia: A Final Warning*, Lovelock said: "global warming may all but eliminate people from Earth."[314]

Lovelock recanted from his doomsday predictions, describing his own predictions as "wrong" and others as "alarmist" – although only holding to the complete annihilation of life would be more alarmist than Lovelock's earlier predictions. At no point did he examine the survival rates of past extinction episodes involving climate change and human survival. Surprisingly enough, Lovelock himself accepted a non-linear model of climate change, described as follows: "Do not expect the climate to follow the smooth path of slowly but sedately rising temperatures predicted by the IPCC [Intergovernmental Panel on Climate Change], where change slowly inches up and leaves plenty of time for business as usual. The real Earth changes intermittently with spells of constancy, even slight decline between jumps to greater heat." Lovelock's recanting was produced because he believes that climate change has not proceeded as fast as the Gaia model would predict. But, so much the worst for his model.

The earlier, pessimistic Lovelock, though, was on the right track and saw the gravest dangers to humanity arising from "starvation, competition for space and resources, and tribal war." He also said that to survive in the harsh world of the future, we need "to prepare ourselves to fight a barbarian warlord out to seize us and our territory." So, he seems to be *logically* committed to the thesis of this book.

Journalists skeptical of the very existence of global climate change have made much of the claims of Kaufmann (et al.) that "global surface temperatures did not rise between 1998 and 2008."[315] These journalists should have read the entire paper, which does not support climate change skepticism. The title of the paper is "Reconciling Anthropogenic Climate Change with Observed Temperature 1998-2008." It presents evidence that the rapid increase in sulfur emissions, primarily by China's coal consumption has been so vast as to mask the increase in radiative forcing (the rate of change of energy or net irradiance per unit area of the Earth relative to the top of the atmosphere) that would have otherwise occurred from rising greenhouse gas concentrations (global dimming). When the sulfur emissions are reduced by technological improvements in the Chinese coal industry, global warming will allegedly return with a vengeance. A paper by Solomon (et al.)[316] puts the position that man-made pollutants may have slowed global warming as aerosol particles from burning coal may reflect sunlight back into space. More will be said about the issue of "the pause" shortly.

Climate change skeptics maintain that there is no direct evidence that 20th and 21st-century warming (if such warming did occur – the skeptic teams are divided on this), was caused by carbon dioxide increases, as ice ages had occurred when the atmospheric carbon dioxide levels were higher than at present.[317] The causes of an ice age are complex and involve more factors than just the atmospheric concentration of greenhouse gases. Factors include Milankovitch cycles (variations in the Earth's orbit), sunspot cycles, volcanism, and other factors. It is possible for an ice age to occur even with a higher than present-day concentration of atmospheric greenhouse gases relative to these other factors.[318] However, there are various "signatures" of human-caused climate change, rather than natural variability, such as cooling in the upper atmosphere, with lower-level warming, nights warmer than days, winters warmer than summers and land warming more than oceans.

The Earth has also experienced a number of past mass extinctions, such as the Cambrian extinction of 490 million years ago and the more recent Paleocene thermal event of 55 million years ago. These were caused by increased carbon dioxide in the atmosphere, leading to changes in ocean currents and circulation patterns, via the disruption of ocean conveyer currents. This disruption led to the massive growth of green sulfur-producing bacteria and other bacteria producing hydrogen sulfide. The gas enters the atmosphere, and over millions of years build up to such a high concentration that the Earth's protective ozone layer is destroyed. The influx of ultraviolet radiation and high concentrations of hydrogen sulfide in the atmosphere kills off most of life on Earth.[319] According to University of Washington paleontologist, Professor Peter Ward, "[t]he present rise in carbon dioxide levels seems to eclipse any other rate of increase from the past" and once CO_2 levels rise above 450 parts per million (ppm) (May 15, 2019, atmospheric CO_2 levels are at 415.64 ppm, NOAA-ESRL data) "we head irrevocably toward an ice-free world, which will lead to a change in the thermohaline conveyer belt currents [which] will lead to a new greenhouse extinction."

Professor David Battisti of the University of Washington, however, sees CO_2 levels reaching 800 ppm by the end of the 21st century and rising to 1,100 ppm shortly after that, melting the world's ice sheets and setting in motion the next greenhouse extinction.[320] Some authorities believe that adding CO_2 levels from other greenhouse gases means that we may already be at the tipping point of 450 ppm, so humanity is already on the highway to extinction.[321]

While climate change skeptics maintain that global temperatures have not risen since 1997,[322] other climate scientists have said that the past decade is the warmest on record. For example, Professor Richard A. Muller was once one of the world's leading climate change skeptics and was skeptical because of the poor quality of data from temperature stations, with temperature uncertainty of 2-5 C or more. This margin of error is due to the stations being in cities, which are typically hotter than rural areas (known as the "heat island effect"). Muller chaired the Berkeley Earth Surface Temperature Project, which obtained over 1.6 billion measurements from over 39,000 temperature stations across the world. The urban-heating bias was avoided by using rural locations. It was concluded that: "The changes at the locations that showed warming [⅔ showed warming, ⅓ did not] were typically between 1-2°C much greater than the IPCC's average of 0.64°C."[323] Muller concluded that global warming is real.

James E. Hansen, director of NASA's Goddard Institute for Space Studies, has said that his predictions in 1988 about increasing global temperature have been proved true, but he was too optimistic about the speed at which temperature changes would result in an increase in extreme weather.[324] His research team's analysis of six decades of global temperature statistics found a statistically significant increase in the frequency of extremely hot summers. The analysis shows "that, for the extreme hot weather of the recent past, there is virtually no explanation other than climate change."[325] Plotting the temperatures of the world overtime on a Gaussian or bell curve, showed that the extremes of unusually cold and unusually hot are changing so that they *both* become more severe and more common. Thus, in the period of 1951 to 1980, extremely hot temperatures covered 0.1-0.2 percent of the Earth, but since that time, the extremes now cover around 10 percent of the Earth.[326] The European heatwave of 2003, the Russian heatwave of 2010, the droughts in Texas and Oklahoma in 2011, the extremely hot 2012 US summer, and perhaps the 2018 droughts across the US, all have probably been caused by climate change or the intensity of these events influenced by climate change.[327]

In 2013 the Intergovernmental Panel on Climate Change (IPCC) released its latest scientific report from Working Group I, which is said to constitute the "consensus" view on climate change.[328] The report states that the atmospheric concentrations of greenhouse gases such as carbon dioxide, methane, and nitrous oxide are at an unprecedented level compared to other times over the past 800,000 years.[329] A 5,000-year long-term cooling trend has been reversed; the period 1982-2012, for example, in the northern hemisphere was *very likely* the warmest 30 year period in the past 800 years and *likely* the warmest 30 year period for 1,400 years.[330] The average temperature for the 20th century was approximately 0.4 C higher than the average temperature of the past five centuries.[331]

From 1901 to 2012, almost the entire planet experienced warming.[332] There was a warming trend of 0.85 C for 1880 to 2012, with respect to the globally averaged combined ocean and land temperature. The total increase between the average of the 1850-1900 period and the 2003-2012 periods is 0.78 C. Most of the Earth's heating has been in the oceans; the 1971-2010 estimate of energy gain being 199×10^{12} W, equivalent to 0.42 Wm-^{2} of heating over the Earth's surface and 0.55 Wm-^{2} warming over the ocean's surface. Such warming has led to both an annual multi-year and perennial decrease in Arctic sea ice extent from 1979-2012 of about 3.5 and 4.1 percent per decade. In the period 1971-2009, the total mass loss from all glaciers (except those on the periphery of ice sheets) was very likely 226 gigatonnes/year (range, 91 to 361 gigatonnes/per year). The Greenland ice sheet has lost ice at an accelerating rate since 1992, and it is very likely that the increase is 34 (- 6 to 72) gigatonnes/per year for 1992-2001. Earthquakes of magnitude 4.6 to 5.2 have occurred in Greenland due to large icebergs breaking off from tidal glaciers, forcing the glaciers backwards. There has been an increase of seven-fold of such earthquakes since the 1990s.[333]

Most ice loss in the Antarctic ice shelf has been in the northern Antarctic Peninsula and Amundsen Sea, from the melting of outlet glaciers, with the average rate of ice loss increasing from the 1992-2001 period of 30 gigatonnes/per year to 147 gigatonnes per year in the period 2002-2011.[334] However, in 2015 sea ice in Antarctica averaged 14.93 million square kilometers, and in June 2015, this was the third-highest June extent in the records. This was thought to be due to strong atmospheric wave-3 patterns, rather than from a reversal of climate change impacts.[335]

The IPCC accepted that there had been something of a "pause" or "hiatus" in global mean surface temperatures from 1998 to 2012. As already mentioned, this "pause" has been taken by climate change skeptics as showing that global warming is not occurring or has ceased. The rate of warming from 1998 to 2012 is lower than the trend from 1951 to 2012; the 1998-2012 trend was 0.05 C (-0.05 to 0.15 C) per decade, compared to the 1951-2012 trend of 0.12 C (0.08 to 0.14 C) per decade.[336]

Even granting the reality of the "pause," the decade of the 2000s is the warmest decade in the record of global mean surface temperatures.[337] The World Meteorological Organization regarded the period 2001-2010 as the warmest since records began in 1850.[338] The World Meteorological Organization said that 2014 was tied with 2010 as the hottest year on record, with the global average temperature for January to October being 0.57 C above average, and in their January 18, 2018 statement, this claim was also revised to claim that 2016 was the warmest on record, 1.2 C above the preindustrial era.[339] Average global temperatures were the highest in 136 years in July 2015 due to the record warming of the oceans. The combined sea and land temperature in July 2015 was 16.61 C, 0.81 C above the 20th century average of 15.8 C.[340]

There is considerable scientific controversy about the cause of the "pause" and even if it really existed. The IPCC, for example, says that it is real but due to natural variability, with reduced radiative forcing because of volcanic eruptions and a less-active phase of the sun.[341] However, if a time series of unweighted 11-year average temperatures are used, with a removal of year-to-year variations caused by volcanic eruptions, a global warming trend exists.[342] The alleged "pause," based on a short time frame, may not be statistically significant.[343] Others believe that the "pause" may indicate that estimates of climate sensitivity (the equilibrium temperature in response to a doubling of CO_2) need to be revised down,[344] but many authorities disagree.[345] There is debate about the idea that the deep oceans have absorbed the "missing heat," with one research team at the Lawrence Livermore National Laboratory, claiming to have identified an "anthropogenic warming signature" in the upper (0-700 meters) of the ocean, with one-third of the accumulated heat occurring below 700 meters.[346] Evidence of an increase in the acidity of the oceans from pre-industrial times is but one argument for CO_2 being absorbed by the oceans.[347]

Scientists, including those of NOAA's Pacific Marine Environmental Laboratory, see ocean warming from climate change as "unstoppable."[348] Recent research also refutes the notion that it will take decades for the climate system to respond to an increase in CO_2 – maximum warming may occur in as little as one decade.[349] The evidence from ocean heating has led to some climate researchers, such as Kevin Trenberth of the National Center for Atmospheric Research, to believe that the "pause" is now over and that a period of rapid warming is now beginning.[350]

Victor and Kennel have proposed that the measure of global average temperature is not a good measure of climate stress.[351] It is beyond the scope of this book to evaluate this debate further, but – none of the scientists believe that global warming is not occurring. Indeed, there is a weighty opinion that the IPCC consensus on climate change is far too conservative.

In August 2008, the former chair of the IPCC Bob Watson said that the world should work on mitigation and adaption strategies for a 4 C warming, as the world has probably surpassed CO_2 limits.[352] Sea levels could rise by one meter per century, destroying land now occupied by 145 million people. Abrupt climate change, triggered by positive feedback mechanisms, such as tundra methane release, could melt the ice of Greenland and Antarctica, ultimately leading to a catastrophic sea-level rise.[353]

James Hansen (et al.) notes that ice sheets in contact with the ocean face non-linear disintegration from ocean warming, and they predict a sea-level rise of up to 3 meters by the end of the 21st century, rather than the 0.9 meters predicted by the IPCC. A sea-level rise of + 5-9 meters occurred in a prior interglacial period less than 1 C warmer than the present, and human-caused climate change forcing is greater than this.[354] Hansen (et al.) concluded that "[i]t is not difficult to imagine that conflicts arising from forced migrations and economic collapse might make the planet ungovernable, threatening the fabric of civilization."[355]

The OECD's *Environmental Outlook to 2050*, hardly a radical "green" publication, predicts that global greenhouse emissions will rise by 50 percent by 2050 on a business-as-usual scenario, and CO_2 emissions by 70 percent, leading to a rise in global average temperatures of 3-6 C by 2100.[356] These changes are likely to exceed tipping points, leading to abrupt climate change and runaway greenhouse effects. This "catastrophic climate change" will lead to 2.3 billion people facing severe water stress, and air pollution alone is likely to mean that 3.6 million premature deaths occur in China and India. A global average temperature rise of 4 C would see the "lungs of the world," the Amazon rainforest, shrinking by 85 percent, which in itself could constitute a positive feedback mechanism accelerating even further climate change.[357]

BP in its *Energy Outlook 2030*[358] predicts that by 2030 there will be 15 percent more oil, 26 percent more coal, and 46 percent more natural gas being consumed than at present, leading to 4 C warming in the 21st century. The International Energy Agency (IEA) in *Redrawing the Energy-Climate Map* (2013),[359] sees growing use of fossil fuels, such as coal, leading to global temperatures rising in this century from 3.6 C to 6 C; 3.5 C, over pre-industrial levels by 2040; 4 C by 2050 and 6 C by 2100. After 2017, (and it is now 2019), it may be impossible to reverse trends because "our energy system—power plants, the industry sector, the transport sector—will be locked into the capital investments in a way they will use fossil fuel energies."[360] The International Energy Agency believes that the development of low-carbon energy systems will be too slow to stop this extreme global warming.[361]

PricewaterhouseCoopers' report, *Too Late for Two Degrees?* (2012), doubts that warming can be held to 2 C and may reach

4 C or even 6 C. Leo Johnson says in the foreword to this report: "Even doubling our current rate of decarbonization, would still lead to emissions consistent with 6 degrees of warming by the end of this century. To give ourselves a more than 50% chance of avoiding 2 degrees will require a six-fold improvement in our rate of decarbonization."[362] The 2 C carbon budget requires world cuts in carbon intensity by 5.1 percent each year from now until 2050, but as Johnson says, this "required rate of decarbonization has not been seen in a single year since the mid-20th century when these records began."[363] Hence, it is unlikely that global warming will be limited to 2 C.[364] Climatic doomsday is inevitable.

The assessments just considered are highly pessimistic, "doomsday" of course, yet they are not from environmentalist groups, but from respectable business organizations. Those who dismiss climate change as a "conspiracy" (conservatives, many Christian groups, Big Business groups) should hesitate to do so, because the support for climate change comes from a wide range of sources, while opposition is largely from Big Business groups who have the most to lose. Cult-like Christian conservative groups, who oppose climate change because of "New World Order" concerns, are strangely silent on most other NWO-like issues that are far too difficult for their over-spiritual worldview. Don't tell anyone, but there has been a globalized world, a rule of the corporate elite, more constraining than any world government, for some time, a spawn of the liberal/conservative's cherished capitalism.

I can also mention the report by the World Bank, *Turn Down the Heat* (2012),[365] the National Research Council, *Climate and Social Stress* (2012)[366] and the National Intelligence Council, *Global Trends 2030*,[367] all of which give a much more alarming view of climate change than the more conservative IPCC. In other words, there is a weighty Establishment opinion supporting a climate disaster thesis. In general, these reports assume a "business-as-usual" approach, where fossil fuel use increases, primarily through the use of "dirty" sources such as unconventional oil and gas.

One critique of this is that such large temperature increases are unlikely as there is too little oil/fossil fuel left.[368] Thus, peak oil theorist K. Alexlett predicts a 21st-century temperature rise of 1.5 to 2 C.[369] However, even at the upper end of this prediction, extreme climate change could still occur.

The idea that peak oil will save us from climate change is wrong. There are still abundant masses of hydrocarbons, not sufficient to sustain the global consumer society for much longer, but enough to cause, if all or most are used, the worst-case climate catastrophe.[370] Carbon-based fuel, according to most authorities, will continue to meet world energy demands.[371] China is building coal-fired power plants like there is no tomorrow – because there is not likely to be. An average global temperature increase of 2 C is considered to constitute dangerous climate change where tipping points are reached, such as the complete loss of Arctic summer sea ice and the melting of the Greenland ice sheet. A 4 C change will make many already hot regions of the world simply unlivable, and lead to events such as extensive melting of the West Antarctic ice sheet and global sea-level rise of up to 5 meters. A 6 C rise will melt all polar ice[372] and could spell by itself the end of human civilization, with a massive die-off of the world's population.[373]

The other argument against the idea that peak oil will save us from climate change (even though it would itself lead to a collapse of a civilization perhaps more catastrophic in the short-term than climate change), is that positive feedback mechanisms which accelerate climate change are already beginning to act; such mechanisms include vegetation changes, ice sheet changes, ocean circulation, and biogeochemical cycling and other mechanisms.[374] For example, a study by Eric Rignot of the retreat of ice in the Amundsen Sea sector of West Antarctica has concluded that the collapse of the Western Antarctic Ice Sheet has already begun and is now "unstoppable."[375] Glacier grounding lines are retreating by kilometers each year. A sea-level rise of one meter worldwide from this will trigger the loss of the rest of the ice (over a period of two centuries) and a sea-level rise of between three and five meters.

However, there are some positive feedback mechanisms that may reduce the two-century period.

Of particular concern is the so-called "methane bomb" wherein the relatively shallow East Siberian Arctic Shelf, methane fields of an unprecedented scale have been detected, with plumes of a kilometer or wider, with a methane concentration up to 100 times higher than normal.[376]

Can technologies such as geoengineering save us? Carbon-capture and storage methods are costly and take decades to implement, and proposals such as the stratospheric injection of sulfate aerosols could lead to ozone loss and changes to rainfall patterns, particularly in Asia.[377] Rainfall in the tropics could be cut by 30 percent.[378] Kleidon and Renner, based on their climate model, have concluded that even if geoengineering succeeded in reducing surface warming, "it cannot undo differences in hydrologic cycling and convective mass exchange at the same time."[379]

Clive Hamilton is right, in my opinion in seeing climate change as signaling the end of orthodox social sciences, humanities, and philosophy, which in itself is a good thing. He quotes US climate scientist Kevin Trenberth who has said: "The answer to the oft-asked question of whether an event is caused by climate change is that it is the wrong question. All weather events are affected by climate change because the environment in which they occur is warmer and moister than it used to be."[380] The separation of the "Human" and "Nature," taken to be the defining quality of modernity, is thus an illusion Hamilton says, as climate change "shatters the self-contained world of social analysis that is the terrain of modern social science, and explains why those intellectuals who remain within it find it impossible to "analyze" the politics, sociology or philosophy of climate change in a way that is true to the science. They end up floundering in the old categories, unable to see that something epochal has occurred, a rupture on the scale of the Industrial Revolution or the emergence of civilization itself."[381]

Or, the coming collapse of civilization.

Conclusion

Guillaume Faye, in *Convergence of Catastrophes*,[382] predicts a collapse of global civilization by around 2020, which is already too late to stop, although he has probably jumped the gun slightly in the early time frame. Nevertheless, even if the evil date of collapse is a more likely 2030, societies will return to a state similar to the Middle Ages, but more destructive. This is due to converging forces of environmental destruction and climate change, global financial collapse, world pandemics, the depletion of fossil fuels, the destruction of agricultural land, the depletion of fishing resources, civilizational clashes with Islam, the aging of Western populations, terrorism and nuclear proliferation, and ultimately, nuclear war. He says:

> [...] war is coming and announcing itself with unheard-of violence: war in the streets, civil war, widespread terrorist war, a generalized conflict with Islam, and very probably, nuclear conflicts. This will probably be the face of the first half of the twenty-first century. And we have never been less prepared: invaded, devirilised, physically and morally disarmed, the prey of a culture of meaninglessness and masochistic culpability.[383]

Western societies, Faye concludes, believe in "miracles," seduced by egalitarian, humanitarian and liberal dogmas, believing that no matter what, an "invisible hand" will continue to produce harmonious equilibrium. But, there are no miracles in this cold (or, rather, hot) brutal world; hence the planet faces a series of converging ecological, economic, cultural, religious, and ethnic crises. Facing so many threats means that one or more is almost certain to nail us and polish us off.

In a nutshell, the collapse of techno-industrial civilization is inevitable. It is possible that the human race itself, if not most life on the planet, faces extinction in the more distant future, but that is less probable than the end of the world as we know it. The post-apocalyptic landscape, a world of violence, disease, bloody death, and heat (if not radioactivity) is just around the corner. What now?

5. EMBRACING SURVIVALISM

Even if a few people manage to survive worldwide population collapse, civilization will not. The complex association of cultural traits of which modern humans are so proud is a consequence of abundant resources and cannot outlive their depletion. [...] And the spiralling collapse that is far more likely, will leave, at best, a handful of survivors. [...] After a few generations, they might come to believe that the rubble amid which they live is the remains of cities built by gods.

-David Price[384]

At this crunch-point [...] Western civilization will undergo a sea change. Political correctness will finally expire. Straightforward Darwinism will replace it, with all the selfishness, corruption, dirty tricks and cheating that distinguish the genuine struggle to survive, in which the well-being of one individual or group can only be achieved by frustrating or vanquishing another individual or group. The underdog no longer attracts sympathy; he is weak, and liable to be eliminated.

-William Stanton[385]

Here I offer what I take to be the only viable response to the converging and compounding catastrophes discussed above. There are, of course, many lengthy responses that could be given, but here I will keep to basics and essentials, reducing the discourse to one discussion rather than a spiraling book. The following material is intended as only an introduction and not the last word on a vast topic, perhaps the most important topic remaining for humanity, or at least, for those remnants wanting to survive: survivalism.

The need to embrace survivalism, and hard survivalism at that, with a focus upon weaponry, will be mandatory for those who strive to survive the collapse and engage in the struggle for life in post-apocalyptic times. A "mere" economic collapse is likely to kill 25-50 million Americans in the first 90 days, from starvation, disease, and murder, and what has been presented here is a wide-ranging cascading collapse of even greater severity.[386] Of particular concern for those who choose to stay in cities will be the outbreak of disease when the shit not only hits the fan but floods into the water supply so that there will be an instant return with a vengeance of old favorite diseases such as typhoid, cholera, dysentery, cryptosporidiosis, schistosomiasis, polio, hepatitis A, from lack of sanitation.[387] Higher temperatures in some regions, if combined with wet conditions, may result in a ready over-supply of mosquitoes, carrying traditional diseases such as malaria and yellow fever, but now also, western equine encephalitis and eastern equine encephalitis, zika, chikungunya, and dengue.[388] In the sort of SHTF scenario envisaged here, cities will become fetid morgues.

Apart from the disease aspect, social breakdown, as has been argued in this book, will ring in a hyper-violent world as people revert back to the Hobbesian state of nature due to the shortage of resources.[389] Much of the prepper and survivalist literature is not geared towards such possible near-term extinction threats, often addressing economic collapse situations, rather than a systematic undermining of the biological and ecological life support systems of the planet. It may well be that there is no ultimate solution beyond escape from the planet itself, as the late Professor Stephen Hawking proposed,[390] but that is not an option for us ordinary people, even if it was technologically viable.

Thus, we are left with the survivalist/prepper material on hand to face what is coming. In this part, I will focus primarily upon the individual physical transformation needed to have a fighting chance. I am not discounting community/tribal survival strategies, but these have been discussed by others, and there is not much I can add.[391]

To get into the spirit of things, here is an inspired article for newbies to read: Daisy Luther, "Here's How You'll Die When SHTF (and How to Prevent Your Untimely Demise)."[392]

Most prepper/survivalist literature which accepts some type of catastrophic collapse, recommends a retreat away from the cities to either small country towns, or to homesteads, where families can create what Piero San Giorgio calls in his comprehensive overview book, a "Sustainable Autonomous Base,"[393] which is something of a generalization of leading US survivalist James Wesley Rawles' notion of the "American Redoubt."[394] Rawles and many others, including Boston T. Party,[395] have advocated for Americans who want to survive, moving to the mountain states of Idaho, Montana, Wyoming, East Oregon, and Eastern Washington, for both agricultural sustainability and defense. In general, this movement essentially builds on both the 1960s "back-to-the-land" and nuclear retreatism movements. The core idea is for "rootedness, autonomy, permanence," based upon water, food, hygiene and health, energy, knowledge, defense, and the social bond/community. San Giorgio's book is an outstanding introduction to people new to all of this, which I take to be who I am addressing now, since hardened survivalists would not be reading this sort of book, but prepping anyway. So, there is your first book to acquire, and the Kindle version is good and will save valuable dollars, although I hope you do support this good guy because few books in this genre offer so much. I will suggest a number of books needed as reference texts to keep for the dark times to come, but many should be read now and digested, and the vast majority can be got on the interlibrary loan systems of your countries, if like me, you are cash-challenged. In fact, this service can get overseas books, so there is no limit to knowledge acquisition by the sincere.

At the present time, it is well worthwhile spending all free time educating and training for what is to come, rather than wasting time on pointless Hollywood mind-numbing "entertainment," whatever is left during the outbreak freak-out. One subject matter to begin acquiring books and internet literature on is that of homesteading, "country wisdom" and food self-sufficiency. *Mother Earth* news and *Earth Garden* give good introductions to most topics.[396] One can then use the internet to search out further information, such as how to raise, say, meat-line chickens and protect them from predators,

95

etc. For convenience here are some books to consider looking at to get your feet moving, and I put these as in-text references for convenience: Simon Dawson, *The Self-Sufficiency Bible*, (Watkins Publishing, London, 2013); Editors of Storey Books, *Country Wisdom and Know-How: Everything You Need to Know to Live Off the Land*, (Black Dog and Leventhal Publishers, New York, 2004); Carla Emery, *The Encyclopedia of Country Living*, (Sasquatch Books, Seattle, 2012); Abigail R. Gehring (ed.), *Back to Basics: A Complete Guide to Traditional Skills*, 4th edition, (Skyhorse Publishing, New York, 2014); Abigail R. Gehring (ed.), *The Homesteading Handbook*, (Skyhorse Publishing, New York, 2011), and no such list would be satisfactory without John Seymour, *The New Complete Book of Self-Sufficiency*, (Dorling Kindersley, London, 2009), with its magnificent art work, and a foreword by *Small is Beautiful* author, E. F. Schumacher. These will serve as a good foundation for beginning survivalists to conduct their own education while the internet is up and running.

The vast majority of people are not going to have a retreat or a Sustainable Autonomous Base; indeed, people will be struggling to pay off the homes that they have, or trapped in the rent noose, made worse in the present crisis. However, that does not mean that when the time comes, it will not be possible to "bug out" to some remote locality, which you simply "settle." I am not implying taking someone's property, which is an invitation for being shot but to find suitable sustainable land, with water, where you, your family, and maybe a tribal network of families could settle. People will die of fright and commit suicide when the system collapses, so there will be some space created for those who can hang on. It is not contemplated that millions of people will even attempt to retreat, since we are supposing that the vast majority of people are going to die and rot, largely *in situ*. It is hardly unreasonable to suppose that some diehards could hold out and start anew. After all, there are cases where lone humans have been raised by wolves, as in the case of Marcos Rodríguez Pantoja, who lived alone in the Sierra Morena mountain range in southern Spain with wolves, after he was abandoned at age 7 in 1953.[397] Further, there could well be better opportunities outside your present country, if it is a shithole: Fernando Aguirre, *Bugging Out and Relocating: What to Do When Staying is Not an Option*, (2014), is a good book on this topic, clear and no bullshit.

People lacking a Sustainable Autonomous Base will need to bug out and find one, hopefully, some locality that has been found prior to collapse. Survival chances are therefore lower than if one was living in one's rural retreat, but that is just as it is going to be for most people. Hence, the issue of bugging out, Get(ting) Out of Dodge (GOOD), is going to be of vital importance for most people. That means that would-be survivors are going to need to also beef up on issues associated with bugging out. In general, the idea is to get the hell out before the shit hits the fan, and thus, hopefully, some large vehicle will be available, a van or truck, perhaps with a trailer. If one has this, then one can work out what needs to be taken, in your modern version of the pioneer's covered wagon ("prairie schooner"); if they did it, so can you, and more easily given the vast quantity of consumer goods available. To organize your stuff, it would be good to look at John Wesley Rawles' *How to Survive the End of the World as We Know It*, (Penguin, New York, 2009), which introduces the meta-organizational principle of having a list of lists. Basically, the idea is to put into what space you have, apart from spare fuel (who knows what could happen to availability), (1) weapons (firearms, ammunition, melee weapons); (2) clothing to last the years which is adequate for the weather conditions one will face, or may have to face if fleeing Mutant Zombie Bikers (e.g. both cold weather and hot weather clothes), and a supply of strong, suitable footwear to last the years; (3) water to last the trip, or at least until some can be found and water purification systems (even if just by filtering and boiling, and hence a large pot, and numerous fire starting methods from waterproof matches to flint and carbon steel strikers/magnesium fire starters, tinder (cotton balls soaked in petroleum jelly), so fire will be able to be made in the worst conditions); (4) a stockpile of long lasting food, as much as can reasonably be taken, consistent with having other essential items; (5), some sort of sleeping system, including sleeping mats, and a synthetic sleeping bag, adequate for the coldest climate you are likely to face; (6) a large supply of non-hybrid seeds of nutritious vegetables that will readily grow in the area that you are going to; (7) various hand tools for the garden, and for building a shelter, such as hand saws, that can be resharpened, at least one axe, hammers, nails, files (to sharpen blades and cutting tools) machetes and as much hardware items such as duct tape that can be reasonably packed; (8) medical and first aid supplies, especially antiseptics (Betadine, Mupirocin, band aids, bandages dressings etc., dental care products, painkillers etc.); (9) a sewing kit for clothes repair; (10) kitchen utensils, knives, forks, spoons, bowls, cups, plates, that are not breakable, cooking pot and fry pan, just to name some basic items; (11) odds and ends such as paracord, and any items that can be fitted in the remaining space that you now need to get by (non-electrical, perhaps grooming products, comb, hair cutting scissors etc.) fishing gear (assorted hooks, swivels, shot, fishing line), snares, snare wire and trapping gear, space blankets, tarps, raingear, hats, sunglasses, extra-large garbage bags, a tent, and so on, until the available space is gone.

Essentially the car evacuation scenario will encompass the standard, on-your-back bug out bag, spread over the space of the vehicle, and includes the bigger items that one could not practically be taken on one's back, or in a small cart, such as the garden tools. The articles "75 Essential Items for Bug Out Bag Packing List"[398] and "100 Items to Disappear First After the SHTF"[399] are very helpful. They should be printed off as guides. To take things even further, consult Mark Puhaly and Joel Stevens, *Everyday Survival Kits: Exactly What You Need for Constant Preparedness*, (Living Ready Books, Iola, 2014), which has an ultimate bug out bag (pp. 149-162), that could be useful for TEOTWAWKI, and John McCann, *Build the Perfect Survival Kit*, (Krause Publications, Iola, 2005), is excellent.

The situation of bugging out on foot is one of the worst-case scenarios, but it could happen, even if one leaves by vehicle. Roads could be blocked, or one may need to abandon the vehicle if attacked, taking emergency gear, prepared earlier. This scenario reduces to the backpacker's trip from hell, and it would be well worthwhile to gain backpacking knowledge before TSHTF. The unquestionably best book on this is Chris Townsend, *The Backpacker's Handbook*, 4th edition (McGraw Hill, New York, 2012). This is still the bible for backpackers and has information to prepare one for foot trips lasting months. If you cannot find a new home by then, you will probably die anyway. The book covers in detail footwear, the best types of backpacks, clothing, shelter food and water, and safety issues (e.g., wild animals).

Some notes made from Townsend's book: don't go cheap on footwear for walking, you need boots that are designed for treks, with protection of your feet and long-term comfort. Work boots and runners will not deliver over long trips. This is like tires for your car. Socks are important as well, and need to wick moisture, to prevent tinea and other foot problems; merino wool socks are good. Backpacks, if poor quality, will over a long journey of weeks, kill your back, so it is worth spending some hard-earnt dollars on getting a large heavy-duty pack, with a good fit, a frame that puts the weight on the hips, and has an overall good suspension system. I am no expert on brand choice, so consult Townsend.

For clothing, the layer system for cold weather has now become standard, rather than just one big, thick coat. In a nutshell, there is an inner layer of underwear to wick moisture (but not cotton, unless in the heat, as it will become soaked, fine merino wool is good): a thicker mid-layer for insulation, and an outer shell which is breathable, waterproof and windproof. In colder weather, probably a suitable parker is needed, along with waterproof, windproof pants. For cold weather use: wool or fur hats, with a leather or synthetic covering to deal with rain. Shelter: a lightweight tent with fabric that is both waterproof and breathable (Gore-Tex, Cuben Fiber, eVent), otherwise you will wake up at 3 a.m. with water dripping down your nose from the roof of the tent. There are other options, such as the Australian bush swag, which is a waterproof canvas sleeping "bedroll," usually insect-proof, and with a built-in foam mattress.

The swag is lightweight, but still a bit heavy for most people to take on foot. As well, one is gift-wrapped in a confined space, which may not be the best thing to do in the fields of North America, compared to the relative safety of Australia. Those going ultra-light may opt for a Bivouac bag, also waterproof and breathable. This would require a sleeping pad or air mattress or a self-inflating pad. Sleeping bags should be good quality synthetics, which usually can still keep one warm when wet (up to a point), for down bags will certainly lose their insulating qualities when wet.

It would be a good idea to take up backpacking now, before The Great Collapse, to get a taste of what life in the great outdoors is like, to experience its pitfalls. That said, though, it is one of the good things in life that should be enjoyed now before our descent into hell. Hence, one can have fun, while preparing for the collapse and Getting Out of Dodge, or wherever, whatever.

Closely associated with backpacking is wild country survival, the sort of thing which Bear Grylls and Les Stroud have made damn entertaining TV shows from. There is serious literature on these bushcraft survival skills, such as making fire, purifying water, trapping, fishing, and building shelters. This material is covered in a number of superb books, the granddaddy of them all being by former British SAS soldier, John Wiseman, *SAS Survival Handbook: The Ultimate Guide to Surviving Anywhere*, (Collins, London, 2009). This book will bring you up to speed on bushcraft survival skills, such as fire-making, and purification of water, two absolutely essential skills needed for bugging out survival. My only point of disagreement is the claim on page 49, that a normal diet includes 10 g daily of salt if I read this correctly; way too much, with the American Heart Association recommending 2.3 g a day as the limit, and 1.5 g being better.[400] Otherwise, an excellent book. Along the same lines is Chris McNab, *SAS and Elite Forces Guide: Wilderness Survival*, (Amber Books, London, 2011).

Very detailed wilderness survival essays are compiled in A. Rost, *Survival Wisdom and Know-How: Everything You Need to Know to Subsist in the Wilderness*, (Black Dog and Leventhal Publishers,

New York, 2007). With a North American focus, topics covered are food, hunting, and fishing, drinking water, fire, shelter, travel on land, travel on water, navigation, dealing with weather and climate, first aid, and much more. There is even an informative discussion of black and brown bears. Overall, 480 pages in a large format, double-column book, complete with a very good index.

There are two books taking a "minimalist" approach to survival, doing it with just the clothes on one's back and knife on one's belt. Of course, if there was a choice, no sane person would go this way, but gear can be lost or stolen, so you could wind up in this situation and thus should be ready. See Bob Holtzman, *Adventure Survival Handbook: How to Stay Alive in the Wild with Just a Blade and Your Wits*, (New Burlington Books, London, 2012) and M. Elbroch and M. Pewtherer, *Wilderness Survival: Living Off the Land with the Clothes on Your Back and Knife in Your Belt*, (Ragged Mountain/McGraw-Hill, Camden, 2006).

Obtaining safe water while traveling could be the most challenging problem, next to self-protection. Typical water sources may be highly contaminated, perhaps with floating, badly decomposed corpses. Some very good articles on water treatment are AJS, "Water Treatment Options: How to Avoid Poisoning from Toxins" Part I and Part II.[401] These articles, written by a Ph.D. scientist, are the most insightful that I have seen about the difficulty of obtaining uncontaminated water in a grid down, bug-out situation. It offers a strong case for bugging out more quickly, but as I have recognized, most people will not be able to do this. Hence, some serious research time needs to be devoted to the water purification issue.

One of the key areas that would-be survivors should start educating themselves about is survival and collapse medicine. I am well aware of the standard prepper wisdom of having a doctor, dentist, or at worse, a nurse in one's survival group, but seriously, how many people know medical professions well enough to invite them into the group, if they are interested at all? Having worked "around" the medical field, I can say that most doctors, let alone surgeons, care only for money, and at a personal level, would probably die off quickly in a grid down situation anyway. Obviously, if you have a good doctor, well, good luck to you. But most people are going to be on their own regarding health and medicine.

Thus, individuals need to take responsibility for their health immediately, not merely attempting to achieve excellent levels of fitness, with no smoking, drugs, or alcohol at all, and with the diet described in this book, but also by educating themselves about medical matters. One can start doing this by researching a particular medical problem that comes along. Practice diagnosing the problem, read up on it from reliable medical sources on the internet, such as peer-reviewed medical journals (abstracts, if not the full articles are usually available to the general public, and medical textbooks from the library (if one is still open), and have detailed knowledge before going to a GP, if one is still available. After a while, you will begin to get a feel for diagnosing your medical problems, and not get taken for a sucker.

This knowledge should be enhanced by detailed reading. The iconic beginner's text is by David Werner, *Where There is No Doctor* (2017). There are probably still old PDFs lurking on the net, but the 2017 edition is substantially updated. Along with this, dental problems are very important as well. The introductory text is Murray Dickson's *Where There is No Dentist* (2018). Again, there are older versions available as PDFs, but you need the new one, and you need a hardcopy of this. You will need to know how to pull teeth when there is no possibility of getting professional service in a SHTF/ collapse situation, not, of course, to be tried now.

In general, even if no other books recommended here are purchased (and this reading can be done using local library interlibrary loans), having hard copies of medical books could be the difference between life and death for you and your family. Speaking of families, childbirth is usually neglected by preppers, so if you plan on dipping your wick, have on hand, Susan Klein's (et al.), *A Book for Midwives* (2013). These books were all written for people in the Third World, but a collapse situation will capture those levels of poverty and degradation, and beyond, so the books will be relevant.

Regarding collapse medicine, there are numerous prepper survival medicine books on Kindle, but most of these, while having some merit, are too superficial to put much faith in. There is a free downloadable 614-page book worth printing off: *Survival and Austere Medicine: An Introduction*, 3ʳᵈ edition, (2017), by the Remote, Austere, Wilderness and Third World Medicine Discussion Board Moderators, dealing with grid-down medicine.[402] The book discusses topics not dealt with in-depth in other survival medicine books, including nursing care in a grid down situation, and dealing with the health threat of nuclear, biological and chemical warfare.

On collapse medicine, Joseph Alton and Amy Alton, *The Survival Medicine Handbook: A Guide for When Help is Not on the Way*, (Doom and Bloom, 2013), is excellent, and a paper version needs to be purchased for the medical reference library. The approach to primarily orthodox medicine, but more traditional herbal and complementary treatments are mentioned where relevant. The book has a good index, and a survivalist would do well to work through the book, using it as a basis for one's own research. This can be supplemented with information at the doom and bloom website.

Ralph La Guardia, *The Doomsday Book of Medicine: What Will You Do When There Are No Doctors or Medicine?* (Mindstir Media, New Hampshire, 2015), is a similar book to *The Survival Medicine Handbook*, but with a more complementary medical orientation, since La Guardia sees a grid down situation as leading to no doctors, and no conventional medicine. So, for example, honey might be used for wound healing. Conventional antibiotics are going to run out no matter how much is stored because they have a shelf life. Thus, research renewable medical resources, such as herbal antibiotics: see Stephen Harrod Buhner, *Herbal Antibiotics: Natural Alternatives for Treating Drug-Resistant Bacteria* (Storey Publishing, North Adams, 2012), which is extensively referenced. As well, get some good texts on herbal medicines: Alfred Vogel, *The Nature Doctor: A Manual of Traditional and Complementary Medicine* (Keats Publishing, 1991), David Hoffman, *Medical Herbalism* (Healing Arts Press, 2003), and Rosalee De La Foret, *Alchemy of Herbs* (Hay House, 2017), are good starting points. Natural news.com, also has numerous articles on this topic.

I like Gerard S. Doyle's *When There is No Doctor: Preventive and Emergency Healthcare in Challenging Times* (Process Media, Port Townsend, 2010) and James Hubbard's, *The Survival Doctor's Complete Handbook: What to Do When Help is Not on the Way* (Reader's Digest, New York, 2016), which, while not being as comprehensive as the other books listed above, do try to get you to think in a problem-solving medical diagnostic way, and getting a taste of medical methodology and thinking in a problem-solving fashion, is just as important as having a mass of medical facts at hand. Facts need to be ordered by theories to be of much use. While not collapse medicine as such, these two books are also useful: William Forgey, *Wilderness Medicine: Beyond First Aid*, 6th edition (Falcon Guides, Guilford, 2012), and Hugh Coffee, *Ditch Medicine: Advanced Field Procedures for Emergencies* (Paladin Press, Boulder, Colorado, 1993).

What about surgical procedures? The standard book cited here is *Emergency War Surgery: NATO Handbook* (Pacific Publishing, 2011), which presupposes that even in battle conditions, there will be on-going links to modern medical technology and resources. Thus, there will be a supply of inhalational anesthetic gases such as isoflurane, sevoflurane, and desflurane, which will not occur in a long-term grid-down situation. Previously used anesthetics such as halothane will ultimately suffer the same fate. There are, of course, opioids that can be used as anesthetic agents, so pain control is not hopeless. As well, maintaining surgical conditions to minimize the risk of sepsis, will be a challenge. But, the main difficulty will simply be that even the ordinary GP has limited surgical knowledge, and will only be good for relatively simple surgical procedures. The medical autodidact will probably be fine with simple things, such as wound suturing (stitches), extracting foreign objects from the skin, removal of ingrown toenails/fingernails, and activities like that. But, most surgery that is taken for granted now, such as precision eye surgery (e.g., pterygium excision with conjunctival autograph), will be beyond the capabilities of all but qualified surgeons. As for heart surgery, brain surgery, and transplants, forget it; if you need this in a long-term grid-down scenario, kiss your ass goodbye. Accept the inevitability of death.

It would be wise to get whatever surgery you have been putting off (e.g., say a carpal tunnel nerve release operation) done before it all falls apart. That goes for things like wisdom teeth, which usually cause problems at some point. You do not want to have someone try and pull these out, which will be like having your throat pulled out via your mouth. Getting all dental problems fixed now, practicing sound dental care, with a diet free of cane sugar, maybe the wisest thing you can do in preparation for the end. Toothache will come back to haunt the remnant as a true curse of mankind. Don't be afraid of having any problematic teeth removed, for it is better that a dentist does it safely now than Aunt Gertrude with her trusty, rusty pliers. Trust me; you do not need too many teeth to get by. And, go for extraction over root canal treatments for reasons detailed here.[403]

The Philosophy of Survivalism

Many people have expressed opposition to survivalist ideas and its core philosophy, even while accepting that a collapse of techno-industrial civilization is coming. American ecological writer and former Grand Archdruid of the Ancient Order of Druids in America, John Michael Greer, has been critical of survivalism in his books *The Long Descent: A User's Guide to the End of the Industrial Age*[404] and *The Ecotechnic Future: Envisioning a Post-Peak World*[405] and other writings. As a caveat, Greer's more recent book *Dark Age America*[406] is more along the lines of this present work being more pessimistic than his previous works in this genre.

Greer starts from the plausible enough position that at this point, "it's almost certainly too late to manage a transition to sustainability on a global or national scale, even if the political will to attempt it existed – which clearly it does not." Consequently, "we are headed at a breakneck pace toward a future of narrowing options, dwindling resources, and faltering technology." For Greer, there will be no crash or a massive catastrophe, but rather a gradual process of decline, a "slide down statistical curves that will ease modern industrial civilization into history's dumpster." This process of decline and fall will take between one to three centuries and end in a Dark Age.

The West will be subject to epic migrations (or invasions) as the industrial age ends and military forces dependent on fossil fuels, fail. Mexicans will pour across the border faster than they do today, transferring the United States into "something else," i.e., greater Mexico. Mass migration of Asians will occur by sea and will result in the English language itself "only [being]spoken in a few enclaves in the Pacific Northwest." Millions of Indonesians and other Asians will land off the coast of Northern Australia and swamp Australia. He could be describing the world now, especially the present refugee deluge upon Northern Europe, and here in the US.

The *Mad Max/Road Warrior* society scenario is dismissed by Greer, even though the very thesis of *The Long Descent* is that in the long march to a Dark Age, most of the technology and knowledge of today will be lost. But, he also inconsistently says that even if a mass die-off of humanity occurred, the survivors could still use today's culture and resource base, and before long, the internet would be working! He also says: "Everyone alive after the collapse would have grown up in the pre-collapse world and learned the skills needed to operate a modern society." This is certainly wrong because a society of the technical sophistication and complexity of ours requires millions of specialized technicians to function, and after the death of these technicians, society grinds to a halt, as has been said previously. Most people lack the skills and know-how to be able to repair even relatively simple electronic or mechanical devices or even light a fire using only sticks.[407]

Greer has a comic book view of survivalists as generally lone madmen hiding in a cabin in the woods with stockpiles of food and firearms, while the outside world burns. This is the same view held by the founder of the transition town initiative, Rob Hopkins, who believes that cities such as the mega-developed Sunshine Coast, Queensland, can make a transition away from fossil fuel use and become sustainable ecocities.[408] No, they are not pulling our greens. Greer criticizes survivalists for believing in the myth of apocalypse, but the real myth-makers are those who believe such communitarian/ socialist fairy tales. A few people planting "community gardens" and holding hands and chanting, or praying, does not a revolution make. Nevertheless, the opposition to survivalism is made clear by Hopkins in his article "Why the Survivalists Have Got it Wrong,"[409] which makes the misguided critique that survivalists seek to live in isolation while, "peak oil and climate change, and the challenge that they present, are a call to return to society" and that most beloved of entities, "community." All of this assumes, of course, that a *Mad Max/ Road Warrior* die-off situation will not occur, and that a rapid collapse is not going to happen, assumptions which we have seen are questionable.

Greer also makes specific and weak criticisms of survivalism: "Isolated survivalist enclaves with stockpiles of food and ammunition would be a tempting prize and could count on being targeted" by roaming brigands. That, of course, is if they find them. Perhaps the attention of these roaming gangs will be taken up targeting the green socialist "communities" who have plenty of food, but no guns and no will to resist. *The Walking Dead* TV series gives good examples of this, especially Alexandria. To this challenge, it could be said: "However, many you kill, there will always be more – and eventually, your ammo will run out." All the more need for truly massive stockpiles of guns and ammo and the use of melee weapons, going medieval, using weapons that won't run out, as will be discussed later in book 2. Call it "sustainability."

Hopkins says that survivalism is a distinctly anti-social and irresponsible creed. However, the survivalist movement has never strictly been about *lone* people or even *isolated* families preparing for disaster in all its forms and retreating to safer ground.[410] Safety in numbers, as far as that is possible, is accepted by survivalists. Survivalists, though, by contrast to back-to-the-landers, (deep) ecologists, and preparedness retreaters, are robust and rugged individualists who are ready, willing, and able to go it alone if necessary, come what may, even if the sewers of hell are opened and flood the earth. The spirit of self-reliance, self-sufficiency, independence, and overall toughness is repugnant to many. Survivalism is about raising a defiant "rude finger" up to the Establishment's modernist way of life, that of urban helplessness and dependence upon the crusty teat of Big Sister, the modern boss of Big Brother, in our estrogenic welfare-based society.

Kurt Saxon, who coined the term *survivalist*,[411] also notes that survivalists, generally unlike back-to-the-landers, (deep) ecologists and preparedness retreaters, are ready, willing, and able to fight if necessary, because self-protection is taken to be a primary component of self-reliance.[412] Kurt Saxon was not anti-community by the way; because of insurmountable problems of the future survival in cities, he thought that the most reasonable survival strategy was for people wanting to live, to get out of the cities and head to small rural towns and "become part of the community."[413]

Rawlesian survivalists, followers of the survival philosophy of James Wesley, (comma intentional) Rawles,[414] although also concerned with self-defense, believe that survivalists by stockpiling resources are in a position during a crisis to dispense charity to people in need; hardly an anti-social and irresponsible creed, contrary to Hopkins. Rawles sees it as practical Christianity in action. My view of Christianity is detailed elsewhere; I regard it as a form of metaphysical brain cancer, and it has no monopoly on kindness and charity.

In a debate/dialogue with Richard Heinberg, Hopkins was asked whether a focus on emergency planning should be made just in case dire things happen during the "transition."[415] Hopkins' response was that "in terms of visioning, there isn't a positive potential outcome to use to inspire and engage people. Transition is very deliberately designed to be non-threatening, to be inviting and engaging."[416] A vision of collapse preparations could make the movement look like a "survivalist cult" – a politically incorrect fate-worse-than-death.

However, just when it seems that all hope is lost, Hopkins says that there is merit in putting together bushcraft training, bioregional studies, bio-intensive horticulture, traditional allotment gardening, and emergency response organization.[417] Even in terms of "positive thinking," as Peter Sandman has said, it is calming for people to prepare, giving a sense of control, which builds confidence and hopefully gives a greater capacity to cope with fear.[418]

Chris Martenson in *The Crash Course*, argues that personal preparation is not selfish because it is one less person drawing on community resources, so putting one's survival affairs in order, is the best thing an individual can do for the community: "If you do, you'll have a stable foundation to utilize, and you'll be in a better position to add valuable resources and skills to community efforts. A strong community begins with strong household."[419]

Surviving the Coming Collapse of Civilization

Apart from a number of excellent books dealing explicitly with the zombie apocalypse,[420] where zombies are conceived as the living/ walking dead, little has been written about surviving the coming collapse of civilization, the multi-generational scenario. Most cinematic treatments of this are worse than useless unless these items are viewed as catalogs of mistakes, as, for example, *The Walking Dead* and *Fear the Walking Dead*, are.

Christ Lisle, a former US Army Ranger in an often-cited online article "Prepare for Peak Oil on a Budget,"[421] saw peak oil leading to billions of people dying and leaving large quantities of stuff behind. He adopted a minimalist approach and recommended not buying survival items (bar one item), but that one should "pick up off the ground when others leave it behind." For many lacking wilderness survival skills, such a minimalist approach could guarantee a place among the billions dying. Nevertheless, Lisle recommends purchasing a high-quality synthetic (not down) sleeping bag, rated down to -20 C. The synthetic bag, unlike the down, can still keep you warm when wet, and is a "mobile shelter." Lisle said: "I've slept comfortably in the snowy Italian Alps and Alaska with no fire, no tent, and no ground pad – all I had was a good sleeping bag. I've spent many nights outside, and I am here to say that a good sleeping bag can keep you cozy warm in any climate under any conditions, be it rain, sleet or snow." Well, maybe, but a tarp, groundsheet, and tent/swag would be an improvement – and why not treat yourself, for this is TEOTWAWKI! Put a good synthetic sleeping bag on the shopping list, and if you haven't got one, get one soon. Or buy two.

James Ballou's *Long-Term Survival in the Coming Dark Age*[422] is an excellent introduction to new Dark Age collapseology. The foreword is by Ragnar Benson, a leading survivalist author. Neither Ballou nor Benson speculates about the most likely cause of The Great Collapse, and the book plunges straight into strategies and tactics for long-term survival. Long-term survival differs from shorter-term disaster preparedness insofar as there is going to be nobody coming to rescue you because there is *no rescue*. All has been lost. Cites will become "violent slum areas for the most part plagued with disease,"[423] as with no government and no government support services, human waste, and human violence will not be contained. Hence, there is a need to retreat/bug out from cities to rural areas, and ultimately live much simpler lives, with tribal living for protection. There will be stalking, killing, and butchering game (what is left) for meat, along with gathering wild foods, with horticulture and agriculture, the main food sources. Until, or while, such practices are being put in place, short-term survival will be by drawing on food stockpiles accumulated before the Great Collapse.

Ballou's book discusses bugging out (also discussed below[424]), but the most important sections of the book deal with life in the post-collapse world. Pre-collapse, there is an urgent need for people to acquire extensive self-defense skills (with firearms and other weapons) as well as practical skills, e.g., medicine over arts, blacksmithing over the humanities, mathematics and philosophy, woodworking skills over the law. The world of paper and computer work, the world of talking, chattering, and whinging, will be replaced by a practical, hands-on, can-do world – or death. A survival workshop, using hand tools as was done in the 19th century, needs to be established at one's retreat, and I will discuss the issue of tools later in this chapter.[425] Survivors will recycle and salvage everything because as Chris Lisle noted, the great die-off of the bulk of humanity will leave mountains of resources (e.g., scrap metal, timber, and other materials) that can be used by salvaging parties, once the formerly-populated areas are no longer a disease and security threat. Nevertheless, consumer society itself supplies many useful items that people throw away each day, such as containers to use for storage during the Dark Age. Rubbish dumps are a source for scrap timber and building materials that can be scavenged from the trash.[426] Indeed – on "hard rubbish days," consumers throw out great treasures for scroungers, such as old tools and scrap material that could be used for clothing. And, taking clothing as an example, in the "short-term," for about 50 years, I estimate, stockpiled clothing and clothes made from stored cloth and scavenged materials will sustain the survivors, but in the longer-term clothes and footwear will need to be made first hand from fibers, animal hides, and leather.

Ballou's *Long-Term Survival in the Coming Dark Age*, and related books, are a useful starting point for one's survival framework of knowledge. I suggest that it can be supplemented by further books and information organized under the following topics:

1. Bug out and survival retreats.

2. Wilderness and backwoods survival philosophy.

3. Disaster preparedness philosophy.

4. Self-reliance and self-sufficiency philosophy.

5. Tools and the craftsman.

Bug Out and Survival Retreats

Although some survivalists believe that urban survival is possible in situations of much less severity than a collapse, in general, survivalists such as Ragnar Benson, Bruce D. Clayton, Jeff Cooper, Cresson Kearny, James Wesley Rawles, Kurt Saxon, Joel Skousen, and Mel Tappan, have favored bug-out locations (BOLs) or survival retreats.[427]

Piero San Giorgio in *Survive the Economic Collapse*[428] writes of the need to find a "Sustainable Autonomous Base" (SAB), a "secure space" with "rootedness, autonomy, permanence," "where one cannot merely survive, but hopefully thrive, living perhaps more simply, but well."[429] SAB is based on seven fundamental principles discussed in their own chapters in his book and are (1) water; (2) food; (3) hygiene and health; (4) energy: (5) knowledge; (6) defense and (7) the social band, creating a tribe (a genuine "community" rather than a socialist hippy commune) for genetic and socio-cultural reproduction. Some of the basic aspects of the SAB will be discussed in this chapter and in this book.

Mel Tappan in *Tappan on Survival*[430] argued that population density is a major factor in choosing a retreat because retreats less than a tank of gas away from population centers face the real risk of being overrun by systems-dependent people. Apart from the problems of hungry mobs and roaming bands of looters, there is the problem of disease. Tappan listed other factors affecting retreat locations, such as whether nuclear power plants are in the vicinity (in case they are abandoned and not shut down and go into meltdown). Locating near military bases or National Guard armories may prove problematic, in case the troops ultimately decide to be the new warlords in a collapse, or maybe worse, they desert to be with their families leaving the ghouls and associated scum to feast on highly destructive weapons that will ultimately be unleashed against you.

Nuclear war targets are also another matter of concern. Radiation fallout patterns need to be considered. The site also needs to be farmable with good soil and water, and ideally hunting, trapping and or fishing should be available. It is a matter though of trade-offs and balancing factors in decision making, and single-family retreats were not regarded by Tappan as desirable given that if the retreats are found by looters, the superior force will win. Thus, he believed that long-term survival in a post-collapse world, especially in the light of the problem of facing organized gangs of vicious looters, murders, rapists, and cannibals—MZBs—would come from living in a small rural community up to about a population of 5,000 people, engaged primarily in agriculture, not industry.

Tappan felt, and I agree with him, that many people think that they can live, say, in a city and work, and when really stinky, lumpy excreta hits the fan, bug out to their retreat, just in the nick of time. The series *Doomsday Preppers* was full of these feet-in-both-camps bug-out types. He said that there might be no clear warning at all and unless one is already living at one's retreat, the odds are that one will never reach it. Living in such a "community" (that word again) has clear advantages over bug out options such as a boat or mobile land retreats or isolated wilderness retreats, insofar as it is no longer necessary to guess correctly when the collapse will occur (the timing-problem) and it avoids the problems and dangers of bugging out travel, e.g., safely getting to your retreat through the "zombies." It also means that there is adequate time to prepare for the post-collapse world, stockpiling food, clothing, tools, seeds, firearms, ammunition, bladed and bludgeon melee weapons, and other supplies. There is time to settle into the "community," and perhaps when confidences and trust are reached, begin preparing defenses ready for when TSHTF.

It takes considerable time to convert an existing farm into a self-reliant post-apocalypse retreat, so having as much lead time as possible before the end is important. For example, it may take a number of years to get fruit trees and crops established. The last thing that a survivalist wants is to be in a post-apocalyptic situation and find crop failure (because of pests, diseases, or personal incompetence), or find that soils are lacking in fertility.

Fernando "Ferfal" Aguirre, in his excellent book *The Modern Survival Manual*,[431] has presented a survival treatise based on his first-hand experience of living through the 2001 economic collapse in Argentina. He differs from survivalists such as Tappan and Saxon in being critical of the approach of retreating to the countryside.[432] Aguirre argues against this based on surviving Argentina's economic collapse. He sees governments surviving and coming to the countryside to confiscate food. As well, most people can't bug out and live off the land given large population numbers, so they will stay in cities. A similar position has been taken by "Survival Mom."[433] And isn't "Mom" always right? Well, no.

To this much can be said in reply, due respect to motherhood and all that. It is true that governments may survive a partial economic collapse as Argentina periodically has done, but a complete collapse where the army and police do not get paid and hence desert their posts is one where the government *does not survive*. Further, there is no reason why, if a government survives, it won't confiscate food from people *in* the city: it has and will, with the disintegrated US Army becoming a barbarian gang essentially. Further, as described in *The Modern Survival Manual*, cities become highly dangerous places during an economic collapse, with gangs conducting block-by-block home invasions, and although violent crime in the US had gone down in the past few years, 2020 has seen a surge of homicides in several US cities, with some cities' homicide rates, such as Baltimore's, "exploding."[434]

Thus, almost everywhere becomes dangerous in a collapse, but the larger number of people in the city makes the probability of attack greater than in the country. Those considerations are based solely on an economic collapse scenario, and consideration of pandemic disease spread makes a general case against city-based survivalism, although, of course, circumstances could dictate otherwise if terrorists decided to attack rural areas first. The terrorist group Boko Haram, for example, has attacked rural targets in Nigeria, (killing 86 people in late January 2016, with children being burnt alive), but most of its attention has been on city targets, such as with its bombing of the United Nations office in Abuja. Ferfal, in his book, does not consider the possibility of a more general collapse involving ecological variables, as discussed here and in Piero San Giorgio's equally as admirable treatise *Survive the Economic Collapse.*

While Ferfal is critical of "off-grid," presumably isolationist survivalism, he does say: "I recommend basically what I later learned Mel Tappan recommended as well: live in a small town or community. This community or subdivision should be close enough to a moderately-sized city with enough job opportunities, education, and entertainment."[435]

However, there can be a case made even for isolationist survivalism in the classic lone family/tribe or even individual sense. A global pandemic, a "zombie apocalypse" disease of a flu with high mortality, will spread quickly in a large city where people live like hens in a chicken coop. A small town could more easily practice quarantine, and an isolated doomster essentially exists in perpetual quarantine. Consequently, context decides everything; in some desperate survival situations, there is merit even in an isolationist approach. Certainly, in a classic *The Walking Dead* zombie apocalypse, where even in a small town an infection could occur, isolation, like silence, would be golden.[436] And it can be done — Soichi Yokio, a Japanese WW II soldier who refused to surrender after the end of the war, lived in a cave in the jungles of Guam from 1945-1972—alone, and with much fewer resources than we have.[437]

There is a large quantity of literature available about bug-out locations for the United States, Canada, Europe, New Zealand, and Australia, but relatively less for Asia and South America.[438] Joel M. Skousen has published respected books in this field, including *Strategic Relocation: North American Guide to Safe Places,*[439] which in its third edition gives a comprehensive guide to the threats that North Americans and Canadians face, from economic collapse to nuclear war, with associated strategic analyses. For example, there are considerations of the most dangerous areas for earthquakes, the top ten most economical US states to live in, and states with no sales tax, and so on. Skousen also offers, I believe, paid consultation for those seeking special contingency retreat plans.[440] Joel Skousen has also published *The Secure Home*,[441] which tells you how to construct high security, fortified retreats, both in terms of construction of such retreats as well as remodeling existing retreats. He has also produced Special Reports, such as *How to Implement High Security Shelter in the Home* (1996)[442] and *How to Fortify a Closet*, for those on a budget who cannot afford to build a vault room.

James Wesley, Rawles has published the excellent *Rawles on Retreats and Relocation*,[443] and there is some discussion of retreatism in his survivalist novel, *Patriots: A Novel of Survival in the Coming Collapse*,[444] although a more detailed discussion is given on the fortification of retreats, reinforcing houses, constructing anti-vehicular ditches, obstacles, and so on. (Of course, the ballistically-protected house can also integrate a fallout shelter as well.) Rawles' Survival Blog.com has a superb discussion of recommended retreat areas in North America, favoring Idaho, Montana, Oregon, Washington, and Wyoming, as the top five US retreat states, and Kalifornication as the worst. Interestingly enough, Alaska is not an ideal retreat location because although it is the US state with the lowest population density, it has the second-highest crime rate of the US states per capita, and most goods, even food, are transported in. Those most likely to survive are seasoned backwoodsmen and native tribal folk having outdoor skills and able to live self-sufficiently, from hunting and fishing. Much of the land is covered with ice and snow at least half of the year. By contrast, California has a mild climate and long growing seasons, but an appalling socio-political climate and draconian gun control laws, and most other factors that will make, post-collapse, California the zombie apocalypse capital of America. One contributor to SurvivalBlog.com's discussion of retreat areas said that when TSHTF in California, "it will make Katrina's aftermath look like a kindergarten dance."[445]

By way of summary: there is no easy answer to the question of where do you go, if anywhere, when TSHTF. Beyond generalizations, such as leaving large population centers, each person will need to make informed decisions on the basis of their own personal circumstances and what resources are available. It, therefore, may not be possible to follow Tappan's advice and move to an ideal location now. In Australia, there may be no ideal location at all; properties meeting the standard conditions of being an ideal survival retreat in the sense of having adequate water and good soils, could still be overrun in a type of "condition 4" doomsday zombie apocalypse (with either Hollywood zombies or your unfriendly neighborhood types).[446] Bugging out, getting out of Dodge, always needs to be considered as a Plan B option.

A good place for beginning survivalists to start in exploring the theory and practice of bugging out is Scott B. Williams' *Bug Out: The Complete Plan for Escaping a Catastrophic Disaster Before It's Too Late* (2010).[447] Williams is not primarily concerned with the situation of the "lost hiker" (although the advice in his book would clearly help such a person), but rather with shit hitting the fan and TEOTWAWKI scenarios. Fixed position survivalism is not pursued, as most people lack the financial resources to invest in a retreat, he argues. But even so, for a collapse of civilization scenario, ultimately, one will need to find such a retreat to grow food. Owning the land is now ideal but not essential, in my opinion, given the coming high mortality rates. One could attempt to bug out to that location post-apocalypse after the death of the masses. Williams is right in saying that there are dangers in putting all of one's resources in one location because of the difficulty in hiding and defending stockpiles. Agreed: but there will be clear limits in stockpiling resources, which will be bugged out as well. What one needs, if at all possible, is a pluralistic response: a fixed, defensible position as Tappan advocated, plus resources cached securely, safely and sustainably underground, as well as putting into place a bug-out procedure to deal with the worst-case scenario: that is, fleeing your retreat post-collapse. Williams rightly notes that there is enough land in the US for survivalists to bug out and thrive, but not for the entire US population. But, most people are not survival-minded and will wait for Big Sister Government to save them. They will die and rot, producing epidemic disease in the cities.

Williams gives a comprehensive discussion of bug-out locations right across our great and wonderful United States, and in my opinion, the material is accurate. Certainly, any serious US survivalist should study this material and make up his/her own mind.[448] Williams, for example, gives a very comprehensive outline of the bugout bag, which covers the major survival bases of clothing, shelter and fire, food and water, hunting and fishing, and tools. By way of summary, the *bug-out bag and clothing* comprise an internal frame backpack, fanny pack; lightweight mesh bag; leather and Gore-Tex waterproof hiking boots to wear; river shoes; moisture-wicking socks and outer wool socks; wool cap; Tilley sun hat; three bandanas; pants; long underwear; Gore-Tex rain pants; heavy-duty belt, two T-shirts; long underwear shirt; polar fleece long sleeve; Gore-Tex parka; gloves and cammo poncho. For specific survival categories:

Shelter and Fire: camping hammock; paracord; synthetic sleeping bag; disposable butane lighters; Fire Steel Scout x2; fire sticks; cotton balls soaked in Vaseline for tinder.

Food and Water: three-day supply of lifeboat rations or MREs; trail mix; protein bars/power bars; beef jerky; bag of oatmeal; seasonings; water bottles; Polar Pure water disinfectant; filter straws.

Hunting and Fishing: takedown .22 rifle; 200 rounds .22 LR ammo; .357 magnum revolver + holster + speed loaders + 100 rounds ammo; .357 lever action rifle; fishhooks and fishing line; spool of line for drop hooks; wire shares for small game.

Tools: machete with sheath; Bowie knife; multitool; small mill file; diamond sharpener; hand-bearing compass; GPS; cooking pot; stainless-steel spoon; sewing needles [and thread].

Miscellaneous Items: include maps, insect repellent; 50+ sunblock; sunglasses and case; sailmaker's thread and needles; first-aid supplies; extractor snakebite kit; cortisone cream; Benadryl; EpiPen; Imodium; ibuprofen; field guide to edible plants in region; passport/driver's license; cash, gold, and silver coins; tooth care (tooth-brush, toothpaste/salt, dental floss), toilet paper; comb; LED torch; duct tape; gun oil; gun-cleaning tool. William also lists a number of optional items (e.g., water purification filter and reverse-osmosis desalinator).

Along with Williams' book, Fernando "Ferfal" Aguirre has produced another extremely good book which is well worth consulting: *Bugging Out and Relocating: What to Do When Staying in Not an Option.*[449] This book is a comprehensive overview of all of the main aspects of bugging out and relocating and has a sensible and balanced view of the relative advantages and disadvantages of overseas locations for relocation. The author has relocated to Ireland from Argentina (and then to Spain) because of the violence and poor quality of life in Argentina.

For my generalist purposes, the most relevant part of the bug out literature book is the discussion of the bug out bag, which one will need wherever one goes. All survivalists in the know recommend that people not buy generic survival kits but tailor a survival kit to suit their personal circumstances.[450] All items should be essential, durable, and dependable, because whether the bugging out is by foot, horse or a vehicle, space and weight are principal concerns. For example, there is no point taking with one in emergency situations, survival and preparedness books. This material *must be* absorbed into your very being long before the collapse. It is what you should be doing now. It would be insane to suppose that say, one will begin to learn how to light a campfire without matches, fire starters, or any modern technology, by consulting a wilderness survival book when the time comes. Hello hyperthermia. No doubt, pages of the book would be useful for fire-starting purposes, and specialist books, such as an illustrated guide to a region's edible plants, are an exception and could be taken.

The bug out bag should be rugged and easy to carry long distances – hence a backpack big enough to take "everything." And what is "everything"? Cody Lundin, an American teacher of aboriginal survival skills, says that the bug out bag or survival kit "is a distillation of the most simple and effective means of staying alive. It's your lifeline in terms of need, the components within possibly being your only chance of living through your present crisis."[451] The bug out bag should, therefore, address fundamental human needs: (1) *shelter,* including clothing; (2) *water* and the means of purifying water; (3)

the technology for making *fire*; (4) *food* and items for *cooking* it (e.g., a cast iron cooking pot, a plate, cups, and utensils); (5) *clothing* to deal with a range of environments; (6) a *sleeping* system including perhaps a swag (eliminating the need for a tent) and definitely a good synthetic sleeping bag; (7) *health, medical and hygiene* beginning with a basic first aid kit and hygiene (e.g., toothpaste or even salt, toothbrushes and dental floss); (8) *basic tools*, beginning with a knife at a minimum and arguably including much more such as paracord, duct tape, and a machete/hatchet and/or saw and (9) *weapons and security*, firearm(s), and a bladed weapon. All of the specific items are subject to debate because individual circumstances, climate, and environmental resources vary. Nevertheless, the correct approach to take to prepare a bug-out/ survival kit is to address the areas of fundamental human need: without backup, what do *you* need to survive *your environment*?

There are many excellent books which give insightful "shopping list" approaches to preparing a bug out bag, rather than starting with a general human needs approach. The authors of these books have already done the hard thinking for you. I would suggest that people who, for one reason or another, do not want to think all of this through from first principles consult these texts and make up their own "shopping list" by process of mixing and matching.

To begin, former lightweight champion of Ultimate Fighting Championship (UFC), Forrest Griffin (with Erich Krauss) in *Be Ready When Shit Goes Down*,[452] a joyful masculine book of ribald humor and absurdity, presents a sound, but basic bug out bag of (1) canned food (could be a possible weight issue for loner treks); (2) tent; (3) sleeping bag (rated to minus 20 C) and wool blankets (wool retains heat when wet); (4) a propane stove; (5) guns (a semi-auto rifle or a pump-action shotgun); (6) machetes; (7) books on native plants; (8) first aid kit; (9) pick and shovel (presumably a small army folding version); (10) axe; (11) fishing line/gear; (12) boots.[453] Forrest has a "go pack" for getting out quick, consisting of (1) pistol; (2) ammo for said pistol (50 rounds); (3) multitool; (4) Meals Ready to Eat (MREs) (three per day plus some spares); (5) peanut butter (an excellent, sustaining survival food); (6) water; (7) water purifier; (8) map of bug out area; (9) compass; (10) waterproof matches; (11) goggles; (12) gloves; (13) wool socks; (14) boots; (15) wool blanket; (16) flashlight and (17) toothpaste (brush and dental floss).[454] This is the tough approach to the apocalypse: grab the basics and piss-off fast. I would add that a good manual can opener should be in every bug out bag even if you don't take any canned food. You may get lucky and find the odd unopened can of baked beans, clutched in the hands of a decaying corpse. As well, for both sunny and snowy environments, good sunglasses should be added but occur on a few survival lists. They should, because, in some environments, glare will make your eyes feel like they are popping out of your head. A pair of strong leatherwork gloves could also prove useful to minimize cuts to one's hands and possible infections.

Along the same lines, this time from Australia, we have bushman Bob Cooper, who, in his distinctly Aussie approach to survival *Outback Survival*,[455] has put together a survival kit light enough that you actually take it with you wherever you go. The dimensions are 13 x 8 x 5 cms, allowing for the addition of a basic medical kit comprising: antibiotics, diarrhea tablets, anti-nausea tablets, antihistamines, ear/eye ointment, and any personal medications.[456] Bob's Mark-III survival kit, which has saved his hide in the tough Aussie outback is: (1) plastic container; (2) compass; (3) flint and striker; (4) hacksaw blade; (5) cotton pad (first-aid, tinder); (6) whistle; (7) knife; (8) mirror; (9) tweezers; (10) large plastic bags (for obtaining water); (11) needle; (12) fishing line; (13) fishing hooks; (14) brass swivel (stop fishing line twisting); (15) sinkers; (16) trace wire; (17) stock cubes (soup and fishing lure); (18) paracord; (19) tea bags; (20) coffee; (21) glucose tablets; (22) water purifying tablets; (23) Condy's crystals (potassium permanganate, antiseptic, antifungal, fire-making); (24) plasters; (25) scalpel blade; (26) sewing kit (clothes repairs) (27) alcohol swabs; (28) antiseptic wipes; (29) magnifying glass; (30) torch; (31) multitool; (32) playing cards (amusement); (33) pencil; (34) instruction sheet.[457] Note that toilet paper is not on the list – Forrest and Bob are so tough that they don't need it! Toilet paper takes up a lot of space and will quickly run out. In the longer term, post-apocalyptic bum cleaning will be done as people did before toilet paper, using either a cloth and water or one's hand and water. You, too, will get used to it.[458]

Les Stroud in *Survive!*[459] states that one should have for survival situations a personal survival kit carried with you at all times, on your person, so that it is not separated from you or lost, as well as a complete survival kit. The personal survival kit comprises; a sharp belt knife; bandana; small LED flashlight; two large garbage bags; a butane lighter; strike-anywhere matches in a waterproof case; a magnesium flint striker; metal cup; multitool and/or a Swiss Army knife; painkillers; parachute cord; protein bar/snack bar; space blanket and a Ziploc bag.[460] The complete survival kit comprises a sharpening stone for the knife; a candle; dried food; duct tape ("can repair just about any outdoor equipment); fire-starting devices and tinder; fishing lures, hooks, sinkers, a leader and fishing line; flares; small LED flashlight; GPS; map; compass; garbage bags; small hand lens; marker tape (bright colors); money; multitool; needle and thread; Personal Locator Beacon (PLB); Emergency Position Indicating Radio Beacon (EPIRB); parachute cord; pencil and notebook; safety pins; folding saw; signal mirror; snare wire; space blanket; SPOT satellite messenger; water purification tablets; water purifying straw; whistle and Ziploc bags.[461] A basic first aid kit includes antidiarrheal tablets, pain killers; antihistamines; bandages; antiseptic ointment; butterfly sutures, any prescription medicine, surgical blades, and triangle bandages. Stroud does not mention dental gear (toothbrush, toothpaste/salt, dental floss), all of which could be improvised, but the thought of toothache in the field justifies the inclusion of a dental kit, especially toothache drops. In summary, Stroud presents an excellent selection of survival items, as one would expect from a leading wildness survival expert.

The US army has survival kits for cold climates, hot climates, and over water.[462] The basic items are as follows.

1. *Cold Climate Kit* – food packets; snare wire; smoke illumination signals; waterproof matchbox; saw/knife blade; wood matches; first-aid kit; MC-1 magnetic compass; pocket knife; saw-knife-shovel handle; frying pan; illuminating candles; compressed trioxane fuel; signaling mirror; survival fishing kit; plastic spoon (metal would be better); *Survival Manual (AFM 64-5)*; poncho; insect head net; ejector snap; attaching snap; kit, outer case; kit, inner case; shovel; water bag; packing list; sleeping bag.

2. *Hot Climate Kit* – canned drinking water; waterproof matches; plastic whistle; smoke illumination signals; pocket knife; signaling mirror; plastic spoon; food packets; compressed trioxane fuel; fishing tackle kit; MC-1 magnetic compass; snare wire; frying pan; wood matches; insect head net; reversible sun hat; tool kit; kit; packing list; tarpaulin; *Survival Manual (AFM 64-5)*; kit, inner case; kit, outer case; attaching strap; ejector snap.

3. *Overwater Kit* – packing list; raft boat paddle; *Survival Manual (AFM 64-5)*; insect head net; reversible sun hat; water storage bag; MC-1 magnetic compass; boat bailer; sponge; sunburn-preventive cream; wood matches; first-aid kit; plastic spoon; pocket knife; food packets; fluorescent sea marker; frying pan; seawater desalter kit; compressed trioxane fuel; smoke, illumination signals; signaling mirror; fishing tackle kit; waterproof matchbox; raft repair kit.

Items in the various medical packets include a surgical razor, tweezers, insect repellent, sunscreen lotion, soap, surgical adhesive tape, aspirin tablets, adhesive bandage, gauze, elastic bandage, diphenoxylate hydrochloride, atropine sulfate tablets, sulfacetamide sodium ophthalmic ointment, and iodine water purification tablets.

Zombie apocalypse writers have also put together some good, basic survival packs. F. Kim O Neill, in *The Ultimate Guide to Surviving a Zombie Apocalypse*,[463] has the following zombie bug out bag: (1) maps and compass; (2) a gun and at least 100 rounds of ammo, magazines and maybe a cleaning kit; (3) multitool; (4) utility knife; (5) short sword-kukri or sheathed gladius; (6) flashlight, batteries and spare bulbs; (7) food rations; (8) small quantity of water (weight problem) plus water purification tablets; (9) fire-making gear; (10) first-aid kit; (11) warm clothes; (12) space blanket; (13) rope/paracord; (14) radio; (15) personal hygiene kit (sunblock, toothpaste, dental floss, towel); (16) shovel and for zom poc, armor such as gauntlets.[464] If the zom poc is a metaphor for pandemic disease, this could be useful.

A similar sound list is given by Michael Thomas and Nick Thomas in *Zompoc: How to Survive a Zombie Apocalypse:*[465] (1) drinking water; (2) first-aid kit; (3) antibacterial wipes; (4) antibacterial hand sanitizer; (5) toilet paper; (6) feminine hygiene products (for the ladies and wound dressing); (7) clean towels and face cloths: (8) fuel stove and cooking pot; (9) toothpaste, toothbrush and dental floss; (10) hydrogen peroxide; (11) isopropyl alcohol (12) flashlight and batteries; (13) candles; (14) green emergency glow sticks; (15) survival whistle; (16) compass; (17) signal mirror; (18) flint fire starter, waterproof matches, lighter; (19) waterproof containers and bags; (20) warm jacket (also waterproof and breathable); (21) multitool/knife; (22) working gloves; (23) nylon rope, at least 45 feet; and (24) gaffer tape.

Max Brooks' bestselling book, *The Zombie Survival Guide: Complete Protection from the Living Dead,*[466] also contains items, which by now we see as standard: (1) backpack; (2) hiking boots; (3) two pairs of socks; (4) water bottle; (5) water purification tablets; (6) waterproof matches; (7) bandana; (8) maps of area; (9) compass; (10) flashlight; (11) poncho; (12) signaling mirror; (13) bedroll or sleeping bag; (14) sunglasses; (15) first-aid kit; (16) Swiss Army knife or multitool; (17) radio; (18) knife; (19) binoculars; (20) firearm, rifle, 50 rounds of ammo; (21) cleaning kit; (22) pistol (Brooks favors a .22 rimfire, 25 rounds); (23) hand weapon and (24) signal flares.[467] Brooks recommends for a group that one person carry maps, a compass, radio, binoculars, cleaning kit, and signal flares.[468] He recommends for groups: (1) silent ballistic weapon, e.g., crossbow or silenced firearm plus ammo (a good thing to have even without Hollywood zombies); (2) telescopic sight; (3) medical kit; (4) two-way radio; (5) crowbar and (6) water-purification pump.[469] Again, all sound ideas.

Be sure that your bug out bag/ survival kit has multiple means of starting a campfire, including waterproof matches, flint and steel, and a number of magnesium block fire-makers, Swedish fire steels, and even cigarette lighters. Learn how to start a fire in wet weather.[470] Embers could be carried to start the next fire as the Australian Aborigines did, and survivalists could do this using their cast iron cooking pots.

There are two excellent disaster preparedness books by women that give detailed bug out/survival kits: Kathy Harrison, *Just in Case: How to be Self-Sufficient When the Unexpected Happens*[471] and Peggy Layton, *Emergency Food Storage and Survival Handbook: Everything You Need to Know to Keep Your Family Safe in a Crisis*.[472] Apart from these being overall good books, especially in the area of food storage and preparation, the flavor of the books and writing style appeals to women and gifts of these books to your female partner and daughters should be considered. Both books also have discussions of emergency kits, and some important information can be found, not explicitly mentioned in most of the books written by those with testicles, such as dealing with children or babies. Harrison, for example, mentions that cast iron is the only cookware material able to withstand the high temperatures of wood fire cooking, and most other cookware material will not last as long.[473] This is an important consideration for apocalyptic bugging out, as a cooking pot will be essential for boiling water as part of your water purification rituals, as well as carrying embers.[474]

Earlier I mentioned Cody Lundin, US Aboriginal skills expert. His two must-read books are *98.6 Degrees: The Art of Keeping Your Ass Alive!*[475] and *When All Hell Breaks Loose: Stuff You Need to Survive When Disaster Strikes*.[476] Both books are written with earthly humor; Lundin cites a note from Col. Jeff Cooper, who refused to endorse *98.6 Degrees*: "Sorry, but Anglo-Saxon vulgarisms give evidence of lack of imagination and limited vocabulary, and are not to be taken seriously." On the contrary, the literary device of "vulgarisms," the zany drawings, especially of hot babes, gets Lundin's message across to his intended audiences; the books are "blokey," but in no way show limited knowledge. Lundin exhibits considerable knowledge of human physiology and biochemistry, as he clearly explains the dangers of hypothermia and hyperthermia, for example. He shows how hypothermia, the drop of one's core body temperature below 98.6 F (37 C), and hyperthermia, the raising of core body temperature above these base temperatures, can be prevented by the use of clothing, shelters and making a fire, for the case of hypothermia. It is not the point of the present book to examine all of these details and reinvent the wheel. Regarding, for example, hypothermia prevention, he gives a fine outline of the modern layering system for cold environments (base layers, insulation layers, and environmental layers). Stated simply, the *base layer* is worn against the skin and must wick away sweat, but in cold weather, keep you warm. The mid-base layer provides basic insulation and warmth when conditions are mild. The insulation later supplements the mid and base layers for colder conditions. The outer or environmental layer is breathable to allow sweat and heat to escape but provides a waterproof barrier against wind, rain, and snow. Having faced the prospects of hypothermia once myself on a hunting trip, I greatly appreciated these books.[477]

Specific details about clothing, sleeping bags, and tents can be found in a classic backpacker's book, such as Chris Townsend's *The Backpacker's Handbook*, which is now in its fourth edition.[478] Townsend is an experienced backpacker and has traveled across the world, and experienced all matter of climates. His book goes into detail about the best brands of hiking boots, sleeping bags, tents, and so on. This is another must-get, must-read book by an author who is a world expert on this topic.

The basics: as you do not know where you will end up, a person bugging out after a collapse will need to have a synthetic sleeping bag rated to at least -20 C and adequate warm clothing in the layer system to survive if and when it snows. One should have sound wet wear-pants and a jacket or poncho, waterproof and breathable and a snow parker, also waterproof and breathable, and when not in use, it can be rolled up, and a cotton work shirt can be put over it to make a pillow. Clothing systems also need to be able to deal with hot weather, and while cotton is a "death cloth" for cold, wet weather, the fabric works fine in hot, dry climates, wicking moisture.

Headgear is essential: a waterproof, wide-brimmed hat for winter travel, plus a woolen cap or balaclava for sleeping. In the summer, especially areas with a diminished ozone layer, such as Australia and Chile, a wide-brimmed sun hat plus bandana is reasonable. However, as the sun gets "lower" on intensive UV days, one can still get burnt even if wearing a hat and bandana. Here in Texas, I usually stitch cotton side protection to a hat that can be clipped in the front to resemble Arab headgear. When I was working in the Australian bush, as well in desolate areas of Chile, I have labored outdoors in 43 C + heat with eye-frying UV radiation, and with good wrap around glasses, have not gotten sunburnt. I have fashioned sun hats with cotton side and front covers from cheap straw hats (two or three placed over each other creates strength and resistance from moderate strikes from vegetation/light tree branches when cutting) and in the winter I take off the covers and put duct tape on the surface of the hat to make a rain hat for less than US $6.

Lightweight tents will not see out the distance in any longer-term survival event. Usually zips fall apart, or the fabric tears. Tarps are a good fall-back when the tent ultimately dies. Otherwise, bugging out could become a form of buggery by Nature.

There are other things to be said about equipment that I leave to the section below on wilderness and backwoods survival philosophy. Rounding off this discussion on bugging out, it is important to note that all of the discussions in bugout/survival kits are heavily influenced by "lost in the woods/bush/desert" scenarios. Not much thought has been given to "bugging out forever" where one takes all that one can carry, and like the first settlers, our pioneering ancestors, makes a new home from scratch. The reason for this is that most preppers are not preparing for the zombie apocalypse. Indeed, it would be extremely difficult for one person or a small survival group to survive with just the gear on their backs. We are assuming here the worst-case scenario of say evacuation from one's retreat because of climate change, disasters, or a range of other factors. Eco-refugees, we assume as well, will travel on foot, perhaps because of the presence of cannibals, predators, and associated MZB scum and filth on the roads, as in the movie and book, *The Road*, or if roads are simply clogged with the debris of cars. In the alternative, bugging out may occur in the distant future because of climate change and other ecological disasters, long after cars have deteriorated.

In the worst-case scenario, assuming again that one has at least enough time to bug out, an individual or group needs a survival cart with tires that are from a mountain bike, with a repair kit and bike pump, or solid rubber tires. Each person can carry a basic survival backpack with their clothes and personal items in case they get separated from the group. Thus, each person has everything they need for bugging out on an individual basis. The survival cart will be a small version of the pioneers' covered wagon. Waterproof, extra-large duffel bags will be arranged to a human's needs survival theme. One bag can be full of *medical, surgical, and health supplies*; another, small hand *tools*; another to *self-defense*, with spare parts to guns (if you have any left), cleaning kits, and ammunition. There should be at least one large food bag with compact, nutritious, long-life foods. MRE's are a possibility, although there are problems for many people with long-term use, such as digestive issues, as MRE's have ingredients similar to most highly processed food, being high in salt and low in fiber, and they are not lightweight.[479] But, perhaps one could have dried goods, beans, legumes, grains, powdered milk, protein powder, multivitamins, powdered "superfood" supplement, and freeze-dried foods, to construct one's own healthy MRE's.[480] Tin food would be unsatisfactory because of the weight of the tin and liquid content. Food to be taken must have a high nutrition energy to weight ratio, and one can't eat the tin. It is true that tin foods in having water already in the food do not need to have water added, but you are simply not going to be able to carry sufficiently more than a few days' supply of water, so obtaining water will become, along with preventing hyper- and hypothermia and security, your main concerns in bugging out.

I will discuss wilderness survival shortly. My view on "living off the land" is that if what is meant by this phrase is heading into the woods or outback scrub with no bushcraft skills, or poor ones, you will probably starve to death or get eaten by predators. Much depends on what wild food is in the environment where you choose to make your, perhaps, last stand. If game is available and you have a firearm, your chances of survival improve. Living entirely on gathered wild foods is difficult. This is well illustrated by the documentary *Alone in the Wild* (2009, Channel 4), where the likable bloke Ed Wardle attempted to last three months in the wild at Dog Pack Lake and Tincup Lake, Yukon, Canada. He lasted a respectable 50 days, breaking down because of loneliness ("I miss people too much") and lack of food. Although he had a rifle and a pump action shotgun, Canadian socialist law prevented him from shooting game, which was available. He reflected, in one segment of the documentary, while hungrily eyeing a juicy moose, that if he could have shot the beast, hunger would be gone.

However, long-term survival will involve more than just hunting and gathering. Simple agriculture will need to be practiced. This means that a survival bag needs to be devoted to non-hybrid seeds for vegetables (and fruit trees that can be grown realistically from carried seeds rather than nursery-prepared seedlings, which as pot plants will not be practical to carry), with adequate stocks to prepare for a possible failed first or even second crop. Some basic hand tools will need to be taken. To clear scrub, it would be useful to have a cutting-edge mattock or bushhook, which by the way, can double-up as an excellent MZB melee weapon. It would be nice to have a "slasher"—an old-style tool which is essentially an agriculture version of a pole axe weapon (or vice-versa)—a thick blade on a pole (say a long shovel handle), for scrub clearing. You will probably need to make one if you have blacksmithing skills or get one made up before the collapse. A long-handled spade, with a flat rather than curved blade, can also be sharpened on the edges for scrub clearing, and in a WROL situation, MZB clearing as well.

Wilderness and Backwoods' Survival Philosophy

Wilderness survival has been exhaustively covered in two broad genres of books. First, there are army/navy/air force survival guilds such as the *US Army Survival Manual* FM 21-76,[481] the Royal Australian Navy, *The Survival Manual*,[482] and the Royal Canadian Air Force Survival Training School, *Down but Not Out*.[483] This school of thought has flourished into a large number of SAS and commando-type books, which cover the same basic topics of the psychology of survival (positive can-do attitude and all that), shelter, water, food, and dangerous animals and poisonous plants. These books outline primitive skills to help one live off the land (or maybe even the sea), including hunting, trapping, and fishing. The classic book in the field is John Wiseman's *SAS Survival Handbook*.[484] But, more recently, there have appeared a number of other superb texts,[485] with the *SAS and Elite Forces Guild* series by Chris Mc Nab being particularly good.[486]

The second genre of wilderness survival is the backwoods, or for Australia, bushman traditions.[487] The great American magazine *The Backwoodsman* ("The Magazine for the 21st Century Frontiersman") has been published for over 30 years, and all of this wealth and knowledge and wisdom can be purchased on DVD – to be done before "power down.[488] There are many informative books[489] and websites.[490]

For example, Bob Holtzman's *Adventure Survival Handbook: How to Stay Alive in the Wild with Just a Blade and Your Wits*[491] gives a minimalist approach to wilderness survival, showing the importance of a good knife for making shelter and in fire and food preparation. He discusses the advantages and disadvantages of fixed blades and folders, and plain vs. serrated edges. (I prefer a fixed blade plain edge and a serrated edge folder to have the best of both worlds). Holtzman gives a guide to sharpening knives and axes, as well as basic axe use, such as how to fell a tree, climbing, sectioning, splitting and hewing.[492]

After decades of chopping wood, preparing fire breaks and clearing feral trees on my folk's Texas ranch and then my own, I prefer a good handsaw to an axe, and even to a chainsaw, especially on slippery hillsides and in the wet. I don't agree with the machete school of wood chopping either, for anything beyond a basic campfire. If you need to cut up literally masses of timber by hand, don't use an axe, use a biomechanically superior saw. And, *a fortiori*, using a Bowie knife for wood prepping, as is common to many entertaining knife testing YouTube videos, can be done, but is not long-term efficient, compared to saws.

A great wilderness survival book from the editors of Stockpiles books is *Survival Wisdom and Know-How: Everything to You to Know to Subsist in the Wilderness.*[493] This is a large-format book with three columns of print per page and fully adequate line drawings giving 7,845 skills and instructions on topics including animals, insects, and plants for food; packing and cooking food; water; hunting and fishing; fire; shelter traveling on land and water; weather and climate; navigation and first-aid – principally for a North American and Canadian audience. This book is essentially a wilderness survival encyclopedia and is a clear "must-have," as is John and Geri McPherson's *Ultimate Guide to Wilderness Living,*[494] which deals with surviving with just your bare hands and what you can scab in the woods. Here you will learn about making primitives tools, working flint and stone, and making wooden bowls and plates and primitive pottery and cordage. The McPherson's deal with the construction of basic shelters such as lean-tos, wickiups, and more complex shelters. I have given this book to my three youngest kids to make up shelters for themselves in the hills on the farm while I have been scrub-clearing. They did fine in making both summer and winter shelters for themselves, although they got all manner of crap on the book.

Tom Brown's Field Guide to Living with the Earth[495] and Tony Nesters' *The Modern Hunter-Gatherer,*[496] also cover wilderness survival fundamentals, such as traps and snares, fire making, shelter construction, bow and arrow making, weaving stone and bone tools, hides and tanning (making buckskin), clay pot making and living simply without the trappings of civilization. These are classic books, well worth obtaining and studying.

Tony Nester in *The Modern Hunter-Gatherer* has given a very useful dot point list of the bushcraft skills which a complete survivalist will need to know. They are:

- "How to make a fire in any weather (wind, snow, rain) using modern fire-making devices.

- Be proficient with a knife, axe and saw.

- How to dress properly and understand the insulative values of different garments and footwear.

- How to handle common backcountry injuries and deal with trauma.

- How to construct natural and improvized survival shelters as well as hogans and cabins for long-term living.

- How to ID, harvest, and know, how to use a dozen of the common edible plants of their region.

- How to use medicinal plants for healing injures and have made an herbal first-aid kit.

- Able to cook delicious (or at least, edible) meals over the campfire using a variety of modern and primitive cooking methods.

- ID common animal tracks and have the ability to follow the trail of a wounded animal.

- Be skilled in hunting small game with a pistol and rifle.

- Able to make primitive deadfalls and snares and successfully procure wild game with them.

- How to skin, clean, and process wild game and fish.

- How to preserve meat and fish through smoking and air-drying into jerky.

- Be proficient at primitive methods of fire-making such as the bow-drill and hand-drill.

- How to use at least ten bush knots for lashing.

- Be skilled at navigating with map and compass, GPS, and barehanded/ celestial methods.

- How to read the clouds and forecast inclement weather up to 72 hours away.

- Make improvised containers for cooking and know how to coal-burn utensils.

- Skilled at basic tailoring for mending gear and clothing.

- How to make improvised hunting weapons such as bows, atlatls, and throwing sticks.

- How to make quickie stone-tools and improvised cutting edges from natural materials.

- Be proficient at living in the deep snow and extreme cold weather.

- How to sleep well in the wild."[497]

It is a good, sensible list, especially the last point about the value of being able to sleep soundly outdoors. But, as a bushman who has lived in the driest states on the driest continents on Earth, and the driest parts of West Texas, I would like to add to this list: be proficient at living in the extreme heat and how to find and purify water. Short-term survival methods of finding and obtaining water are well covered in the wilderness survival literature and include dew and rainwater collection; condensation methods using plants; water from plants especially plant roots; the solar still and improvised distillation. For both short-term and long-term survival, purification of water is needed to protect human drinkers from waterborne diseases caused by parasites, protozoa, bacteria, and viruses. Prior filtering of the water will remove large particles of dirt and mud and material that may protect bugs from disinfecting agents. Bleach and tincture of iodine can be used, along with stabilized oxygen products. Boiling for about one minute at low altitudes, and for several minutes at higher altitudes is a time-proven method of killing waterborne pathogens. Distillation—boiling water and collecting the steam—is also a way of dealing with salts, chemicals, and heavy metals. Solar water disinfection, exposing water in plastic PET bottles to the sun's UV rays, can be used to kill the organisms causing diarrhea, including viruses, bacteria, and parasites.

Disaster Preparedness, Philosophy

The disaster preparedness literature, primarily manuals and information handouts from government organizations such as FEMA and emergency services organizations, is, of course, useful for general emergency preparation. In the disaster preparedness genre, Dr. Arthur T. Bradley's *Handbook to Practical Disaster Preparedness for the Family*[498] is outstanding for its stated purpose of meeting "likely" threats rather than TEOTWAWKI or the zombie apocalypse. Where I disagree is that one of our likely future threats is, in fact, TEOTWAWKI and the zombie apocalypse. Dr. Bradley had more recently published *Disaster Preparedness for EMP Attacks and Solar Storms*,[499] a truly superb, much-needed book alerting us to this threat and showing how vulnerable modern technological society actually is to TEOTWAWKI. Consequently, his *Handbook to Practical Disaster Preparedness for the Family* should not be your only reading in this field, but it is an excellent place to start because the book is written as if you were with him out in the shed having a few cold beers.

Mathew Stein has published two books *When Technology Fails*[500] and *When Disaster Strikes*.[501] The latter book is more in the conventional disaster preparedness genre. Definitely an "A" like Bradley's book, and you would do well educating yourself with either. *When Technology Fails* through should be given an "A+" because this 439-page book in double columns essentially gives a synthesis of the disaster preparedness and self-reliance, self-sufficiency traditions, the later traditions originating from the "back-to-the-land" movements of the early 20th century and particularly in the 1960s. Stein has an engineering background and has hands-on experience with most of the technologies discussed in his book. The basics are covered including fire-starting; food; shelter; water; first-aid; what to do when high tech medicine fails (holistic health, herbs, etc., the holistic health section is objected to, predictably enough, by some on the net); clothing and textiles, heat and energy; metalworking; blacksmithing; utensils and storing; not-so-modern chemistry and engineering, machines, and materials. Each chapter concludes with a set of references with a synopsis and a brief discussion of a wide number of topics, such as the selection of sleeping bags that gets one column (but the information is correct as he favors fiber-filled synthetic bags). Obviously, other books mentioned earlier can offer further information. Nevertheless, *When Technology Fails* is highly recommended because it puts much information between two covers and it does so with the explicit recognition that our present society is unsustainable, and that we are facing a "long emergency."

I have already mentioned the work of leading US survivalist James Wesley, Rawles on retreats, and his novel *Patriots*. *Patriots* may not be great literature but would be more helpful to a novice survivalist than a work of great literature. The novel is concerned with a group of patriots, who ultimately organize themselves as a militia, who face the socio-economic collapse of America because of crippling US debt and deficit problems. I won't spoil the plot. The most interesting read for me were long sections on survival preparations, including a discussion of survival knives and fighting knives, firearms selection; fuel storage; and how to fortify a house. There is a mention of the need for farming, but most of the book deals with the action part of retreatism rather than more monotonous manual labor. The preparation of explosives, Molotov cocktails, and thermite use occurs.

Rawles' *How to Survive the End of World as We Know It*,[502] is essentially the distillation of the wisdom of his survivalblog.com between covers and one of the outstanding books on this field. If budget constraints for a reader were great that only, say, ten books could be purchased, I would definitely put this book in the top 10 list, along with Stein's *When Technology Fails*, which jointly cover most of the bases including firearms and self-protection. Rawles adopts the original approach to developing survival lists, giving a master "list of lists" from which people work on making up their own survival lists. Thus, the list of lists would cover the basic areas of water; food storage; food preparation; personal items; first-aid/ minor surgery; chemical/nuclear/biological/pandemic defenses; gardening; hygiene/sanitation; hunting/fishing/trapping; power, lighting, batteries; fuels; firefighting; tactical living; general security; security/firearms; communications and monitoring; tools; survival books; barter and charity. Rawles then goes into dot point details under each of these sub-categories.

Rawlesian survivalism embraces sound principles which I see as worthy of acceptance: lower populated areas are preferable to higher populated areas; exercise restraint, but be prepared to use lethal force if necessary; there is strength in numbers – retreat groups should ideally make use of a number of families for 24/7 security; the need for skills over technology; wealth in tangible goods rather than fiat currencies; seek good soil, clean water and adequate rainfall for agriculture; store adequate and surplus supplies; food storage is needed as crops may fail; undertake proper training with all tools including guns; use of "appropriate technologies"[503] such as a blacksmith's forge in collapse situations; the better-prepared one is, the more can one help others; some technologies offer advantages in the short term (e.g., night vision gear and communication equipment), and some in the longer term (e.g., barbed wire and razor wire); seek out skilled, reliable friends with practical knowledge; fortify your retreat, which ideally you should at live at all year round; and in living, live simply and frugally.

Before moving on to consider worthy self-reliance and self-sufficiency books, nuclear war survival skills should be briefly mentioned. Dr. Bruce Clayton's *Life after Doomsday*[504] is a still-relevant classic, and his more recent *Life after Terrorism*[505] updates things with a consideration of more recent horrors including biological and chemical warfare and much more. Available online is a respected book by Cresson Kearney, *Nuclear War Survival Skills* (1986).[506] The US Armed Forces, *Nuclear, Biological and Chemical Survival Manual* (2003)[507] is also worth consulting, as mentioned earlier.

After the media image of survivalists as crazies tramping through the scrub with guns, comes the image of survivalists as stockpilers of supplies and food. So, let us not disappoint them. There are a number of excellent books available to help you get started on food stockpiling and preserving grown food. Kathy Harrison's *Just in Case*[508] and Peggy Layton's *Emergency Food Storage and Survival Handbook*[509] have already been mentioned, and both books provide a wealth of information on food storage and preparation. Harrison introduces the OAR system: organize, acquire and rotate, where you actively manage your food stockpile, keeping track of "use by dates" and using food then replacing it. The food stored will be foods that one's family actually eats. Another take-home message is that while you can't live on bread alone, bread and soup are a possibility: soups and casseroles are excellent foods. Tin soup, mixed with rice or soup mix, can make a quick meal.

Jack Spigarelli's *Crisis Preparedness Handbook*,[510] gives a comprehensive guide to emergency and survival preparations, including survival tools to store and stockpile; clothing; heat; cooking and light; sanitation; medical and dental; home preparation and management; communications; preparations for a terrorist attack (biological, chemical and nuclear), but focuses largely on food and water stockpiling, food production and food preservation in chapters 5-19 of the book. Spigarelli, also says that one should store the types of foods that a family will normally eat, because children faced with an absolutely boring diet may starve. Adults too may lose interest in food if it is "oh no, not fuckin' baked beans again!" even if the mistake of my friend with the fatty, salty meat mentioned in the paragraph above is avoided.

There is merit in putting aside a large stockpile of the Mormon "basic four" of wheat, sugar (honey), powdered milk, and salt. It is possible, if you know what you are doing, adding variety to these staples by making from gluten, the protein part of flour, a meat substitute that can be made into various dishes. But, as said, you will need to know how to prepare this and be a good cook. Further, the narrower the base of foods you have, the greater the risk of starvation if you or your family develop allergies to a particular item, such as wheat and wheat products (gluten) and cow's milk (lactose). As well, this diet is lacking in fats and vitamins, although vitamins could come from fresh fruit and vegetables, and bush/wild foods to be added to it. But, even then, the diet is lacking in essential fats such as omega 3 fatty acids. At a minimum, the Mormon basic four should be expanded to include as well as the four – oils (especially olive oil), a variety of grains and legumes, multi-vitamins and micronutrients such as selenium supplements, protein powder, herbs, seasonings, and leavening agents. Olive oil trees can be grown both for oil and use can be made of olive leaf extracts, an excellent herbal treatment for a range of heart and respiratory conditions.

Stored food will deteriorate at various speeds, depending on storage conditions, losing nutrients, palatability, and in the case of foods like yeast, thickeners and gelatines, their functional properties.[511] There is, surprisingly enough, little scientifically based knowledge on the shelf life of various foods, and most of the figures cited in various books are estimates.[512] There is general agreement that salt and maybe sugar under ideal (moisture-free) storage conditions last indefinably, but beyond that, there is little agreement. Some figures for illustration are: canned goods, two years (although under ideal conditions, canned fish, three to five years); dried dairy products, five years; dried fruits and vegetables, seven years; dried beans and legumes, seven years; grains (other than wheat, e.g., oats), ten years; wheat 10-20 years; Meals Ready to Eat (MRE), 3 + years; dehydrated food, 10-15 years; freeze-dried, 7-25 years.

Spigarelli cites a study that found that 40-year-old canned cream corn, fruit cocktail, and green peas were about nutritionally equivalent to some freshly canned foods.[513] He says that canned goods retain, even after a number of years, 50-90 percent of their vitamin content, and all of their proteins, fats, and carbohydrates.[514] Spigarelli puts the shelf life of canned food at 2 ½-7 years. However, I have tried to store tin food under "ideal conditions" (cool, dry, etc.) and have never kept a tin of canned food "alive" more than about four years, especially with tomatoes in it (i.e., baked beans = acid) My bad luck! Thus, Lundin's advice is good advice: "take all prophetic advice about how long your vittles' will be vital with a grain of salt. The sure way out of this dilemma is to *rotate your food by storing what you eat and eating what you store.*"[515]

Dehydrated, air-dried, freeze-dried and canned foods, all have their advantages and disadvantages, especially with respect to cost, with freeze-dried and air-dried foods generally costing substantially more than canned food. On the principle of not putting all of one's eggs in the one basket, it is ideal for building up one's food reserves using a variety of these types of foods such as freeze-dried meats, dehydrated foods like powered milk, potatoes, cheese, eggs and soups and canned foods like fruit, vegetables, and ready-to-go soups. There is no "one size fits all perfect food storage plan;" rather, each individual survival unit, typically a family, will need to devise a plan to best suit their ends and tastes. In a collapse situation, food will be one of the few remaining pleasures in life and, for the purposes of morale, needs to be something to look forward to and keep one, keeping on.

It is important to properly store food in food grade storage containers that protect the food from insects and pests such as rats and mice. It is amazing what rats can get into, so beware and prepare!

In a nutshell, what food items should be put away by people on a tight budget, who just cannot think through all of these issues for themselves because they are so time-strapped from working long hours for minimal pay, just to keep body and soul together? "Health Ranger" Mike Adams has put together a shopping list of 50 items.[516] Adams makes the point that salt will be hard to come by in a collapse situation, so sea salt (which has iodine) should be put away in large quantities. It lasts indefinitely under ideal conditions, and it is possible to store enough, in suitable *glass* containers, to last generations. There is almost nothing written on the ultra-long-term storage chemistry of food-grade plastics because these things haven't existed long enough to judge their stability over a few hundred years. Will chemicals leak into the salt after 50 or more years? What about 100 years? Ideally, for ultra-long-term storage, use glass containers.

In the distant future, salt can be obtained from journeys to the oceans.

Self-Reliance and Self-Sufficiency Philosophy

The self-reliance/self-sufficiency and ecology movement has produced a range of useful works for the survivalist. Zachary Nowak in *Crash Course: Preparing for Peak Oil*,[517] gives a useful review of books and lists many useful websites, as does Ted Trainer's "Simpler Way" website aimed for small scale self-sufficient local economies, the abandonment of consumerism and adoption of simple living.[518] Some key books to consult are Carla Emery, *The Encyclopaedia of Country Living*,[519] John and Martha Storey, *Storey's Basic Country Skills*,[520] and A. R. Gehring (ed.), *Back to Basics*.[521] Today the living simply/ organic/permaculture/minimalism traditions are "mainstream," and newsagents often hold an array of magazines such as *Mother Earth News* and *Permaculture, Grass Roots, Earth Garden*, and *Warm Earth*. f course, many more US-produced magazines will be available. There are also many excellent "off-grid" living books, worthy of considering, because long-term survival in the future will definitely be off-grid, or rather, no grid.[522]

The late John Seymour, the father of self-sufficient living, wrote some books of lasting value including *The Fat of the Land*,[523] *The Self-Sufficient Life and How to Live It*,[524] and *The Forgotten Arts*.[525] This latter book gives an outline, albeit a brief one, of a variety of traditional crafts, including some surprising ones such as wooden fork and rake making. The production of various tempered blades by blacksmithing is covered as well, including the slasher which I mentioned earlier (and wherever else I can fit it in), which could serve the dual purpose of a land clearing tool, far superior to any machete, as well as a pole axe weapon for pruning the zombie herd.[526]

Seymour's masterwork is *The New Complete Book of Self-Sufficiency*,[527] which in its 2009 publication by Darling Kindersley, compiles material from two of his older books, *The New Complete*

Book of Self-Sufficiency (1976) and *The New Self-Sufficient Gardener* (1978). "Why should we all labor to enrich the banks?" he asks. Yes, screw the banks and the global financial conspiracy and all that. Instead, self-sufficient living, through moving from the cities to the countryside, is a way of regaining our lost humanity: "[s]elf-sufficiency does not mean "going back" to an acceptance of a lower standard of living. On the contrary, it is the striving for a higher standard of living, for food which is fresh and organically grown and good, for the good life in pleasant surroundings, for the health of body and peace of mind which comes with hard, varied work in the open air, and for the satisfaction that comes from doing difficult and intricate jobs well and successfully."

Seymour advocated the method of "high farming" used in Europe centuries ago, which involved a balance of plants and animals, e.g., plants feed the animals, and animal wastes fertilize the soil. Crops are rotated, and there are no monocultures, to control pests. Animals are free ranged. He felt that a five-acre holding could easily supply all the food necessary for a large family, and has already been mentioned, it can be achieved with less than that. The color illustrations alone are almost works of art in themselves and far more productive to view than much of the toxic sludge filling our modern art galleries. There is useful information about how to butcher a pig; chicken and rabbit breeds; clearing, draining and irrigating land; hedging and fencing; using working horses; preparing land and sowing; harvesting; how to make butter and cream; cheese, bread; bottling; pickles and chutney; jams and syrups; brewing and wine-making; compost; dry composting toilets and a wide range of crafts and skills.

Small scale, largely organic farming, without electricity, and using horsepower, has been practiced by the Amish in America. Life there has involved lighting and cooking with a wood stove; water without an electric pump; washing clothes without a washing machine; entertainment without TV or video games; communication without a phone or texting; transport without a car; farming without a tractor and running a farm and woodworking shops without electricity. As Scott and Pellman put it: "Unlike many North Americans, the Amish value simplicity and self-denial over comfort, convenience, and leisure. So they try to discern the long-range effects of innovation before deciding whether to adopt it."[528] Electricity was seen to lead to a lifestyle contrary to church and family life (although some battery-powered devices are used). The Amish see "folly in a lifestyle that avoids physical labor, then creates an exercise in the form of jogging or aerobics." For the Amish, the adoption of a self-sufficient lifestyle was done for the purposes of preserving their culture; but for us non-Amish, it will be needed to preserve our lives. The fact that a group of people has lived and strived to live this way indicates that it is possible, in the midst of our insane techno-industrial societies' death throes, to live an alternative life.[529]

Tools and the Craftsman

One topic sometimes mentioned in survival books is the need to have a supply of hand tools for a grid-down situation. Today, whether it be those who work with wood, stone, metal, or the garden, most work is done with power tools. Land clearing of feral trees and vegetation is done with a chainsaw, whipper-snipper/brush cutter instead of an axe/handsaw and machete, slasher, and scythe. It is said that these tools are faster and more efficient than their hand equivalents. I have cleared many acres of territory of blackberry, olive, and other weeds using a hand saw, slasher, machete, and even a "don't care" katana. Here are my conclusions from a lifetime of hard sweat.

Petrol driven chainsaws, if they are a quality brand and regularly serviced, usually work well. They are about three to five times faster than a good saw or axe man. However, on steep land, they can be extremely dangerous, and I have seen one chainsaw accident (a co-worker) and don't want to see another. The axe and handsaw are much quieter and safer and do not require fuel beyond muscle power. Also, you don't breathe fumes. One government site on weed control says that chain saws and mechanical slashers "create high levels of soil and vegetation disturbance."[530] Chopping and sawing wood is one of the best forms of exercise, having immediate spin-off benefits for melee weapon combat. If one can use a wood chopping axe well, using a fighting axe (say a Viking short axe) or a tomahawk, is not too difficult. Hand-sawing is an excellent triceps developer. Hence, the art of the axe and saw needs revival. Further, one could bug out on foot with an axe or a good quality (sharpenable) handsaw, but it is impractical to lug around while bugging out, a chainsaw, brushcutter, and fuel. Consequently, the art and science of the axe and saw need revival among survivalists.[531]

In terms of clearing weeds such as blackberry on relatively flat land, the modern handheld brushcutter is not used and a tractor with a slasher attachment, rules. There is no contest against it – assuming that you own a tractor and can maintain it. But, the wheeled tractor becomes dangerous on very steep slopes (tractors with tracks are better, but have their limits as well), and both cannot be used on extremely swampy land. The hand-held brush cutter, though, is inferior to the manual tool equivalents of a slasher/machete/sword/ parang for tough scrub and a scythe for grass. I have worked with many guys who have used a brushcutter or a string trimmer and have always beaten them in terms of the amount of scrub cleared per unit of time, using hand tools.[532] Much time is wasted clearing crap stuck in the whirly bits, not so for a scrub katana/machete.

The survivalist/prepper/doomsteader needs to stockpile various types of hand tools, general tools, and supplies. For the shorter term, tools needed for automotive and electrical repair and maintenance are needed, e.g., oil filler, wrench, a range of sockets, spanners, compression tester, battery charger, fuse wire, etc. However, the concern in this book is for long-term survival in a coming dark age, and our thoughts are for tools that are man-powered only. In general, one will need gardening tools, metalworking tools, woodworking tools, masonry tools and a range of basic supplies, including such items as duct tape (the more the better), PVC electrical tape, safety goggles, dust masks, sunglasses, hearing protection, parachute cord (can't have too much), rope (can't have too much), plastic sheets, water containers, buckets, tarps, barbed/razor wire, fencing materials (e.g., star droppers, wire mesh), hacksaw blades, fire-starting mechanisms (matches, flint, and steel, etc.), bleach, flashlights, work gloves, hoses, water pipe, chain, scales, paint, paintbrushes, plumber's tape, wood and general purpose glues, massive quantities of nails and screws of various sizes, silicone sealant, washers, tire wire (the more the better), cement, WD-40, oils and lubricants, and sandpaper, to name but a few items.

Woodworking tools include hand saws, rubber, and wooden mallets, hammers, nuts & bolts, screwdrivers, chisels, adze, files, Stanley knives, drawing knives, squares, tape measures, planes, dividers, and axes. Metalwork and blacksmithing tools include a workbench, wrecking bar, nails, vice clamps, spanners, ball-peen hammers, files, (various types), hand-crank forge, bellows, grinding wheel, sledgehammer, forging tongs, a heavy-duty vice, punches, pliers, tin snips, leather apron, wire brushes, welder's gloves, work gloves, pliers, hack saws, safety goggles and so on. Masonry tools include shovels/spades, trowels, bolsters, manual mortar mixer, builder's square/tape measures, float, bricklayer's hammer, spirit level, and cement edger and joiner. Garden tools include a slasher, machetes, spades and shovels, rakes (including a fork rake), forks (including a pitchfork), saws, axes, hatchets, block splitters, wheelbarrows, crowbars/fencing bars, sledgehammers, post-hole diggers, mattocks (with both pick-end types and axe-like end types), pruning shears, pruning saws, sharpening stones, wedges, and picks, among many other items.

Many, but not all commercially made tools are somewhat fragile, especially cheap Chinese made garden tools. I have purchased chipper hoes whose blade ends bend after hitting a few rocks, a problem due to either inferior slag-ridden steel incorrectly heat-treated, low carbon steel, and/or thin hoe blades. Spades and shovels tend to be better, so to make up hoes, I have often cut up a spade and welded on a section to put a handle. Fork rakes can also be made up of garden forks. Anvils can be made from sections of heavy I-beams, railway iron, or engine blocks. Knives can be made from old files, although they will be somewhat brittle as an impact tool or weapon, and thus need reforging and re-heat treating. Car (older models) and truck leaf spring steel is much better.

One could, of course, purchase hand-forged tools made by local blacksmiths, but this may be costly, and the extra life needs to be balanced against the cost. For the longer-term, a survival workshop centered on blacksmithing needs to be constructed now for the use of present and future generations.[533] There is likely to be enough scrap metal in the decaying cities of the future to supply all the metal that remnant blacksmiths will need, perhaps for centuries. However, most of the steel in such cities is soft, low-carbon mild steel that can be case hardened (on its surface), but not hardened by heat treatment. To make tools and edged weapons, a supply of high carbon steel needs to be secured before the collapse as it may be hard to find in Post Apocalyptica under the masses of decaying humanity and their garbage.

Tools, along with weapons, are items that can and should be stockpiled now at one's "Sustainable Autonomous Base," if one has one, or at least acquired now for early bird bugging out via a vehicle such as a light truck.

The use of hand tools was once an important part of manhood, replaced by industrialism and consumer culture. The idea of craftsmanship was abandoned, to be replaced by mass production.[534] But, in Post Apocalyptica, this ancient ideal, once a philosophical aid in living one's life, will once more return.

Manhood: Getting Lead Back in Your Pencil

The stakes of the game, for true men, will soon be to *survive*. That's all – to survive [...] [f]or one day, when the machine has exhausted all the possibilities of its original élan, it will totter and fall. Then, for us, it will be enough to be numerous, to maintain solidarity, so as collectively to regain control of our earth after we have fiercely defended our few areas of retreat. It is in order to be there, at that decisive moment, that we must survive now. So, do not be ashamed: let us build our refuges! Remember that a rebel wins if he can hold out one hour longer than his adversary. Let us organize ourselves to do so.

- Michel Drac[535]

Apart from engaging in a massive education program about the survival aspects discussed in the last section, a person who intends to give it his best to survive the coming collapse needs the right mental attitude, philosophy, and mindset. This is a difficult topic to approach since, even though there are writers who have been through economic collapse situations, the sort of global cascading converging and compounding catastrophes discussed here are only now beginning to be experienced, and we have not seen anything yet.

Nevertheless, it is clear that survival will require a return to masculine values associated with warriorhood. The American Psychological Association has labeled traditional masculinity, the core values being strength, courage, mastery, and honor (per Jack Donovan), as "harmful."[536] Never mind that it is only masculine values embodied in the potential for violence, through police forces and the defense forces, which stand as a foundation for the protective structure of society, enabling thin-armed pencil necks to philosophize about the nonsense that they do.[537]

Apart from the political attack upon traditional masculinity, men face a wide-ranging environmental assault from endocrine-disruptors, estrogen-mimicking chemicals (xenoestrogens), and phytoestrogens found in "foods" such as soy,[538] caffeine, lignans (cereal brans and beans), coumestans (split peas, pinto beans, lima beans) and even beer (8-prenylnaringenin). These chemicals can have ill-health effects for both men and women, but for men, there is the problem of lowering testosterone, something which is already crashing in the West, along with sperm quality.[539]

There are numerous steps that can be taken to minimize contact with endocrine-disrupting chemicals, but it is not possible to eliminate them completely, and some damage is inevitable. What one can do is to minimize one's consumption of phytoestrogens in one's diet, and at least for men, move to a "testosterone-increasing" diet, as described in numerous books, but these are exceptionally good: Dr. Martin Katahn, *The T-Factor Diet*, (W. W. Norton, New York, 2001), and Chad Howse (with Dr. Stephen Anton), *The Man Diet*, (Chad House, 2018). This involves moving right away from a grain-based diet, as depicted in the food pyramid, and consuming high-quality protein from meats, carbs from anti-oxidant-rich vegetables and fruits, and correct levels of fats. The T-diet genre significantly overlaps with the paleo diet revolution, which has arisen in response to the obesity epidemic, and an array of other diet/lack of exercise epidemics, including diabetes, irritable bowel syndrome, and various food allergy reactions, often produced by the chemicals used in processing and flavoring foods. The paleo diet maintains that we should eat like a caveman, high protein, high fiber, and whatever fats come with it, but with low carbohydrate: Dr. Sarah Ballantyne, *Paleo Principles*, (Victory Belt Publishing, 2017). Refined sugar, and even fructose in excess, must be avoided as being worse than the plague: sweet poisons,[540] so even fruits, especially fruit juices, need to be carefully monitored, as fructose can worsen insulin levels.[541] Excessive sugar consumption can have a wide range of ill-health effects, being linked to breast cancer and metastasis in the lungs.[542] However, there needs to be balance here, as whole fruits do contain numerous anti-oxidants and other beneficial chemical compounds. Natural news.com, is a good source for examining the health benefits of fruits, such as, for example, the anti-aging effects of pterostilbene in blueberries.[543] Obviously, completely abandon the consumption of alcohol, all recreational drugs, cigarettes, and other poisons.

A study of the isotopes of bones of deceased people from the 15th to 17th centuries in Northern Ostrobothnia, Finland, found that 70 percent of the diet of these Nordics, was fish such as Baltic herring.[544] Today, men in Iceland live longer than even the Japanese, thriving on a manly diet of mainly fish, with few vegetables and little grains.[545]

The paleo-T diet amounts to eating foods such as quality meats, especially Omega 3 rich oily fish, organic vegetables with a focus upon those high in antioxidants, and anti-cancer nutrients (e.g., broccoli rather than potatoes), and the elimination of all grains. Little has been written about diet in a long-term collapse situation; the general assumption is that grains will continue to be grown after all stores have been used up. But, growing, say, wheat, assuming that one does not develop a gluten allergy over the long term, is not an efficient use of agricultural land, compared to growing vegetables, or even many nuts. In the long-term, survivors will return to a paleo style diet of meat and fish and vegetables, with some in-season fruits to finish a meal. There will be no metabolic diseases, obesity, diabetes, or the other horrors of life in the modern human battery hen coops. Life will be short and sweet, instead of long and bitter.

However, in a collapse situation, it may not be possible to store enough correct food to sustain one's family, given the vast quantities of food that people need. It should be possible for people having a Sustainable Autonomous Base (SAB), to preserve meats, fruits and vegetables in quantities to see them over most hard times; there are numerous books on Amazon on this, simply search for "prepping, canning and preserving," or just "canning," and "preserving." The Organic Prepper is also a very good website. Despite this, it may be necessary to also stockpile dried foods such as beans and various grains, simply for long-term security, as these foods last a long time, and are calorie-dense. Even if these are sub-optimal foods in ideal conditions, sub-optimal foods are better than starving.[546]

Before moving on from the diet issue, there are some foods with a long shelf life that should be in a survival stockpile. Protein powders used in bodybuilding and powerlifting present a concentrated source of protein, dead easy to prepare (mix with water), with a long shelf life, providing that the powders are stored out of direct sunlight in a cool, dry place. Along with vitamin tablets, these items can keep one going in hard conditions. Olive oil is a neglected survival food too; an old Italian who survived World War II told me that he, as an old man (the story dates back to the 1960s), had hidden some large bottles of olive oil, and that helped keep him alive during the food shortages. It is good for one's cardiovascular health, as well.

Thus, getting one's diet in shape, right now, if the would-be survivor is carrying excess fat, is the first thing to do, even before physical training. One needs to rebuild oneself. This is especially important since obese people have, on average lower brain volumes.[547] While it could be argued that people with smaller brains may be more susceptible to becoming obese, it is more likely given the obesity crisis, that brain shrinkage could be caused by obesity.[548] If that is not so, then there must be more dumb manure-makers out there than was previously thought.

There is also an ideological dimension to all of this, with weaker types of men often having testosterone levels of 85-year-old normal men. So, stay away from both soy.[549]

Now, with your diet under control, what next? We need to prepare for self-defense and fighting.

6. PHYSICAL TRAINING:
SELF-DEFENSE AND UNARMED COMBAT

Every normal man must be tempted at times to spit on his hands, hoist the black flag, and begin slitting throats.

- H. L. Mencken (1880-1956)[550]

Those who live are those who fight.

- Victor Hugo (1802-1855)[551]

Physical training is something that should be undertaken as soon as possible by the would-be collapse-survivalist. As Jean Raspail says in his book *The Camp of the Saints* about the end of the European world: "Did you ever see the lamb attack the wolf and gobble it down?" Physical training has as its sole aim, the desire to make people more wolf-like and not to remain in a lamb chop state. While it is important to lose weight, it is not necessary to reduce body fat to six-pack levels. In fact, bodybuilding does not aim to primarily produce strength and athleticism but to generate a "cut" profile. This obsession with a ripped look is dangerous from a collapse perspective. Most professional bodybuilders, and sadly power athletes, produce their phenomenally cut bodies by hard training, but also with chemical supplements including various cocktails of steroids and maybe growth hormone and who knows what else, to transform their bodies into something once described by, I believe, comedian Clive James, as a "condom full of walnuts." They consume enormous meals, throwing down a quantity of food that will not be

151

available on a sustainable basis. Needless to say, the said chemical additives will not be around for long, and the large muscles will soon atrophy.

Strength training, done right, which is drug-free, is one of the best things a person can do to get ready for the hard times to come. There is the obvious physical dimension, which I will write about, but strength training combined with a practical self-defense unarmed combat system can improve one's mental attitude, making a person tougher. I say this, not from research work from journals, but from training people and seeing personal transformations, even in my own sons and daughters. Pumping iron can lead to being more like iron than soggy pasta.

Certainly, from a physical perspective, humans have been in decline for the entire duration of the modern world, and even with nutrition, they have lacked the harshness of life that made people like the Vikings, Romans and Spartans, men to be feared.[552] For example, in the 4th century BCE, Greek author Xenophon wrote a matter-of-fact account of how Greek soldiers rowed an Athenian warship on a journey of 236 km from Byzantium to Heraclea in a day. This was an average of 7-8 knots over a 12-16-hour trip. Modern rowers can only manage 6 knots, and then only for an hour before conking out. Hence, if this account is accurate, and there is no reason for thinking that it is not, as it was reported in a matter-of-fact way, the average Greek soldier was fitter than a contemporary elite rower. These soldiers sustained themselves on a sub-optimal diet of barley mixed with olive oil, washed down with wine. Genetic changes may or may not have occurred, but these are not significant enough to account for the differences, which are more likely due to the average premodern exercising intensely from an early age.[553]

The elements of fitness include muscular strength and related, bone density, cardiovascular fitness, and flexibility.[554] There are numerous modes of training nowadays in gyms/fitness centers, offering a plethora of different approaches to achieving fitness and the body beautiful. There is High Intensity Interval Training (HIIT), Pilates ("Contrology"), yoga, Zumba, and many more. Screw them!

For the apocalypse one needs hard-core barbarian training that is totally dedicated to developing fighting fitness, attempting to be the men that the Spartans, Romans, and Vikings were. So, okay, you need flexibility, and all the stretches you will ever need are covered in the iconic stretching book by Bob Anderson, *Stretching*, (Shelter Publications, Bolinas, 2010), now in its 30th year of publication.

For strength development, nothing beats old school classical weight training using predominately barbells but spiced with dumbbells and maybe kettlebells. Basic compound exercises are performed, such as the squat, bench press, deadlift, power clean, bent over rows, calf raises, sit-ups with weights, and maybe for entertainment, biceps curls, but usually it is more efficient to train large muscle groups, so the biceps are better hit with heavy rows and chin-ups. These basic exercises are detailed in numerous places on the internet, but a good beginner's book is Mark Rippetoe, *Starting Strength Training: Basic Barbell Training* (Aasgaard Company, Wichita Falls, 2017). Next up, have a look at Bobby Maximus and Michael Easter, *Maximus Body* (Rodale, 2018). This will give all of the weight training routines you will need to get moving, and get results.

I spoke of "barbarian" training, and this approach is represented well by Steve Justa in *Rock Iron Steel: The Book of Strength* (IronMind Enterprises, Nevada City, 1998) and *High Plains, Heavy Metal, Iron Master, Super Strength Bible!* (Strongerman Productions, 2012). This is but one example of the old school strongman approach to strength athleticism. A book with even more relevance to unarmed combat training is Bud Jeffries, *Super Strength and Endurance for Martial Arts* (Strongerman Productions, Lakeland, 2005). The thesis of these books is that there are various types of strength, all of which interact in a holistic fashion, so a great variety of hard-core training methods is necessary to produce the well-rounded strength athlete, who can do more than simply bench press substantial weight. As Bud Jeffries says, the "formula" is "the combination of low reps, high reps, overloading movements, off-balance movements, and conditioning." (p. 19)

Thus, to be considered in addition to the conventional barbell, dumbbell, and kettlebell lifts, are activities such as walking with heavy weights (classic farmer's walk), dragging or pushing weights, such as cars or trucks, barrel lifting, log lifting, sandbag lifting, rock lifting, log throwing/caber tossing (as in the Scottish Highland games), flipping large truck tires (if available), and numerous functional grip strength exercises. A book which goes into great detail about this type of old school training is Brook Kubik, *Dinosaur Training: Lost Secrets of Strength and Development*, (The Author, 2006), and for lifters over 40 years, *Grey Hair and Black Iron: Secrets of Successful Strength Training for Older Lifters*, (Brooks Kubik Enterprises, 2010). Indeed, the later book is well worth reading even by younger lifters, as there is a sensible material on a number of dangerous lifts that often result in injury. Old Time Strongman[555] relives the tradition and philosophy of the strongmen of the past such as Arthur Saxon (1878-1921) (training with abbreviated, intense drug-free section). For a taste of the wisdom of the past, consult, Arthur Saxon, *The Development of Physical Power* (1931).[556]

The next thing to consider is the enormously controversial topic of martial arts training, primarily unarmed combat. This is an area that I have been interested in for most of my life, and I have come to have heretical thoughts about this. Bruce Lee (1940-1973), expressed doubts about the efficiency of classical Asian and Western martial arts systems in the 1960s and early 1970s, essentially arguing that all such systems have limitations built into their framework, such as classical Wing Chun, with its preoccupation with close-range fighting and largely straight attacks. He put all of this down in his posthumous book, *Tao of Jeet Kune Do* (Black Belt, 2011).

Along the same lines are the objections made by John Perkins (et al.) in *Attack Proof*, (Human Kinetics, Champaign, 2009):

Whether by plan or accident, self-defense training on almost all levels has become inadequate, overstylized, unnatural, and in many cases, too sportive. To teach large numbers of people in a short time, instructors boil down defensive moves into simple regimented, robot-like techniques that bear no resemblance to actual fighting. Similarly, some originally authentic systems of fighting have developed into highly artistic and dance like art forms that are appropriate for demonstration purposes only. (p. xi)

James LaFond's book *The Fighting Edge: Using Your Martial Arts to Fight Better*, is the best book I can recommend on exposing the mythology of the martial arts. Apart from the limitations of the "martial arts," there has been a much more practical tradition of unarmed combat coming from World War II systems, as seen in the works of people like William Fairbairn and Rex Applegate, *Kill or Get Killed*, (Paladin Press, Boulder, Colorado, 1976). This has, in turn, led to many military hand-to-hand combat systems being marketed. In general, this is a vast improvement upon classical Asiatic approaches. However, as has been pointed out in the article, "The Myth of Military Hand-to-Hand Combat Systems,"[557] beyond the sound fundamentals, the special combat units in the military do not have the time to develop high skill levels in unarmed combat, since they have other teaching priorities for soldiers who will be fighting with weapons. Sure, bullets run out, and this has often happened, but it is rare for soldiers in any era to go immediately for unarmed fighting, unless there is no weapon available. Usually, a fighting knife would be resorted to in the last pitch effort. As Sgt Rory Miller has said: "Possibly the most overlooked aspect of power generation in the martial arts is one of the most effective: use a tool. I will take a hickory baseball bat over the hardest fist on Okinawa."[558]

Even with the rise of Mixed Martial Arts, which has shown the limits of the standard Asian systems, there are still many stories of superb fighters, capable of beating down multiple attackers, still being defeated, or worse, killed by punks armed with weapons, such as iron bars and knives.[559] And, regarding the present fad of ground fighting, while this is unquestionable effective in the octagon, it was never a good idea in the street, or bar, with sharp objects around, such as broken glass, and the knife of your opponent's buddy.[560]

In conclusion, the basic philosophy of the martial arts and even more practical unarmed combat training is that you will be weaponless, or lose your weapon, or won't have a spare, or any number of other hypothetical scenarios. But, while there are merits in having these unarmed skills, the point remains that the enormous amount of time devoted to becoming proficient in these unarmed skills, does not cash out in real self- defense benefits compared to weapons training. Perhaps that is why the Asian systems, which take years, if not decades to master, bullshit on about spiritual values and all the rest of it. While one can lose a weapon, better-skilled fighters simply do not, have backup and backup to the backup weapons, and other plans. People actually did this in the past, and survived, with only basic unarmed skills, if that, perhaps nothing more than a strong arm and the will to rip out an eye or crush a throat. Therefore, the sort of intense time-consuming effort required for unarmed self-defense training, from an apocalypse perspective, is best channeled into weapons training, firearms first, then melee weapons. If there is spare time, unarmed combat definitely should be studied, but it is not a chief priority. Developing survivalist weapons savvy is much more important. Sure, MMA fighters are touch guys in the cage going up against opponents playing by the same rules, but in the Great Collapse, one needs to throw away the rule book.[561]

There are many good books in the urban survival genre dealing with primarily surviving contemporary urban violence. James LaFond has produced a number of books derived from surviving in one of America' most violent cities, Baltimore, and along with his combative books, he has case studies of predatory violence, including, *When You're Food*, *Waking Up in Indian Country*, and *Thriving in Bad Places*, which take "situational awareness" to a whole new level.[562] Also well worth reading is Tim Larkin, *When Violence is the Answer*,[563]("Your brain is your deadliest weapon"); Marc MacYoung and Jenna Meek, *What You Don't Know Can Kill You* (2018),[564] and Varg Freeborn, *Violence of Mind* (2018).[565] If necessary, from there, the once novice reader can seek out material on his own to digest. It is far better to learn lessons from the stab and gunshot wounds of others, then to learn from firsthand experience, where, as luck will have it, you die.

The main lesson to take on board for the collapse is that the world ceases to be safe in the ways many have taken for granted, for the world will return to a pre-modern state of "constant battles."[566] In the die-off period following the collapse, the adrenaline level will be higher, but even after the bulk of fetid humanity has become food for rats, the remnant will still face danger from other survivors, who will continue to be threats so long as resources are scarce. Thus, the individual would need to live in a state of relaxed vigilance, being aware of one's environment and what is around him, typically described as condition yellow in Jeff Cooper's color code of situational awareness.[567] Condition white is a state of sleepwalking unawareness, a mechanical doing that would leave it up to luck if one survived. Condition orange, next beyond condition yellow, is a focused awareness on something that could become a threat, and condition red, is what it sounds like, red alert, battle stations. Many US police go through this color code awareness (yellow, orange, red, yellow …) each day, and if they can do it, so can you.

A book dealing with the brutality of collapse and cultural war in the Balkans, which does deal with the aspects of hyper-violence, is Selco Begovic, *The Dark Secrets of SHTF Survival*, discussed earlier.[568] This book is particularly good for its hard, gritty realism about the level of degradation that people can fall to, and it refutes liberal-humanist myths of the milk of human kindness, and that the good of human nature ultimately shines through dark situations (my interpretation). There is, of course, a limit from what one can obtain from books, but at least such literature can get one's thinking clearly about the topic, which is a good first step.

Psychologist Richard Logan, writing in the foreword to Les Stroud's *Will to Live*, says that he agrees with Stroud's central thesis that "sometimes the only explanation for why some people survive a hell beyond hell is their steely will to live. Survival often goes so far beyond the capacity of psychologists to explain that there is simply nothing left to say."[569] The will to survive is something which either burns within one or does not, much like other virtues such as courage. Probably it cannot be created *ex nihilo*, but physical training may enhance the flame if it exists.

7. WEAPONRY

Before all else, be armed.

- Niccolò Machiavelli (1469-1527)[570]

Victory belongs to the side
That scores most
In the temple calculations
Before battle.

- Sun Tzu[571]

Firearms, and proficiency in their use, should dominate any present survivalist concern with preparing for the coming collapse. However, the future of private firearms ownership is grim, even for us Americans. Other jurisdictions have severe firearm restrictions, and the "progressive" elites in America are conducting a multi-faceted program to ultimately lead to US gun confiscation, from ammunition sales restrictions to the criminalization of private gun sales, to outright Australia-1996-style confiscation, perhaps using the armed forces to brutalize civilians.[572] The later scenario hypothesizes that the post-Trump Democrat president will use the *National Defense Resources Preparedness Executive Order 13603*, issued by President Obama on March 16, 2012, to declare a "national emergency" over gun violence, with the use of emergency powers to conduct a nationwide gun confiscation program. There are doubts on some sites whether this Order does permit this,[573] but if it does not, surely the "correct" Executive Order will be produced by the post-Trump Democrat president, whose existence is guaranteed by the coming minority. In any case, during the 2020 pandemic, social isolation laws in some jurisdictions ruled that gun shops were not essential businesses (as self-defense was not essential), and were closed under medical martial law.

Facing the coming apocalypse described above will be worse than horrendous without firearms, and even now, in most of Europe, where the bar is set very high to own any firearm, gun ownership is surging.[574] Places such as Venezuela, where the public foolishly allowed gun confiscation, now face threats in both urban and rural areas from gangs, often armed with illegal guns, who are preying upon the vulnerable population, with little protection from the corrupt police force.[575]

In jurisdictions where private firearms ownership is severely restricted, it may still be possible to attend rifle, shotgun, and pistol clubs for novices to get some basic competency with these weapons. It would be important to move beyond merely shooting at paper targets, whether using a rifle, shotgun or pistol, and engage in force-on-force realistic training, to safely simulate real-world firefights, and to attempt to reduce the problem of misses under stress.[576] NYPD statistics for 1994-2000 have a combat situation hit percentage at zero to two yards at 38 percent, with 62 percent misses, due to the effects of adrenaline and fear in general.[577] There is a wealth of information on the topic of realistic firearms training on YouTube and internet sites.[578] A good book to get one's feet moving on close-quarter combat is Shawn Williams, *Armageddon CQB: A Close Quarter Battle Primer for the Apocalypse*, (Outskirts Press, 2018).

If all of the above training is impossible, as seems to be the case in parts of East Asia, there are still internet resources and numerous books to consult, that, while far from perfect, maybe the best possible under the circumstances for learning. Some to read include, Don Mann, *The Modern Day Gunslinger* (Skyhorse Publishing, New York, 2010); Wayne Van Zwoll, *Mastering the Art of Long-Range Shooting* (Gun Digest Books, Iola, 2013); Joe Nobody, *The Home Schooled Shootist: Training to Fight with a Carbine* (Kemah Bay Marketing, Kemah, 2011); Bill Jordan, *No Second Place Winner*

(Police Bookshelf, Concord, 1989) and Jeff Cooper, *The Art of the Rifle* (Paladin Press, Boulder, Colorado, 1997). That would give a beginner a basic introduction, enabling them to then explore other books via Amazon.com, and numerous gun and self-defense sites. There is still a vast amount of excellent information on YouTube on gun-related training, and it should be watched while it is still there. I agree with gun guru the late Elmer Keith (1899-1984), the "father of big bore hand gunning," when he summed up the firearms/self-defense training issue thus: "Anyone can be taught in a couple of hours to aim or point a shotgun, heavy caliber six gun or the .45 Auto at the middle of a criminal, and score decisive hits at the first shot. Aim or point any of these weapons at his middle and shoot as long as he is on his feet. The remaining trouble will then be up to the undertaker."[579] It is ballistics, but not quite rocket science.

Numerous books written since the 1970s have proposed that at a minimum, one needs for self-defense, a military-style semi-auto rifle (e.g., AR-15), a combat pistol, generally a semi-auto rather than a revolver, and a 12-gauge shotgun. This is the position of Dr. Bruce Clayton,[580] Mel Tappan in his iconic *Survival Guns*,[581] and Fred Rexer,[582] to name but a few. That is a basic ideal battery for one person, and primarily for self-defense against a human attacker; Tappan and others also believed that numerous "working" guns are also needed, to deal with hunting small game (.22 LR), or defense against large predators such as bears.[583] There are debates in most gun magazines, or gun comics if you are cynical, about the merits of various semi-auto pistols for self-defense, both brand and caliber, perhaps generated by the intrinsic limitation of most pistols compared to heavy-caliber rifles and shotguns, to have the mythical "one-shot stopping power."[584] For example, many survival savvy people swear by the reliability of the Glock family of semi-auto pistols, such as the Glock 17, with its 17, or even 33 round extended magazines. But, some have abandoned their Glocks and moved to the SIG Sauer camp, such as the SIG P320, allegedly being better for concealed carry.[585] These sorts of debates are somewhat "academic," since pistols are a backup in a grid down situation, where the rifle and shotgun are kings, and most popular commercial brands of defensive pistols are completely adequate for survival self-defense, even if such pistols would not pass an army small arms torture test. One is lucky to have any pistol at all.

Most of the survival gun literature is American and assumes that the Second Amendment will survive. Less dramatically, there is an assumption that semi-auto rifles and pistols will still be legal in civilian hands. Yet, if America goes the way of, say, Australian, New Zealand, or even the degenerate Britain, then Americans will have to make do with whatever repeating weapons are available. As noted by James Ballou in *Arming for the Apocalypse*,[586] survivalists would need to suffice with various hunting rifles, including bolt action and pump action repeaters, and the iconic lever actions from Marlin and Henry. There will be no room here for a "spray and pray" approach that could come from the abundance of riches of the semi-auto, and marksmanship will have to rule. Perhaps this is not all bad, since attacking ferals may "surrender" their possibly semi-auto firearms, so that these guns could be seen as step ladders. But if not, these non-auto guns are highly reliable, not dependent upon gas and other auto-ejection systems, and fire generally more powerful rounds, or at least rounds where there is less controversy about stopping power. These guns could serve the role of a "scout rifle," as conceived by Jeff Cooper,[587] a general-purpose repeater rifle for both hunting and self-defense, powerful enough to put down living targets of up to 1,000 lbs/ 454 kg. Ruger, along with other firearms firms, has marketed an excellent version of the scout concept, the Ruger Gunsite Scout, in .308 caliber. Nevertheless, ignoring dangerous game such as bears, for self-defense against human foes, even lever-action rifles from Marlin, Henry and other firms producing cowboy action guns, such as Uberti and Cimerron Firearms, firing rounds in .357 Mag., .44 Mag., .45 Long Colt, will be adequate. The Browning BLR has a box magazine and comes in a variety of calibers with spitzer bullets (i.e., pointy-nosed), such as in .223 and .308. However, Hornady's LEVERevolution rounds with special tips allow the firing of a spitzer bullet in a rifle with a tubular magazine. The Remington 7600 Police

Patrol pump action rifle comes in .308 and .223 calibers, and the .223 version takes AR-15 magazines, making it a semi-politically correct "assault rifle."

Those who are concerned about gun banning have generally proposed that survivalists have a crossbow, which is far easier for gunmen to use than a compound, long or recurve bow.[588] The bad news is that in some countries where gun bans have occurred, attention has then shifted to crossbows. Australia is an example, which shows that gun control leads to total weapon control. Indeed, in the state of Victoria, Australia, even swords are banned, and all Australian states heavily regulate classical Asian martial arts weapons, ironically the same sorts of weapons that the Okinawans used when disarmed by the Japanese in the 15th century. In any case, while bows have been used for long-distance shots, for self-defense, fast shots are required in many cases. The excellent video, "A New Level of Archery,"[589] featuring Danish archer Lars Andersen, shows how a return to classic shooting, perhaps as practiced by the rapid-fire shooting of the archers of Genghis Khan[590] and the Comanches, can lead to the ability to fire ten arrows in 4.9 seconds, and three arrows in 0.6 seconds. Critics have said that these techniques are only valid for rapid close-range fire, but even so, many of our self-defense concerns are in this basic pistol range. Mastering these skills, even in part, would give one an advantage in a showdown against multiple attackers, perhaps in some out-of-doors bug-out situation where firearms were not involved. Certainly, if one could approach that rate of fire, the bow is viable as a self-defense projectile weapon in gun-banned jurisdictions. As far as I can ascertain, recurve bows have not yet been restricted in jurisdictions where crossbows are now highly regulated.

If one does not have the time to develop such skill, in a firearm-banned society that has not yet banned crossbows, perhaps the recently released fast and accurate Cheap Shot 130 crossbow by Cold Steel[591] may be considered. This delivers shots capable of killing boar and deer within reasonable distances, with a rapid-fire of a demonstrated six shots in 39 seconds, something which could be bettered. The "Buzz Saw" broad head can slice clean through a 200 lb pig carcass. It is probably not possible for most of us to fire arrows at Lars Andersen's rate, but as a ranged weapon against non-armored attackers in a rural environment/outdoors, with no firearms, it would be a devastating range weapon. The Cobra System RX Adder, is a tactical crossbow being a modernized version of the "chu-ko-nu" weapon, having a top-level magazine with five (or six) Ek carbon bolts, which is worth a look.[592]

As far as range/projectile weapons go, if archery falls, following guns, then thrown weapons are a fallback, ranging from homemade thrown spears, such as sharpened sticks if necessary (native peoples did well even with throwing sticks), to a variety of factory-made weapons such as Cold Steel's Torpedo Thrower 80 TOR, a piece of rolled carbon steel, with points at both ends.[593] A little expensive for the apocalypse, in my opinion, where many such weapons will be needed, with most getting "lost." An alternative would be to make one's own, using a thick steel rod, reo rod, sharpened. But, many things can be thrown, and simple rocks have been used since man crawled out of the primal slime, dripping filth, to kill his neighbor and steal his woman, food, and stuff. Here is a video link (in the endnotes) to the infamous Varg Vikernes, of Thulean Perspectives, who makes a convincing case that good old-fashioned rocks can be effective range weapons.[594] Try banning that! One can also cheaply make throwing weapons being essentially arrow-like darts with weighted tips, that will always hit the business end first, and one can hold a number of these in hand.[595] Just for the apocalypse, of course, not now!

As far as melee weapons go in an apocalypse scenario, most of the discussion of their use derives from zombie apocalypse literature and film. I am somewhat tired of the zombie genre, which, like zombies, does not die a natural death. In any case, assuming that killing zombies is a metaphor for fighting post-apocalyptic feral scum, we can do much better in the real world than using baseball bats and crowbars, and a variety of sporting goods, or even kitchen utensils, as some of the zombie books suggest. Yes, many people have been killed by baseball bats, but the sort of bat picked up at the sporting goods store today, really cannot take much by way of zombie head beating, and the relatively lightweight maple bats, that have replaced ash, and before that hickory, often break on the field from hitting mere baseballs, rather than skulls.[596]Aluminum bats, more expensive, maybe more durable, but can still warp, and in torture tests, like demolition events, eventually break, often surprisingly quickly.[597] The synthetic bats produced by Cold Steel (e.g., Brooklyn Crusher and Smasher) are very good and have reviewed well. However, mattock handles, especially synthetic ones are also good and cheaper. Indeed, axe handles are cheap and arguably better weapons than baseball bats and are designed for taking impact.

As for crowbars, these are highly durable, having primary uses as a tool other than as a weapon. But, if they have reach, they will be somewhat weighty and unwieldy. These may be fine for dispatching the odd MZB but will be slow against human opponents who may have superior faster weapons. As for anything found in the kitchen, to make utensils a primary weapon, rather than a weapon of the moment (while cooking), is asking to die, probably unfed too.

The better apocalypse books see the most appropriate anti-MZB melee weapons as being precisely the medieval weapons used against humans in the past, various polearms such as spears, swords, axes, war hammers, and large knives, as last-ditch weapons.[598] There are, of course, many different types of melee weapons, including flexible weapons such as three-section staffs, and various whips, but for ordinary people rather than specialized martial artists, it is best to keep to the tried and proven more conventional weapons, rather than something like a three-section staff, where one is more likely to injure oneself than one's opponent.

For most people, melee weapon choice will involve bladed weapons rather than rigid body impact weapons, such as various sticks and staffs. It was noted by the European masters, such as Joseph Swetham in *The Schoole of the Noble and Worthy Science of Defence*, (London, 1617) and earlier by George Silver, *Bref Instructions Ypon My Pradoxes of Defence* (London, 1599), with all other things being equal, a good quarterstaff man would defeat an unarmored, non-shield carrying, blade-wielding, opponent of "equal" ability. The reach and lightness of the staff gave a speed advantage that would overcome the merits of, say, a blade, or even a heavier pole weapon such as a poleaxe. Still, today, most people are not going to acquire this skill level,[599] given all of the demands facing us, and the collapse will only intensify this. However, pole training can be an important aid to power training for whatever weapon one uses, especially if large thick steel pipes are used as leverage bars to increase upper body and forearm strength. Even in a collapse situation, without barbells and conventional weights, one could still do an upper body workout using such bars, thick scrap iron, or branches from trees or logs. Heavy clubs were used by the Indian wrestlers to increase strength, and the same can be done in a post-apocalyptic environment, using found material. A log can have a handle carved into it to enable a safe grip, and this can be slung as one would if using it as a weapon, making sure not to clout yourself in the head. This will, in turn, increase the destructive power of blows delivered from bladed weapons, even if one does not use sticks as a primary weapon.

Another argument in favor of bladed weapons, if they are available, is that for the average person, it may not be possible to put down some lunatic with one hit from a stick before he is on to you. Remember the Tueller drill, that for someone with a holstered gun, there is 21 feet (6.4 meters) danger zone facing an opponent with a blade, who may bridge the gap before he can be decisively stopped by drawing and firing a holstered pistol.[600] This will also apply to the use of stick weapons. Basically, the knife-wielding opponent could be onto one, if the first attack fails. Of course, unlike the pistol defense, there is always footwork, blocking, and counter-attacks, but these could, in turn, come unstuck. For the moderately trained person who is not going to have the strategic combat sense of decades-trained martial artists, in a post-apocalyptic scenario, there will need to be use made of weapons capable of delivering to an unarmored person a one-shot stop.[601] While that concept may be problematic for firearms, blades can deliver at closer range devastating attacks, including complete decapitation, and cutting off limbs, and slicing a person in halves, head down to the crotch. There are numerous YouTube videos from Zombie Go Boom.com, where synthetic ballistic heads are easily cut in half by bladed weapons, such as swords, and more dramatically, Cold Steel usually tests its bladed weapons by cutting demonstrations using animal carcasses, where even the lighter machetes (e.g., the Latin machete) and knives, go well in slicing through flesh. Just as enjoyable, for those with a Nordic/Germanic/Viking taste, are the YouTube videos by Thegn Thrand, where medieval weapons are put through their paces,[602]with many tests of reasonably priced swords from Australia's Medieval Shoppe,[603] a most reasonably priced business that mail delivers their goodies to us here in America.

Cutting to the chase, my recommendation for the would-be survivor is to obtain a sword that one likes, and a spare, or if swords are illegal in one's jurisdiction, perhaps fighting axes, such as the Viking hand axe. Longer polearm weapons, such as spears, certainly have their place, the spear being man's primary melee weapon defense against wild animals. Some should be retained at one's survival retreat, perhaps duct-taping a fighting knife such as a Bowie to a stout pole. Of course, commercial spears can be purchased, but these are getting pricey for what one gets, but there is likely to be some medieval re-enactment society in your town, with a blacksmith who can bang out spearheads that you then attach to a pole. The quality of workmanship, as the Vikings knew, need not be as precise as that required for swords. Likewise, for axe heads, which may be obtained from the same source.

With swords being banned in various jurisdictions, fighting axes such as the Viking hand axe are an option for melee weapons. So, how good would the Viking axe be as a post-apocalyptic weapon? John Clements sees the fighting axe as having disadvantages relative to the sword, as the long axe allegedly lacks versatility and proper defense and thus could be defeated by a swordsman with a shield.[604] He is probably referring to the two-handed Dane axe here rather than the smaller Viking hand axes, which are even more versatile than swords, capable of being grasped close to the blade for close-range fighting, as well as being able to be thrown, something not usually done with a sword. These light axes can chop better than most swords, if long enough, and are not slow in recovery, as the larger Dane axe, or even a wood chopping axe would be.[605] These small axes feature in the Bayeux Tapestry and other depictions, so the Vikings, Normans, and Germanic warriors must have used them as weapons of war. Further, these sorts of axes are still pretty much under the politically correct radar weapons and can be purchased for much less than any decent sword. A family could arm up with them while obtaining good swords, today, is still an expensive venture. Expense and availability were some of the main reasons for Vikings preferring axes to swords, and for us poor people today, the same argument holds. For axe training, including fighting tomahawks, there is not much good material on YouTube, swords overwhelmingly dominating. For books, D. C. McLemore, *The Fighting Tomahawk: An Illustrated Guide to Using the Tomahawk and Long Knife as Weapons*, (Paladin Press, Boulder, Colorado, 2004), and *The Fighting Tomahawk* Volume II, (Paladin Press, Boulder, Colorado, 2010), can serve as introductory texts. The fighting axe techniques are much easier to learn than sword fighting, and people who have used woodwork axes already have a head start.

Swords have a special place in the dark hearts of doomsters as melee weapons. Indeed, as John Clements has observed, swords are a quasi-mystical weapon of high symbolic significance, often having names, and featuring in epic sagas of light versus darkness and other English lit stuff that we forgot from school.[606] Apart from that, swords deliver truly devastating attacks upon unarmored human flesh, and as has been said above, while there could be problems for the non-expert putting down some drugged lunatic, even with a handgun, a good sword has no such erectile deficiency problems. The Moro suicide attackers, the Juramentados, during the 1899-1913 Moro Rebellion in the Philippines, would often soak up numerous slugs from the US .38 caliber service revolvers of the time, then kill the US soldier with a short sword. Legend has it that this led to the use of the Colt .45 Model 1911 semi-auto pistol, but this service sidearm arrived after the Moro Rebellion. Instead, the Colt .45 Model 1902 and DA Model 1909 revolvers were used, which were better than the .38 revolver, but not perfect against drugged-up crazies.[607] Winchester repeating shotguns fared better. However, the use of a sword, longer than the Moro's one, be it katana, Viking sword, or other European and Asian blades (such as the fearsome Chinese war sword or Dadao[608]), would decisively end the confrontation, since no-one fights on after being decapitated.

It is also interesting to note that today the Philippines' marine corps and Special Forces issue soldiers with short swords such as the bolo and ginunting, with blades up to 51 cms (20 inches). The weapons are useful for fighting in thick jungles in Mindanao, where very close-range fighting can occur. These weapons are quiet and effective in the vegetation, which offers a parallel situation for civilians in a domestic home invasion scenario, where the actual house presents the cluttered environment, that may not be conducive to using a rifle (even a carbine), or shotgun. While swords have long been abandoned from most other armies, in favor of the use of bayonets, that does not necessarily apply to civilian survival use, where the issue of weight and interference with other gear, may or may not be applicable.

The sword which a survivalist chooses for a multi-generational conflict is really a matter of personal style and taste. In general, one would be wise to have a sword which was excellent in stabbing and slashing/chopping, but most swords are good enough here; even the Chinese war sword can stab.[609] The real issue, in my opinion, is not the futile question of "what is the best sword," but rather, what type of sword best fits into your melee combat strategy. For example, there is no question that the huge two-handed "great sword"[610] or the Zweihänder, used by the German Landsknecht mercenaries in the early 16th century to chop the heads off of pikes, would be effective in some outdoor situations, especially in a rural environment. But, in general, such a weapon is going to be clumsy in most applications, and a more practical sword will be needed. I believe that whatever sword one likes, and up to a point there will be a strong element of personal taste and aesthetics in sword choice, the weapon should be capable of effective one-handed use. This is necessary for the use of a shield, even one banged up from marine plywood, to defend against the use of throwing weapons, such as spikes, weighted arrows, throwing sticks, and even rocks. What point is there having a huge blade wielded in two hands if one gets one's skull smashed in by a rock, in a David vs. Goliath deathmatch?

It should be possible to train to be able to use iconic two-handed swords, such as the katana, with one hand. Japanese swordmaster Miyamoto Musashi in *A Book of Five Rings*[611] had a method of two-sword fighting, *Niten Ichi-ryū* (二天一流), "the school of the strategy of two heavens as one." This involved use of the katana and the shorter wakizashi, indicating that the katana could be effectively wielded in one hand and would achievable by strength training and using training "swords" such as iron bars, much heavier than the actual sword. It is not too difficult.

Obviously, if one opts for the use of a sword, a fine weapon is needed, and here is the age-old problem with swords, even for today: expense. A cheap made-in-China knockoff katana is probably going to be unreliable, although I did buy a Damascus steel katana, which cuts very well, but who knows when TSHTF. Cheaper swords bought from on-line shopping sites may be suspect, for your life could one day depend upon their reliability. Thus, if finance is going to be an issue, as I expect that it will for many people today, struggling just to get by, the alternative could be a combat machete. Cold Steel makes numerous permutations of a basic pattern of 1055 carbon steel with a baked-on anti-rust matt finish and 2.8 mm thick blades. There are classic working machetes such as the Latin, but others are along the cheap weapons line, such as the gladius, tactical katana, Chinese war sword, barong, kopis, various Bowies, and kukris, some with neat handguards, such as the Royal kukri. One should go to their website, have a look at what strikes you as interesting, then seek out a store that sells them, try it in your hand, and purchase if satisfied.

Obviously, there are numerous other brands of machetes to choose from, but Cold Steel comes first to mind as giving good bang for the buck. Nevertheless, for workhorses that can double as weapons, the Latin and bolo machetes produced by the Brazilian company Tramontina, maybe even more value for money.[612] MTech's Tactical Combat Machete, with a 25-inch, 4 mm thick blade, and Kershaw's Camp 18, would also be excellent cost-effective choices for machetes that are really short swords, so there is no sharp dividing line between machetes and swords.[613]

A good book to get started on sword/machete training is Fred Hutchinson, *The Modern Swordsman: Realistic Training for Serious Self-Defense*, (Paladin Press, Boulder, Colorado, 1998). This book does not single out any particular type of sword to be used for self-defense, but rather offers general training strategies based on practical methods used in warrior cultures of the past, such as ancient Rome. This involves using a surrogate sword for training much heavier than the battle sword (e.g., steel rod), strikes on a training post or hanging tire or heavy bag, safe sparring with mock weapons and protective gear with a partner(s), and a devotion to physical fitness and all-round athleticism. Weight training for the wrists and forearms should be conducted. Speed training, such as striking a ball on a string, should be done.

Well worth looking at while it still remains on YouTube is Cold Steel's take on machete fighting, which gives useful insights for blade fighting in general.[614] I do not have a high opinion of the Asian martial arts, and so as far as weapons training goes, one needs to get skills taught at a reasonable pace, rather than being made into a cash cow for "the Sifu." Perhaps, if HEMA (Historical European Martial Arts) is in your town, it would be worth checking out. There could even be medieval sword fighting clubs at the local university. Both would supply training partners for free sparring, which is the key thing to getting good in any combat weapons-based activity; you have to fight a lot.

Finally, the knife; about knife fighting, there is no end of controversy. A good book to have a look at to get into the realistic knife-fighting mentality is Don Pentecost's *Put 'Em Down, Take 'Em Out: Knife Fighting Techniques from Folsom Prison* (Paladin Press, Boulder, Colorado, 1988): "Many who thought that they were the "world's deadliest man" laid down when faced with true adversity!" (p. 4) "The traditional martial arts are, in fact, busy perpetuating the most useless shit imaginable." (p. 12) "The martial arts are selling a style. Eastern religion, philosophy, language, tradition, and culture do *not* promote effective self-defense. In fact, most martial artists are neither trained nor proficient streetfighters because simply put, they do not fight." (p. 13) Modern martial arts have been produced for people largely in urbanized societies, and have thus had a preoccupation with empty-handed techniques because that is all that people have outside of pistol carry, if one is lucky, in the United States. As shown in another classic work, James LaFond, *The Logic of Steel: A Fighter's View of Blade and Shank Encounters*, (Paladin Press, Boulder, Colorado, 2001), most knife encounters are sneak/surprise attacks, where the victim may not even see the blade coming. Street knife attacks in the modern urban jungle are not like the classic standoff portrayed in martial arts books, where the attacker approaches in a ritualistic overhand attack (as in the shower scene in the movie *Psycho* (1960)), but are unexpected, and knives come out of seemingly nowhere, and then your guts are in your hands, then slipping through your bloody fingers, gliding onto the street, down the sewer grate.[615]

That being said, I distinguish between possible knife fighting in the modern urban jungle and the collapsed world to come. As I see it, the surprise element may be much less for true hardcore survivors. In the post-apocalyptic world, being alert and battle-ready will be a *sine qua non* of existence. Thus, there are situations where knives could be drawn as last-ditch weapons, possibly if the main weapon has been dropped/knocked out of the hand, or broken. More importantly, the knife in collapse, WROL situations, would be used against unarmed muscle-bound, martial arts-based- psycho-attackers (no doubt multiple invaders), something legally out of bounds now in most situations, barring perhaps multiple attackers. Remember, morality has gone down the toilet at the end of days.

The knife in the hands of a competent fighter is more than enough to take down the trained, unarmed combat person. As Richard Ryan has said: "The hard truth is that you're unlikely to ever control someone who's armed with a knife. You'll never grab or trap the knife hand, you'll never lock or break the arm or wrist, and you'll most certainly never take a knife away from all but the most incompetent attackers."[616] And: "The knife offers no margin for error, so unless your attacker is an idiot, your chances of recognizing, intercepting and controlling him—or his weapon—are about as good as your chances of winning the lottery."[617]

Therefore, what a survivalist would want in such a post-apocalyptic situation as a primary last-ditch melee weapon for up close and personal attacks, is not a tactical folder, or even a superb fighting knife such as the iconic KA-BAR, (Big Brother), or otherwise excellent knives produced by Glock with blades about 6 or 7 inches, but *big* knives, not short sword length, but around the 12-14 inches mark.[618] Any longer and one may as well carry a weapon such as a gladius, which in itself is one clear option. This "big knife" philosophy was the position taken by Bill Bagwell, writing in the "Battle Blades' column in *Soldier of Fortune* magazine from 1984 to 1988, and published in his book, *Bowies, Big Knives and the Best of Battle Blades*, (Paladin Press, Boulder, Colorado, 2000). Along similar lines: Paul Kirchner, *Bowie Knife Fights, Fighters, and Fighting Techniques* (Paladin Press, Boulder, Colorado, 2010), and blade master James Keating: *Gentleman's Steel Reader*.[619] The idea here is simply that if it comes to using a knife, you want to have a badass piece of steel to perforate, chop, slice, dice, or otherwise serve up your opponent. Against a smaller blade, while these may technically be faster, the big blade is not slow and has reach and heft. There are numerous suitable Bowies available, made by almost all leading knife firms, such as the ESEE Junglas and Busse Bushwacker Mistress, a range of Bowies from Buck and Cold Steel (e.g., ranging from the premium quality Natchez Bowie to the machete-style Black Bear Bowie). All are of good quality to have in your hand when the chips are down.[620]

The Bowie is not the only style of big blade, with there being the iconic kukri made by almost as many blade firms as those making Bowies. This weapon is spiritually linked to the legendary Gurkha soldiers and has been used in many battles, an interesting one being when Gurkha Bishu Prasad Shrestha, fought 40 armed men on an Indian train. Armed with his kukri, he killed three, injured eight, and prevented the robbery, according to some reports. He said that he could not have survived without the kukri. While there are numerous manufactures of kukris in the West, especially the United States, one could consider purchasing one straight from the Gurkha homeland of Ex-Gurkha Khukuri House, and/or Everest Blade of Nepal, and/or Kailash blades. I would particularly like to have the money to purchase the "Scourge" modern kukri from Kailash, designed as an ultra-bad ass apocalypse end times melee weapon.[621]

Other big blade options include Asian blades such as the Wing Chun butterfly knives and the Japanese tanto. The iconic tanto need not be discussed in any detail here; it is widely recognized as having superb penetration in stabbing, and massive tissue-destructive potential due to its wicked chisel-shaped edge (in one version), as well as being a fully-adequate slasher. Go for a weapon with a blade length of around 12 inches, whether your choice is the classic Japanese design or more modern tactical variations with polypropylene handles.[622]

Kung Fu Butterfly swords, such as the Wing Chun butterfly knives/swords, are used in pairs, fighting with a weapon in each hand. The blade is about as long as one's forearm, which is to provide protection when blocking, the blade is spun using the trapping guards, like a sai, so that the weapon lies along the forearm, edge out to opponent. Thus, some of the commercial products which have flat trapping guards are difficult to spin, having a flat surface that does not permit smooth hand movement. That may not matter if one is not aiming to be a classical expert. Still, a proper set of butterfly swords are relatively expensive, and so for this reason alone, would not be the best weapons choice for ordinary folk. It is a different matter if one has trained in the Wing Chun system, of course.

With all of this, you will be ready for the end. Good luck, because we are going to need it.

8. CONCLUSION

One of the most dangerous errors is that civilization is automatically bound to increase and spread. The lesson of history is the opposite; civilization is a rarity, attained with difficulty and easily lost. The normal state of humanity is barbarism, just as the normal surface of the planet is salt water. Land looms large in our imagination and civilization in history books, only because sea and savagery are to us less interesting.

- C. S. Lewis.[623]

"It must be stated again and again that this society, in which in our own time the transition from Culture to Civilization is taking place, is *sick,* sick in its instincts and therefore in its mind. It offers no defense. It takes pleasure in its own vilification and disintegration.[624]

- Oswald Spengler (1880-1936)

Western civilization is dying. As Keith Preston observes, "[c] ivilizations die when their elites lose faith in their own civilization to such a degree that the will to survive no longer exists."[625] The situation regarding even this significant existential threat to the West is, as we have seen substantially worse, since the elites, exhibiting pathological altruism at the moron level,[626] actively are permitting brutal crimes to go unpunished, or unpunished until forced to act, with a collapse of social capital. As Gwendolyn Taunton also laments: "Our civilization is dying [...] the chasm of oblivion looms larger than even Spengler predicted for the West. What serves to tie our community together? There are no ties of kindred, no bonds of affection betwixt the masses of faceless individuals that compose our cities – the average man can barely stand to look his neighbor in the eyes. The image of the Nation and the State is shattered beyond repair; we can barely accord our government with credibility little alone trust and respect – thus, does our civilization linger on, opening wide the gates of death to permit the vultures to pick our carcass clean."[627] Nevertheless, as Troy Southgate has also observed, "chaos and disorder […] inadvertently contains the redeeming elements of sanity and redemption, and this unifying spirit will engender a common identity and enable people to pull together and fight back."[628] That is the upside of going down. However, even if this "come together" scenario of circling the wagons does not occur, we still will have interesting times, as we face inevitable death and destruction, of all that oppresses us now, as all burning ships sink.

The late Guillaume Faye (1949-2019) was excited:

> Despair is not appropriate. The end of the world is good news, even if it will occur soon with distress and suffering. After the coming shadows will come the light. Human history is far from reaching its end. Preparing for catastrophe and rebirth means transforming one-self *from the inside*. The tragedy on the horizon is perhaps the will of what is called God or fate. We are ruled by forces which we do not understand and which play dice with us. A new world is about to be born. Man is despairing, but despair is inhuman. The future is thrilling because it is catastrophic. We are dice in God's hands. Who is God?[629]

We are soon going to find out. Hopefully, the material presented above will be an aid in beginning your survivalist education if you are a novice, hence giving you at least a fighting chance.

ENDNOTES

[1]   Albert Camus, *The Plague*, Hamish Hamilton, London, 1948), last two paragraphs.

[2]   https://www.dailymail.co.uk/news/article-8190397/Swedens-Prime-Minister-Stefan-Lofven-warns-citizens-prepare-thousands-deaths.html.

[3]   https://www.dailymail.co.uk/news/article-8202335/Man-NSW-town-Bathurst-fined-1000-taking-morning-walk-without-reason.html.

[4]   https://nypost.com/2020/04/08/california-county-threatens-1k-fine-for-not-wearing-face-masks-in-public/.

[5]   https://www.dailymail.co.uk/news/article-8203631/Police-call-powers-fine-people-driving-second-homes.html.

[6]   https://yougov.co.uk/topics/health/articles-reports/2020/04/08/do-public-think-police-have-gone-too-far.

[7]   https://hnewswire.com/america-is-going-to-be-used-to-invoke-medical-martial-law-the-tribulation-factor-in-play-hell-on-earth/; https://libertarianinstitute.org/articles/this-martial-law-will-end-and-end-badly/.

[8]   https://www.youtube.com/watch?v=DSJzPZCEW4I.

[9]   https://theconversation.com/.

[10]   https://news.trust.org/item/20200408103237-l2epf.

[11]   https://khn.org/news.

[12]   https://aapsonline.org.

[13]   https://www.wsj.com/articles/

[14]   https://www.wsj.com/articles/.

15   https://www.livescience.com/.

16   J. G. Cross and M. J. Guyer, *Social Traps*. (University of Michigan Press, Ann Arbor, 1980).

17   William McNeil, *Plagues and People*, (Penguin Books, Harmondsworth, 1976).

18   https://foreignpolicy.com/2019/11/16/china-bubonic-plague-outbreak-pandemic/; https://edition.cnn.com/2019/11/23/asia/plague-china-history-intl-hnk-scli/index.html.

19   R. Ornstein and P. Ehrlich, *New World New Mind: Moving toward Conscious Evolution*, (Doubleday, New York, 1989), p. 127.

20   https://www.history.com/topics/world-war-i/1918-flu-pandemic.

21   Quentin Smith, "Critical Note of John Leslie, *The End of the World*," *Canadian Journal of Philosophy*, vol. 28, no. 3, 1998, pp. 413-434.

22   "Pandemic Potential Seen in Gene Changes of Bird Flu," at http://www.bloomberg.com/news/articles/2014-02-13/pandemic-potential-seen-in-gene-changes-of-bird-flu; E. Tsang, "Doctor Warn of Pandemic Potential of the New H10 N8 Bird Flu Virus," February 5, 2014, at http://www.scmp.com/news/china/article/1421212/china-scientists-reveal-second-case-h10n8-raising-alarm-about-bird-flus.

23   R. A. Langlois (et al.), "MicroRNA-Based Strategy to Mitigate the Risk of Gain-of-Function Influenza Studies," *Nature Biotechnology*, (August 11, 2013); DOI: 10.1038/nbt.2666.

24   https://thebulletin.org/2020/03/.

25   K. G. Andersen (et al.), "The Proximal Origin of […]," *Nature Medicine*, March 17, 2020, DOI: .https://doi.org/10.1038/s41591-020-0820-9.

26   D. MacKenzie "Why the Demise of Civilisation May be Inevitable," *New Scientist*, April 2, 2008, at http://www.newscientist.com/article/mg19826501.500-why-the-demise-of-civilisation-may-be-inevitable.html.

27   https://rt.com/op-ed/.

28   J. Willick, "How Epidemics Change Civilizations," March 27, 2020, at https://www.wsj.com/articles/how-epidemics-change-civilizations-11585350405.

29   Greg Sheridan, "Globalisation, Open borders and Long-Term Victims of

Disease," March 21, 2020, at https://www.theaustralian.com.au/inquirer/.

30   Rich Lowry, "We are All Restrictionists Now," April 1, 2020, athttps://www.politico.com/news/magazine/2020/04/01/we-are-all-restrictionists-now-160459.

31   As above.

32   https://abcnews.go.com/

33   https://abcnews.go.com/Politics/

34   Ken Klippenstein, April 1, 2020, at https://www.thenation.com/article/politics/.

35   https://www.forbes.com/sites/breannawilson/2020/03/16/.

36   https://edition.cnn.com/2020/04/08/europe/.

37   https://www.zerohedge.com/health/food-banks-warn-theyll-soon-run-out-food-economic-suffering-explodes-all-over-america.

38   https://www.newsweek.com/nearly-60-percent-workers-wont-meet-financial-needs-under-1495364 .

39   https://www.usnews.com/news/economy/articles/2020-04-03/; https://www.shtfplan.com/headline-news/almost-half-of-small-business-will-close-if-they-cannot-reopen-soon_04062020; https://www.shtfplan.com/headline-news/49-percent-of-u-s-companies-expect-layoffs-in-the-next-three-months-as-unemployment-heads-to-great-depression-levels_03312020.

40   https://www.cnbc.com/2020/04/03/[...]-way-worse-than-the-global-financial-crisis-imf-says.html; https://www.scmp.com/economy/china-economy/article/3078519/.

41   https://www.rt.com/business/485025-us-economy-losses-moodys/; https://www.theguardian.com/world/2020/apr/03/;https://apnews.com/b219627e31d87779e5253f9a072be4dc.

42   https://www.naturalnews.com/.

43   https://www.breitbart.com/europe/2020/04/05/.

44   https://www.naturalnews.com/; https://www.zerohedge.com/geopolitical/.

45   https://www.dailymail.co.uk/news/article-8196473/Normal-life-wont-resume-2021-says-scientist-pandemic-preparedness.html; https://www.dailymail.co.uk/news/article-8199977/World-Health-Organization-expert-warns-

against-ending-strict-lockdowns-Europe.html; https://www.telegraph.co.uk/news/2020/04/06/.

[46]   https://www.zerohedge.com/health/some-bad-news-jpm-what-happens-after-we-pass-virus-peak.

[47]   https://www.youtube.com/watch?v=aEubPR36pzk&feature=emb_title.

[48]   https://www.naturalnews.com/2020-04-05.

[49]   https://www.foxnews.com/politics/.

[50]   https://www.technologyreview.com/2020/03/10/916678/; https://medicalxpress.com/news/2019-04-flu-vaccine.html.

[51]   https://www.naturalnews.com.

[52]   https://www.naturalnews.com/; http://fortressdefense.com/sustainability/.

[53]   https://www.zerohedge.com/health/socio-economic-issues-will-erupt-italian-officials-fear-south-turning-powder-keg.

[54]   https://reason.com/2020/03/27/pandemic-related-unemployment-and-shutdowns-are-a-recipe-for-social-unrest/; https://gnseconomics.com/2020/04/08/the-worst-economic-collapse-ever/.

[55]   https://nypost.com/2020/04/04/.

[56]   https://www.breitbart.com/national-security/2020/04/07/george-soros-funded-group-to-governors-release-as-many-prisoners-as-possible/.

[57]   https://www.zerohedge.com/.

[58]   Daisy Luther, "We won't be Getting Back to Normal. Not Soon. Not Ever," April 8, 2020, at https://www.theorganicprepper.com/getting-back-to-normal/.

[59]   https://www.youtube.com/user/CanadianPrepper33.

[60]   https://www.youtube.com/user/TheModernSurvivalist.

[61]   https://www.naturalnews.com/.

[62]   https://www.theorganicprepper.com/about-daisy/.

[63]   https://www.peakprosperity.com/.

[64]   https://www.zerohedge.com/.

65   http://www.finfacts.ie/Irish_finance_news/articleDetail.php?In-the-long-run-we-are-all-dead---John-Maynard-Keynes-159, the full quote being: "But this *long run* is a misleading guide to current affairs. In the long run we are all dead. Economists set themselves too easy, too useless a task if in tempestuous seasons they can only tell us that when the storm is long past the ocean is flat again."

66   https://www.youtube.com/watch?v=toky5tYFMMg.

67   J. Seidel, "Why We have Apocalypse on Our Mind," May 22, 2019, at https://www.news.com.au/technology/science/evolution/why-we-have-apocalypse-on-our-mind/news-story/1071af2ff4942f07c3932f2391f5e00e; https://theconversation.com/we-spoke-to-survivalists-prepping-for-disaster-heres-what-we-learned-about-the-end-of-the-world-118867.

68   https://www.youtube.com/watch?v=JsDhfM7MXqI.

69   https://www.wired.com/story/; https://www.hilltimes.com/2020/04/01/.

70   Willian Ophuls, *Immoderate Greatness: Why Civilizations Fail*, (CreateSpace, 2012).

71   https://richardheinberg.com/peak-denial; https://www.foreignaffairs.com/articles/2020-04-02/oil-collapse; https://www.cnbc.com/advertorial/2019/03/19/is-peak-oil-looming.html.

72   Joseph Alton and Amy Alton, *Alton's Pandemic Preparedness Guide: Dealing with Emerging and Current Viral Threats*, (Doom and Bloom, 2020).

73   Cat Ellis, *The [...] Survival Manual: How to Prepare for Pandemics and Quarantines*, (2020) at https://learn.theorganicprepper.com/cartflows_step.

74   Quoted by W. L. Langer, *The Diplomacy of Imperialism: 1890-1902*, (Alfred Knopf, New York, 1965), p. 86.

75   Thomas Hobbes, *Leviathan*, (Penguin, Harmondsworth, 1968), I, 13, 9.

76   See for example, J. M. Greer, *Dark Age America: Climate Change, Cultural Collapse, and the Hard Future Ahead*, (New Society Publishers, Gabriola Island, 2016).

77   David Price, "Energy and Human Evolution," *Population and Environment*, vol.16, 1995, pp.301-319.

78   As above, p. 315. See further V. Gordon Childe, *Social Evolution*, (Watts, London, 1951).

[79]   Roberto Vacca, *The Coming Dark Age*, (Doubleday, New York, 1973), p. 174.

[80]   Mark Widdowson, *The Phoenix Principle and the Coming Dark Age: Social Catastrophes – Human Progress 3000 BC to AD 3000*, (Amarna LTD, Bedford, UK, 2001), p. xi.

[81]   James Ballou, *Long-Term Survival in the Coming Dark Age: Preparing to Live After Society Crumbles*, (Paladin Press, Boulder, Colorado, 2007), p. 1.

[82]   Alan Weisman, *The World Without Us*, (Picador, New York, 2008).

[83]   D. M. Raup, *Extinction: Bad Genes or Bad Luck?* (W. W. Norton, New York, 1991).

[84]   D. M. Behar (et al.), "The Dawn of Human Matrilineal Diversity," *American Journal of Human Genetics*, vol. 82, 2008, pp. 1130-1140.

[85]   W. H. Kötke, *The Final Empire: The Collapse of Civilization and the Seed of the Future*, (Arrow Point Press, Portland, OR, 1993).

[86]   Craig Dilworth, *Too Smart for Our Own Good: The Ecological Predicament of Humanity*, (Cambridge University Press, Cambridge, 2010), pp. 453-454.

[87]   Carolyn Baker, *Sacred Demise: Walking the Spiritual Path of Industrial Civilization's Collapse*, (iUniverse; http://www.iuniverse.com, 2009).

[88]   Carolyn Baker, "What if Collapse Happened and Nobody Noticed?" May 3, 2012 at http://carolynbaker.net/2012/05/03/what-if-collapse-happened-.

[89]   Carolyn Baker, *Collapsing Consciously: Transformative Truths for Turbulent Times*, (North Atlantic Books, Berkeley, 2013), p. 45.

[90]   Mike Adams, "How to Prepare Yourself for the Collapse of the Age of Human Delusion (and the Arrival of Human Spiritual Awakening)," NaturalNews.com, July 14, 2014 at http://www.naturalnews.com/045991_age_of_delusion_spiritual_awakening_mental_practice.html.

[91]   Clive Hamilton, *Requiem for a Species: Why We Resist the Truth about Climate Change*, (Allen and Unwin, Crow's Nest, New South Wales, 2010).

[92]   As above, p. 31.

[93]   As above p. viii

[94]   Guy R. McPherson, *Going Dark*, (Publish America, Baltimore, 2013)

95   Will Steffen and David Griggs, "Compounding Crises: Climate Change in a

Complex World," in P. Christoff (ed.) *Four Degrees of Global Warming: Australia in a How World*, (Routledge, London and New York, 2014), pp. 121-138; A. J. McMichael, "Health Impacts in Australia in a Four Degree World," as above, pp. 155-171.

96   Dominique Venner, *The Shock of History*, (Arktos, London, 2015).

97   Guillaume Faye, *Convergence of Catastrophes*, (Arktos, London, 2012).

98   Piero San Giorgio, *Survive the Economic Collapse: A Practical Guide*, (Radix/Washington Summit Publishers, Whitefish, 2013), p. 171.

99   P. McLoughlin, *Easy Meat: Inside Britain's Grooming Gang Scandal*, (New English Review Press, London, 2016); https://childhub.org/en/child-protection-news/one-million-child-victims-muslim-rape-gangs-uk; https://www.mirror.co.uk/news/uk-news/child-sex-abuse-gangs-could-5114029.

100   E. L. Quarantelli, "The Myth of the Realties: Keeping the Looting 'Myth' in Perspective," *Natural Hazards Observer*, March, 2007, at http://www.colorado.edu/hazards/o/archives/2007/mar07/mar07.pdf; L. G. Sun, "Disaster Mythology and the Law," *Cornell Law Review*, vol. 96, 2011, pp. 1131-1208.

101   Brian Thevenot, "Myth-Making in New Orleans," *American Journalism Review*, December/January 2006, at http://www.ajr.org/article.asp?id=3998.

102   See for example: http://web.archive.org/web/20140704005914/http://jtf.org/america/america.hurricane.katrina.htm

103   "At the Train Station, New Orleans' Newest Jail is Open for Business," September 6, 2005, at http://www.komonews.com/news/archive/4163081.html.

104   K. Bishop, "Preparing for THE Worst," at http://www.preparednesspro.com/preparing-for-the-worst.

105   See, "40 Rapes Reported in Hurricane Katrina, Rita Aftermath," http://www.wdsu.com/news/5627087/detail.html. http://www.frfrogspad.com/disastr.htm.

106   Kevin Bailey, *An Evaluation of the Impact of Hurricane Katrina on Crime in New Orleans, Louisiana*, (Master of Public Administration Thesis, Department of Political Science, Texas State University, San Marcos, 2009).

107   S. Vergano, "Report: No Crime Wave among Hurricane Katrina Evacuees," February 15, 2010, at http://usatoday30.usatoday.com/tech/science/columnist/vergano/2010-02-12-hurricane-katrina-crime_N.htm.

108   J. Kennett, "Louisiana Gangs That Fled Katrina Heighten Houston

Murder Rate," March 3, 2006 at http://www.bloomberg.com/apps/
news?pid=newsarchive&sid=az6n8C6gsqfo.

[109]   Sun, as above, p. 1139.

[110]   Rebecca Solnit, *A Paradise Built in Hell: The Extraordinary Communities That Arise in Disaster,* (Penguin, New York, 2010).

[111]   Richard Heinberg, "Conflict and Change in an Era of Economic Decline, Part 2: War and Peace in a Shrinking Economy," December 12, 2012 at http://www.carolynbaker.net/2012/12/12/conflict-and-change-in-the-era-of-economic-decline-part-2-war-and-peace-in-a-shrinking-economy-by-richard-heinberg/.

[112]   Thomas Sowell, "Early Skirmishers in a Race War," October 24, 2013, at http://www.nationalreview.com/article/362030/early-skirmishes-race-war-thomas-sowell.

[113]   Fernando "Ferfal" Aguirre, "Life after an Economic Collapse: The Same… Only Worse, Part I," November 6, 2014 at http://ferfal.blogspot.com.au/2014/11/life-after-economic-collapse-same-only.html.

[114]   http://ferfal.blogspot.com/2020/04/; Fernando "Ferfal" Aguirre, *Street Survival Skills: Tips, Tricks and Tactic for Modern Survival* (2019).

[115]   Dmitry Orlov, *The Five Stages of Collapse: Survivor's Toolkit,* (New Society Publishers, Gabriola Island, 2013).

[116]   John Grey, *Straw Dogs: Thoughts on Humans and Other Animals,* (Granta books, London, 2002), p. 4.

[117]   Harold Bloom, *The Lucifer Principle: A Scientific Expedition into the Forces of History,* (Atlantic Monthly Press, New York, 1995), p. 2.

[118]   Patrick J. Buchanan, *The Death of the West,* (St. Martin's Griffin, New York, 2002).

[119]   S. Le Blanc and K. E. Register, *Constant Battles: Why We Fight,* (St Martin's Press, New York, 2004); Lawrence Keeley, *War before Civilization: The Myth of the Peaceful Savage,* (Oxford University Press, Oxford, 1996).

[120]   Keeley, as above, p.174.

[121]   Nicolas Wade, *Before the Dawn: Recovering the Lost History of our Ancestors,* (Duckworth, London, 2007), p. 151.

[122]   As above, p. 152.

[123]   Keeley, as above, p. 33.

[124]   Wade, as above, p. 151.

[125]   As above, p. 84.

[126]   T. Flannery, *The Future Eaters: An Ecological History of the Australasian Lands and People*, (Reed books, Port Melbourne, 1994).

[127]   F. Chenel (et al.), "A Farewell to Arms: A Deposit of Human Limbs and Bodies at Bergheim, France, c. 4,000 BC," *Antiquity*, vol. 89, December, 2015, p. 1313.

[128]   C. Meyer (et al.), "The Massacre Mass Grave of Schöneck-Kilianstädten Reveals New Insights into Collective Violence in Early Neolithic Central Europe," *Proceedings of the National Academy of Sciences*, vol. 112, 2015, pp. 11217-11222.

[129]   Steven Pinker, *The Better Angels of our Nature: The Decline of Violence in History and its Causes*, (Penguin, New York, 2011).

[130]   See Nicholas Monsarrat, *The Tribe that Lost its Head*, (House of Stratus, Looe, 2000).

[131]   Annalee Newitz, *Scatter, Adapt, and Remember: How Humans Will Survive a Mass Extinction*, (Anchor Books, New York, 2014).

[132]   As above, p. 1.

[133]   Lewis Dartnell, *The Knowledge: How to Rebuild Our World from Scratch*, (Bodley Head, London, 2014).

[134]   As above, p. 22.

[135]   Dartnell, as above, p. 24.

[136]   Fred Hoyle, *Of Men and Galaxies*, (University of Washington Press, Seattle, 1964), p. 64.

[137]   Lewis Dartnell, "Tacit Knowledge and Loss of Reading," at http://the-knowledge.org/en-gb/tacit-knowledge-loss-reading/.

[138]   Ashley Barkman, "Women in a Zombie Apocalypse," in Wayne Yuen (ed.), *The Walking Dead and Philosophy: Zombie Apocalypse Now*, (Open Court, Chicago and La Salle, 2012), pp. 97-106.

[139]   ""ISIS Wants to Impregnate Yazidi Women and Smash our Blond Bloodline": Fears Grow for the 300 Women Kidnapped from Sinjar," *Daily Mail*

Australia, August 14, 2014, at http://www.dailymail.co.uk/news/article-2724658/Were-not-leaving-Yazidis-refusing-come-mountain-300-women-stolen-ISIS-impregnated-smash-blond-bloodline.html.

140   Nour Malas, "Ancient Prophecies Motive Islamic State Militants: Battlefield Strategies Driven by 1,400-Year-Old Apocalyptic Ideas" *The Wall Street Journal,* November 18, 2014, at http://www.wsj.com/articles/ancient-prophecies-motivate-islamic-state-militants-1416357441.

141   A. Lloyd, "Yazidi Girls Dragged into Sex Slavery by Their Hair," *The Australian,* December 23, 2014, pp. 1, 4.

142   Ivan Watson, "'Treated Like Cattle': Yazidi Women Sold, Raped, Enslaved by ISIS," November 7, 2014, at http://edition.cnn.com/2014/10/30/world/meast/isis-female-slaves/.

143   J. Newton, "ISIS Burn 19 Yazidi girls to Death in Iron Cages After they Refused to have Sex with Jihadists," June 6, 2016, at http://www.dailymail.co.uk/news/article-3627063/ISIS-burn-19-Yazidi-girls-death-iron-cages-refused-sex-jihadists.html.

144   "British Female Jihadis Running ISIS "Brothels" Allowing Killers to Rape Kidnapped Yazidi Women," http://www.mirror.co.uk/news/uk-news/british-female-jihadis-running-isis-4198165.

145   John Hall, "'I've Been Raped 30 Times and It's Not Even Lunch Time': Desperate Plight of Yazidi Women who Begged West to Bomb her Brothel after ISIS Militants Sold her into Sex Slavery," *Daily Mail Australia,* October 21, 2014, at http://www.dailymail.co.uk/news/article-2801353/i-ve-raped-30-times-s-not-lunchtime-desperate-plight-yazidi-woman-begged-west-bomb-brothel-isis-militants-sold-sex-slavery.html.

146   Dennis Meadows, quoted from M. Mukerjee, "Apocalypse Soon: Has Civilization Passed the Environmental Point of No Return?" *Scientific American,* May 23, 2012, at http://www.scientificamerican.com/article/apocalypse-soon-has-civilization-passed-the-environmental-point-of-no-return.

147   Pentti Linkola, *Can Life Prevail? A Radical Approach to the Environmental Crisis,* (Integral Tradition Publishing, 2009), p. 157.

148   Donald A. Collins, "Heading for a World Apocalypse? *Journal of Social, Political, and Economic Studies,* vol. 35, no.1, Summer, 2010, pp. 242-254.

149   "Stephen Hawking's Warning: Abandon Earth – or Face Extinction," at http://bigthink.com/dangerous-ideas/5-stephen-hawkings-warning-abandon-

earth-or-face-extinction.

150   S. Motesharrei (et al.), "Human and Nature Dynamics (HANDY): Modeling Inequality and Use of Resources in the Collapse or Sustainability of Societies," *Ecological Economics*, vol. 101, 2014, pp. 90-102.

151   G. Turner, "On the Cusp of Global Collapse? Updated Comparison of *The Limits to Growth* with Historical Data," *Gaia*, vol. 21, no. 2, 2012.

152   Jared Diamond, "Ecological Collapses of Past Civilizations," *Proceedings of the American Philosophical Society*, vol. 138, 1994, pp. 363-370, cited p. 363.

153   Karl W. Butzer and Georgina H. Endfield, "Critical Perspectives on Historical Collapse," *Proceedings of the National Academy of Sciences*, vol. 109, no.10, 2012, pp. 3628-3631, cited p. 3628.

154   https://www.youtube.com/watch?v=OA_CndlBuog.

155   M. Wackernagel (et al.), "Tracking the Ecological Overshoot of the Human Economy," *Proceedings of the National Academy of Sciences*, vol. 99, no. 1, 2002, pp. 266-271.

156   S. Postel, *Pillar of Sand*, (W. W. Norton, New York, 1999).

157   D. R. Montgomery, *Dirt: The Erosion of Civilizations*, (University of California Press, Berkeley, 2007).

158   L. R. Brown, "Could Food Shortages Bring Down Civilization?" *Scientific American Magazine*, April 22, 2009, at http://www.scientificamerican.com/article.cfm?id=civilization-food-shortages.

159   S. Pimm (et al.), "The Biodiversity of Species and their Rates of Extinction, Distribution, and Protection," *Science*, vol. 344, 2014, pp. 1246752-1 – 1246752-10.

160   UN Department of Economic and Social Affairs, *2019 Revision of World Population Prospects*, (United Nations, New York, 2017), https://population.un.org/wpp/.

161   https://data.oecd.org/migration/foreign-born-unemployment.htm; https://www.pewresearch.org/global/2018/03/22/at-least-a-million-sub-saharan-africans-moved-to-europe-since-2010/; https://www.breitbart.com/europe/2019/01/31/germany-majority-refugees-still-jobless.

162   Global Resource Observation, *Climate Change, Resource Scarcity and Conflict*, (Anglia Ruskin University, Cambridge, September, 2014), at http://www2.anglia.ac.uk/ruskin/en/home/microsites/global-sustainability-institute.

html.

163   J. Zalasiewicz (et al.), "Colonization of the Americas, 'Little Ice Age' Climate, and Bomb-Produced Carbon: Their Role in Defining the Anthropocene," *The Anthropocene Review*, vol. 2, no. 2, 2015, pp. 1-11.

164   Lloyd's Emerging Risk Report, *Food System Shock: The Insurance Impacts of Acute Disruption to Global Food Supply*, (2015), at https://www.lloyds.com/~/media/files/news%20and%20insight/risk%20insight/2015/food%20system%20shock/food%20system%20shock_june%202015.pdf.

165   Pascal Bruckner, "Apocalyptic Angst of the Western World," *The Weekend Australian*, April 21-22, 2012, p. 20.

166   Mark Steyn, *America Alone: The End of the World as We Know It*, (Regnery Publishing, Washington DC, 2006).

167   Mark Steyn, *After America: Get Ready for Armageddon*, (Regnery Publishing, Washington DC, 2011).

168   Tim Morgan, *Perfect Storm: Energy, Finance and the End of Growth*, Tullett Prebon, Strategy Insights, Issue 9, 2013 at http://ftalphaville.ft.com/files/2013/01/Perfect-Storm-LR.pdf.

169   Samuel Huntington, *The Clash of Civilizations and the Remaking of World Order*, (Simon and Schuster, New York, 1996).

170   Mark Steyn, *Lights Out: Islam, Free Speech and the Twilight of the West*, (Stockade Books, 2009).

171   Frank Salter, "Germany's Jeopardy: Could the Immigration Influx "End European Civilization"?" January 15, 2016, at http://www.eurocanadian.ca.

172   Lee Harris, *Civilization and Its Enemies*, (Free Press, New York, 2004), *The Suicide of Reason*, (Basic Books, New York, 2008).

173   Patrick Buchanan, *Suicide of a Superpower: Will America Survive to 2025?* (Thomas Dunne Books/ St. Martin's Press, New York, 2011).

174   John Derbyshire, *We Are Doomed: Reclaiming Conservative Pessimism*, (Crown Forum, New York, 2009).

175   Thomas W. Chittum, *Civil War Two: The Coming Breakup of America*, (Lexington and Concord Partners, Ancon, Panama City, distributed in the USA by American Eagle Publications, Inc. 1996).

176 Morris Berman, *The Twilight of American Culture*, (W. W. Norton, New York, 2001), *Dark Ages America: The Final Phase of Empire*, (W. W. Norton, New York, 2007), *Why American Failed: The Roots of Imperial Decline*, (John Wiley, New York, 2011).

177 Berman, *Dark Ages America*, as above, p. 6.

178 Robert D. Kaplan, "The Coming Anarchy: How Scarcity, Crime, Overpopulation, Tribalism and Disaster are Rapidly Destroying the Social Fabric of Our Planet," *The Atlantic Monthly*, February, 1994, pp. 44-76, *The Coming Anarchy: Shattering the Dreams of the Post Cold War*, (Vintage Books, New York, 2000), "Why So Much Anarchy?" February 5, 2014, at https://www.stratfor.com/weekly/why-so-much-anarchy.

179 W. Frey, *The Diversity Explosion: How New Racial Demographics Are Remaking America*, (Brookings Institution Press, Washington DC, 2014).

180 Kaplan, *The Coming Anarchy*, as above, pp. 49-50.

181 R. Harvey, *The Return of the Strong: The Drift to Global Disorder*, (Macmillan, London, 1995); R. Harvey, *Global Disorder*, (Constable, London, 2003).

182 Niall Ferguson, *The Great Degeneration: How Institutions Decay and Economics Die*, (Allen Lane, London, 2012).

183 Alain De Benoist, "La fin du monde a bien eu lieu," *Eléments*, no.146, January-March, 2013.

184 William Ophuls, *Immoderate Greatness: Why Civilizations Fail*, (CreateSpace, North Charleston, 2012). The discussion to follow is greatly in debt to this superb book, especially for some references.

185 Edward Gibbon, *The History of the Decline and Fall of the Roman Empire*, edited and abridged by David P. Womersley, (Penguin, New York, 2001), p.435.

186 As above, p. 435.

187 Will Durant, *Caesar and Christ: The Story of Civilization*, vol.3, (Simon and Schuster, New York, 1994), p.665, cited from Ophuls, as above, p. 4.

188 N. Georgescu-Roegen, *The Entropy law and the Economic Process*, (Harvard University Press, Cambridge, MA, 1971).

189 Chris Hedges, "The Treason of the Intellectuals," March 31, 2013, at http://www.uruknet.info/?p=96437.

[190]   Ophuls, as above, p. 86.

[191]   Jonathon Maberry, "Take Me to Your Leader: Guiding the Masses through the Apocalypse with a Cracked Moral Compass," in James Lowder (ed.), *Triumph of the Walking Dead: Robert Kirkman's Zombie Epic on Page and Screen*, (Smart Pop/Ben Bella Books, Dallas, 2011), pp. 15-34, cited pp. 18-19.

[192]   William Ophuls, *Plato's Revenge: Politics in the Age of Ecology*, (MIT Press, Cambridge MA, 2011), p.208.

[193]   Roberto Vacca, *The Coming Dark Age*, (Doubleday, New York, 1973).

[194]   Mike Adams, "Grid Down Catastrophe Strikes India; Half the Population Stranded with No Electricity," NaturalNews.com, July 31, 2012 at http://www.naturalnews.com/036640_India_power_grid_failure.html.

[195]   American Society of Civil Engineers, http://www.asce.org/reportcard/.

[196]   Alice Friedemann, "A Century from Now Concrete will be Nothing but Rubble," January 19, 2014, at http://energyskeptic.com/2014/enough-energy-left-to-rebuild-concrete-infrastructure.

[197]   "ASCE: Infrastructure Delay Costs Billions Each Year," July 28, 2011, at http://www.think-harder.org/think-concrete-blog/11-07-28/ASCE_Infrastructure_Decay_Costs_Billions_Each_Year.aspx.

[198]   Vacca, as above, p. 191.

[199]   Debora Mackenzie, "Are We Doomed?" *New Scientist*, vol. 197, no. 2650, April 5, 2008, pp. 32-35.

[200]   Joseph Tainter, *The Collapse of Complex Societies*, (Cambridge University Press, Cambridge, 1988).

[201]   As above, pp. 118-120.

[202]   Robin Hanson, "Catastrophe: Social Collapse, and Human Extinction," in N. Bostrom and M. M. Ćirković (eds.), *Global Catastrophic Risks*, (Oxford University Press, Oxford, 2008), pp. 363-377, cited p. 366.

[203]   Mike Adams, "Is the Fabric of Industrialized Society Starting to Unravel? Highly Complex Civilizations are More Vulnerable to Collapse," Natural News.com, December 29, 2011 at http://www.naturalnews.com/034517_complex_societies_collapse_2012.html.

[204]   Sidney Dekker, *Drift into Failure: From Hunting Broken Components to*

Understanding Complex Systems, (Ashgate, Surrey, 2011).

205   P. Bak, *How Nature Works: The Science of Self-Organised Criticality*, (Oxford University Press, Oxford, 1996).

206   M. Schafer (et al.), "Early Warning Signals for Critical Transition", *Nature*, vol. 461, 2009, pp. 53-59.

207   A. D. Barnosky (et al.), "Approaching a State Shift in Earth's Biosphere," *Nature*, vol. 486, June 7, 2012, pp. 52-58, cited p. 52.

208   Alok Jha, *The Doomsday Handbook: 50 Ways the World Could End*, (Quercus, London, 2011).

209   P. G. Brown (et al.), "A 500-Kiloton Airburst Over Chelyabinsk and an Enhanced Hazard from Small Impactors," *Nature*, (2013); doi:10.1038/nature2741.

210   B. McGuire, *Surviving Armageddon: Solutions for a Threatened Planet*, (Oxford University Press, Oxford, 2005).

211   "Geomagnetic Mega-Storm," Spaceweather.com, September 2, 2009, at http://spaceweather.com/archive.php?view=1&day=02&month=09&year=2009.

212   "Great Breach in Earth's Magnetic Field Discovered," December 16, 2008, at http://science.nasa.gov/science-news/science-at-nasa/2008/16dec_giantbreach.

213   As above.

214   H. Abdussamotov, "Bicentennial Decrease of the Total Solar Irradiance Leads to Unbalanced Thermal Budget of the Earth and Little Ice Age," *Applied Physics Research*, vol.4, no.1, 2012, pp. 178-184.

215   P. Farquhar, "Sun Storm to Hit with 'Force of 100 m Bombs," News.com.au, August 25, 2010 at http://www.news.com.au/technology/science/sun-storm-to-hit-with-force-of-100-bombs/story-fn5fsgyc-1225909999465.

216   National Research Council, National Academy of Sciences, *Severe Space Weather Events: Understanding Societal and Economic Impacts*, (National Academies Press, Washington DC, December 2008), p. 77.

217   B. Hoffmann, "Ex-CIA Analyst: Attack on US Could Kill 9 Out of 10 Americans," May 12, 2015, at www.newsmax.com/Newsmax-Tv/Peter-Vincent-Pry-power-grid-attack-U-S-/2015/05/12/id/644144/.

218   Matthew Stein, "Geomagnetic Storms, EMP and Nuclear Armageddon," *Nexus*, February – March, 2012, pp. 21-26, 80; "The Other Electrical Grid Failure

Problem," at http://survivalblog.com/letter-re-the-other-electrical-grid-failure-problem/.

[219]   "Is Class X Flash First Warning of 2012 Solar Storm?" News.com.au, February 8, 2011, at http://www.news.com.au/technology/science/solar-flare-jams-radio-satellite-signals/story-fn5fsgyc-1226007817482.

[220]   T. Phillips, "Near Miss: The Solar Superstorm of July 2012," July 23, 2014, at http://science.nasa.gov/science-news/science-at-nasa/2014/23jul_superstorm/.

[221]   P. Riley, "On the Probability of Occurrence of Extreme Space Weather Events," *Space Weather*, vol. 10, 2012; S02012; doi:10.1029/2011SW00734.

[222]   A. Taggart, "Former CIA Director: We're Not doing Nearly Enough to Protect against the EMP Threat," June 7, 2015, at http://www.peakprosperity.com/podcast/92943/former-cia-director-were-not-doing-nearly-enough-protect-against-emp-threat-.

[223]   C. Pugh (et al.), "A Multi-Period Oscillation in a Stellar Superflare," *Astrophysical Journal Letters*, vol. 813, 2015: doi:10.1088/2041-8205/813/1/L5.

[224]   Y. Notsu (et al.), "Do *Kepler* Superflare Stars Really Include Slowly Rotating Sun-Like Stars? Results Using APO 3.5 m Telescope Spectroscopic Observations and *Gaia*-DR2 Data," *Astrophysics Journal*, May 1, 2019, 876: 58.

[225]   J. Kappenman, *Geomagnetic Storms and Their Impacts on the US Power Grid*, (Metatech Corporation, Meta-R-319, January, 2010), at, http://web.ornl.gov/sci/ees/etsd/pes/pubs/ferc_Meta-R-319.pdf.

[226]   Hannah Parry, "White House is Preparing for Catastrophic Solar Flares which Could Wipe Out Power Around the World for Months – Bringing an End to Modern Civilization as We Know It," November 4, 2015, at http://www.dailymail.co.uk/news/article-3302185/White-House-preparing-catastrophic-solar-flares-wipe-power-world-months-bringing-end-modern-civilization-know-it.html.

[227]   https://www.whitehouse.gov/presidential-actions/executive-order-coordinating-national-resilience-electromagnetic-pulses/.

[228]   https://www.dhs.gov/sites/default/files/publications/NIAC%20Catastrophic%20Power%20Outage%20Study_508%20FINAL.pdf.

[229]   Shut Tomari, "An Urgent Request on UN Intervention to Stabilize the Fukushima Unit 4 Spend Nuclear Fuel," May 1 2012, at http://greenaction-japan.org/en/2012/05/press-release-coalition-sends-urgent-request-for-un-

intervention-to-stabilize-the-fukushima-unit-4-spent-nuclear-fuel/.

[230]   B. Jacobson, "The Worst is Yet to Come? Why Nuclear Experts are Calling Fukushima a Ticking Time Bomb," May 5 2012, at http://carolynbaker. net/2012/05/05/the-worst-is-yet-to-come-.

[231]   "New Evidence of Nuclear Fuel Releases Found at Fukushima," February 18, 2018, at https://phys.org/news/2018-02-evidence-nuclear-fuel-fukushima. html; https://www.scientificamerican.com/article/crippled-fukushima-reactors-are-still-a-danger-5-years-after-the-accident1/; https://video.foxnews.com/ v/5315777703001/#sp=show-clips.

[232]   UN Scientific Committee on the Effects of Atomic Radiation, "The Chernobyl Accident," at http://www.unscear.org/unscear/en/chernobyl.html.

[233]   Yuri M Shcherbak, "Ten Years of the Chernobyl Era," *Scientific American*, April, 1996, pp. 44-49.

[234]   John Vidal, "Nuclear's Green Cheerleaders Forgot Chernobyl at Our Peril," April 2, 2011, at http://www.theguardian.com/commentisfree/2011/apr/01/ fukushima-chernobyl-risks-radiation. Alexey Yablokov (et al.), *Chernobyl: Consequences of the Catastrophe for People and the Environment*, (Annals of the New York Academy of Sciences, New York, 2009), volume 1181.

[235]   https://www.peoplesworld.org/article/eight-years-after-fukushima-nuclear-meltdown-workers-still-facing-radiation-risk/.

[236]   Rich Wallace, "Fukushima Plant 'Set to Collapse' from Another Quake or Tsunami," *The Weekend Australian*, March 9-10, 2013, p. 12.

[237]   BBC News Asia, "Fukushima Radiation Level '18 Times Higher' than Thought," September 1, 2013 at http://www.bbc.co.uk/news/world-asia-23918882.

[238]   Rick Wallace, "Tokyo to Act on Radioactive Leaks," *The Australian*, August 9, 2013, p. 10.

[239]   M. Willacy, "Fukushima Plant Spilling Contaminated Water into Sea 'for Years,'" August 12, 2013, at http://www.abc.net.au/news/2013-08-12/fukushima-plant-workers-raise-safety-concerns/4879960.

[240]   Rick Wallace, "Radioactive Leak at Fukushima," *The Australian*, August 7, 2013, p. 10.

[241]   E. Sukhoi, "Fukushima Radioactive Leak is "the Greatest Threat Humanity Ever Faced," – Expert," Voice of Russia, September 2, 2013, at http://sputniknews. com/voiceofrussia/2013_09_02/Fukushima-radioactive-leak-is-the-greatest-

threat-humanity-ever-faced-expert-3792/.

242 "Fukushima Apocalypse: Years of 'Duct Tape Fixes' Could Result in 'Millions of Deaths,'" August 17, 2013, at http://rt.com/news/fukushima-apocalypse-fuel-removal-598.

243 T. E. Collins and G. Hubbard, *Technical Study of Spent Fuel Pool Accident Risk at Decommissioning Nuclear Power Plants*, (NUREG-1738, US Nuclear Regulatory Commission, February 2011), pp. x and xi.

244 Robert Alvarez, *Spent Nuclear Fuel Pools in the US: Reducing the Deadly Risks of Storage*, (Institute for Policy Studies, Washington DC, 2011).

245 E. S. Lyman, "Impacts of a Terrorist Attack at Indian Point Nuclear Power Plant," Union of Concerned Scientists, September 2004, at http://www.ucsusa.org/nuclear_power/making-nuclear-power-safer/keeping-nuclear-plants-secure/impacts-of-a-terrorist-attack.html#.VYfCQImqqko.

246 C. Wedler, "Defunct Nuclear Power Plant on California Coast is a 'Fukushima Waiting to Happen'" August 17, 2018 at https://www.zerohedge.com/news/2018-08-17/defunct-nuclear-power-plant-california-coast-fukushima-waiting-happen.

247 Matthew Stein, "Four Hundred Chernobyls: Solar Flares, Electromagnetic Pulses and Nuclear Armageddon," March 24, 2012, at http://truth-out.org/news/item/7301-400-chernobyls-.

248 S. N. Padala, "Severe Solar Storms Could Disrupt Earth this Decade: NOAA," August 8, 2011, at http://www.ibtimes.com/severe-solar-storms-could-disrupt-earth-decade-noaa-826351.

249 Rebecca Smith, "US Risks National Blackout from Small-Scale Attack," March 12, 2014, at http://www.wsj.com/articles/SB10001424052702304020104579433670284061220.

250 M. Koren, "How the US Power Grid is Like a Big Pile of Sand," April 8, 2014, at http://www.nationaljournal.com/tech/how-the-u-s-power-grid-is-like-a-big-pile-of-sand-20140408.

251 "Nuclear Weapons Risk Greater than in Cold War, Says Ex-Pentagon Chief," January 8, 2016, at http://www.theguardian.com/world/2016/jan/07/nuclear-weapons-risk-greater-than-in-cold-war-says-ex-pentagon-chief.

252 Ira Helfand, *Nuclear Famine: Two Billion People at Risk?* 2nd edition, (International Physicians for the Prevention of Nuclear War and Physicians for

Social Responsibility, November, 2013) at, http://www.psr.org/assets/pdfs/two-billion-at-risk.pdf.

253   H. Weiss and R. S. Bradley, "What Drives Societal Collapse?" *Science*, vol. 291, 2001, pp. 609-610.

254   J. Beddington, Speech to the GovNet Sustainable Development UK Conference, March 19, 2009, at http://www.gren.org.uk/resources/Beddington'sSpeechatSDUK09.pdf

255   J. Porritt, "Perfect Storm of Environmental and Economic Collapse Closer than You Think," *The Guardian*, March 23 2009, https://www.theguardian.com/environment/2009/mar/23/jonathon-porritt-recession-climate-crisis.

256   L. Brown, *World on the Edge: How to Prevent Environmental and Economic Collapse*, (Earth Policy Institute/W. W. Norton, New York, 2011).

257   Stephen Hawking, "Stephen Hawking: Asking Big Questions about the Universe," TED Talk Series, at http://www.ted.com/talks/stephen_hawking_asks_big_questions_about_the_universe?language=en._

258   D. Cordell (et. al.), "The Story of Phosphorus: Global Food Security and Food for Thought," *Global Environmental Change*, vol. 9, 2009, pp. 292-305.

259   M. King Hubbert, "Degree of Advancement of Petroleum Exploration in United States," *AAPG Bulletin*, Nov. 1967, vol. 51, no. 11, pp. 2207-2227.

260   Patrick Dery and Bart Anderson, "Peak Phosphorus," *Energy Bulletin*, August 13, 2007, at http://www.energybulletin.net/node/33164.

261   Jeremy Grantham, "Be Persuasive. Be Brave. Be Arrested (If Necessary)," *Nature*, vol. 491, 2012, p. 303.

262   Jeremy Grantham, "Welcome to Dystopia! Entering a Long-Term and Politically Dangerous Food Crisis," *GMO Quarterly Letter*, July 2012, at http://f2cfnd.org/wp-content/uploads/2012/09/GMOQ2Letter.pdf

263   As above, p. 3.

264   As above, p. 4.

265   R. B. Gordon (et al.), "Metal Stocks and Sustainability," *Proceedings of the National Academy of Sciences*, vol. 103, 2006, pp .1209-1214.

266   D. Cohen, "Earth's Natural Wealth: An Audit," May 23 2007, at http://www.sciencearchive.org.au/nova/newscientist/027ns_005.htm.

267   "Shortages of Alternative Energy Minerals May Trigger Trade Wars," November 1 2010, at http://www.tgdaily.com/sustainability-features/52283-shortage-of-alternative-energy-minerals-will-trigger-trade-wars.

268   Alice Friedemann, "Peak Oil and the Preservation of Knowledge," *Energy Bulletin*, January 7, 2006 at http://www2.energybulletin.net/node/18978.

269   As above.

270   Friedemann, as above; Thomas E. Hecker, "The Twilight of Digitization is Now," *Journal of Scholarly Publishing*, vol. 35, no. 1, October, 2003, pp. 52-65.

271   Michael C. Ruppert, *Confronting Collapse: The Crisis of Energy and Money in a Post Peak Oil World*, (Chelsea Green Publishing, White River Junction, Vermont, 2009), p. 13.

272   Jeremy Leggett, *The Empty Tank: Oil, Gas, Hot Air, and the Coming Global Financial Catastrophe*, (Random House, New York, 2005).

273   As above, pp. 141-142.

274   As above, p. 191.

275   Matt Ridley, *The Rational Optimist: How Prosperity Evolves*, (Fourth Estate, London, 2010).

276   As above, p. 238.

277   On the unsolved problem of induction see: "The Problem of Induction," at http://www.princeton.edu/~grosen/puc/phi203/induction.html.

278   Alice Friedemann, *When the Trucks Stop Running: Energy and the Future of Transport*, (Springer, New York, 2016).

279   J. Murray and D. King, "Oil's Tipping Point has Passed," *Nature*, vol. 481, 2012, pp. 433-435; Ugo Bardi, *Extracted: How the Quest for Mineral Wealth is Plundering the Planet*, (Chelsea Green Publishing, White River Junction, 2014).

280   W. Zittel and J. Schindler, "Future World Oil Supply," L-B System tecnik, January 2003, at http://www.peakoil.net/files/International-Summer-School_Salzburg_2002.pdf, quoted from R. Heinberg, *Powerdown*, cited above.

281   N. Owen (et. al.), "The Status of Conventional World Oil Reserves - Hype or Cause for Concern?" *Energy Policy*, vol. 38, 2010, pp. 4743-4749, cited p. 4743.

282   As above, p. 4749.

[283] K. Aleklett (et. al.), "The Peak of the Oil Age: Analysing the World Oil Production Reference Scenario in World Energy Outlook 2008," *Energy Policy*, vol. 38, no. 3, 2010, pp. 1398-1414.

[284] International Energy Agency, "Executive Summary," *World Energy Outlook 2010*, (OECD/IEA, Paris, 2010), p. 6.

[285] Alan Kohler, "The Death of Peak Oil," March 28, 2012, at http://www. businessspectator.com.au/article/2012/2/29/commodities/death-peak-oil.

[286] Matt Ridley, "Fossil Fuels are Here to Stay," *The Australian*, March 24, 2015, p. 11.

[287] Brian Walsh, "The Truth about Oil," *Time*, April 9, 2012; A. B. Lovins, "A Farewell to Fossil Fuels," *Foreign Affairs*, vol. 91, 2012, pp. 134-136.

[288] http://www.theoildrum.com/node/9169.

[289] US Legislative Peak Oil and Natural Gas Caucus, *Peak Oil Production and Implications to the State of Connecticut: Report to the Legislative Leaders and the Governor. Addendum: Tar Sands and Shale Oil*, (December, 2007), at http://www. housedems.ct.gov/backer/pubs/TSandOSfina.pdf.

[290] As above, p. 13.

[291] Kjell Aleklett (with Michael Lardelli), *Peeking at Peak Oil*, (Springer, New York, 2012).

[292] https://www.forbes.com/sites/arthurberman/2017/03/01/the-beginning-of-the-end-for-the-bakken-shale-play/#69096dde1487; https://energypost.eu/ bakken-shows-us-tight-oil-production-limits/.

[293] Michael Klare, "The New 'Golden Age' of Oil that Wasn't: Extreme Oil Means an Extreme Planet," October 5, 2012 at http://www.carolynbaker. net/2012/10/05/the-new-golden-age-of-oil-that-wasnt-extreme-energy-means-an-extreme-planetby-michael-klare.

[294] Aleklett, as above, p. 165.

[295] As above. On the limitations of supply of Canadian Oil Sands see B. Söderbergh (et al.), "A Crash Programme Scenario for the Canadian Oil Sands Industry," *Energy Policy*, vol.35, 2007, pp.1931-1947.

[296] Steven F. Hayward, "Obama's Carbon War Running Out of Gas," *The Australian*, June 3, 2013, p. 7.

[297]   J. David Hughes, *Drill, Baby, Drill: Can Unconventional Fuels Usher in a New Era of Energy Abundance?* (Post Carbon Institute, Santa Rosa, February, 2013), at http://www.postcarbon.org/drill-baby-drill/.

[298]   As above, p. i.

[299]   Richard Heinberg, *Snake Oil: How Fracking's False Promise of Plenty Imperils Our Future*, (Post Carbon Institute, Santa Rosa, 2013), p. 79.

[300]   M. Klare, *The Race for What's Left: The Global Scramble for the World's Last Resources*, (Metropolitan Books, New York, 2012); M. Klare, "Oil Wars on the Horizon," *Counterpunch*, May 10, 2012, at http://www.counterpunch.org/2012/05/10/oil-wars-on-the-horizon/.

[301]   Ambrose Evan-Pritchard, "Peak Cheap Oil is an Incontrovertible Fact," August 26, 2012 at http://www.telegraph.co.uk/finance/comment/ambroseevans_pritchard/9500667/Peak-cheap-oil-is-an-incontrovertible-fact.html.

[302]   Energy Watch Group, *Uranium Resources and Nuclear Energy*, (EWG-Series No. 1/2006, December 2006), at http://energywatchgroup.org/wp-content/uploads/2014/02/EWG_Report_Uranium_3-12-2006ms1.pdf.

[303]   T. W. Patzek and G. D. Croft, "A Global Coal Production Forecast with Multi-Hubbert Cycle Analysis," *Energy*, vol. 35, 2010, pp. 3109-3122.

[304]   S. H. Mohr and G. M. Evans, "Forecasting Coal Production Until 2100," *Fuel*, vol. 88, 2009, pp. 2059-2067. See generally R. Heinberg and D. Fridley, "The End of Cheap Coal," *Nature*, vol. 468, no. 7322, pp. 367-369.

[305]   R. Heinberg, *Blackout: Coal, Climate and the Last Energy Crisis*, (New Society Publishers, Gabriola Island, 2009), p. 155.

[306]   R. Heinberg, *Searching for a Miracle: "Net Energy" Limits and the Fate of Industrial Society*, (International Forum on Globalization and Post Carbon Institute, False Solutions Series No.4, September, 2009), at http://ifg.org/v2/wp-content/uploads/2014/04/Searching-for-a-Miracle_web10nov09.pdf.

[307]   T. Trainer, "Can the World Run on Renewable Energy? A Revised Negative Case," *Humanomics*, vol.29, 2013, pp. 88-104.

[308]   B. Lomborg, "Ballooning Cost is Blowing in the Wind," *The Australian*, March 22, 2012, p. 12.

[309]   *The Australian*, February 13, 2012, p. 13.

[310]   See further, "Nuclear Power: The Dream that Failed," *The Economist*, March

10, 2012, at http://www.economist.com/node/21549936.

³¹¹   R. C. Duncan, "America: A Frog in the Kettle Slowly Coming to a Boil," *The Social Contract*, Fall, 2007, pp. 3-13.

³¹²   C. Stager, *Deep Future: The Next 100,000 Years of Life on Earth*, (Scribe, Melbourne, 2011), p. 235.

³¹³   "Scientist Cools on Climate Alarmism," *The Australian*, April 26, 2012, p. 11.

³¹⁴   James Lovelock, *The Vanishing Face of Gaia: A Final Warning*, (Allen Lane, Camberwell, Victoria, 2009), p. 4.

³¹⁵   R. K. Kaufmann (et. al.), "Reconciling Anthropogenic Climate Change with Observed Temperature 1998-2008," *Proceedings of the National Academy of Sciences*, www.pnas.org/cgi/doi/10.1073/pnas.1102467108.

³¹⁶   S. Solomon (et. al.), "The Persistently Variable 'Background' Stratospheric Aerosol Layer and Global Climate Change," *Science*, vol. 333, 2011, pp. 866-870.

³¹⁷   Ian Plimer, "Basic Sciences is the Answer, Not Blinding Ideology," *The Australian*, January 4, 2012, p. 13.

³¹⁸   R. A. Muller and G. J. MacDonald, *Ice Ages and Astronomical Causes: Data, Spectral Analysis and Mechanisms*, (Springer-Verlag, London, 2000).

³¹⁹   Peter P. D. Ward, *Under a Green Sky: Global Warming, the Mass Extinctions of the Past and What They Can Tell Us about Our Future*, (Smithsonian Books/ Collins, New York, 2007).

³²⁰   As above, p. 194.

³²¹   Foundation for the Future, *Humanity Three Thousand: Anthropogenic Climate Destabilization: A Worse-Case Scenario*, (Executive Summary), at http:// www.futurefoundation.org/documents/HUM_ExecSum_ClimateDestabilization.

³²²   J. Leake, "Warming Data Shows Shades of Grey," *The Australian*, February 7, 2012, p.13; B. Stephens, "Climate Zealots, the End Isn't Nigh," *The Australian*, November 30, 2011, p. 10.

³²³   R. A. Muller, "The Case Against Global-Warming Scepticism," 21 October, 2011 at http://www.wsj.com/articles/SB10001424052970204422404576594872796327348.

³²⁴   J. Hansen, "Climate Change is Here – and Worse than We Thought," *The Washington Post*, August 4, 2012, at http://www.washingtonpost.com/opinions/

climate-change-is-here--and-worse-than-we-thought/2012/08/03/6ae604c2-dd90-11e1-8e43-4a3c4375504a_story.html.

[325]   As above.

[326]   J. Hansen (et al.), "Ice Melt, Sea Level Rise and Superstorms: Evidence from Paleoclimate Data, Climate Modeling, and Modern Observations that 2° C Global Warming is Highly Dangerous," *Atmospheric Chemistry and Physics*, vol. 15, 2015, pp. 20059-20179.

[327]   Q. Schiermeier, "Droughts, Heat Waves and Floods: How to Tell when Climate Change is to Blame," *Scientific American*, July 30, 2018, at https://www.scientificamerican.com/article/droughts-heat-waves-and-floods-how-to-tell-when-climate-change-is-to-blame/.

[328]   T. F. Stocker (et al., eds.), *Climate Change 2013: The Physical Science Basis. Contribution of Working Group I to the Fifth Assessment Report of the Intergovernmental Panel on Climate Change*, (Cambridge University Press, Cambridge, 2013).

[329]   As above, p. 1.

[330]   As above, p. 41.

[331]   M. Ahmed (et. al.), (PAGES 2K Consortium), "Continental-Scale Temperature Variability During the Past Two Millennia," *Nature Geoscience*, vol.6, 2013, pp. 339-345, cited p. 339.

[332]   Stocker (et al.), as above, p. 37.

[333]   T. Murray (et al.), "Reverse Glacier Motion During Iceberg Calving and the Cause of Glacial Earthquakes," *Science*, vol. 349, 2015, pp. 305-308.

[334]   As above.

[335]   M. Wegmann (et al.), "Arctic Moisture Source for Eurasian Snow Cover Variations in Autumn," *Environmental Research Letters*, vol. 10, 2015; doi:10.1088/1748-9326/10/054015.

[336]   Stocker (et al.), as above, p. 37.

[337]   As above, p. 61.

[338]   World Meteorological Organization, *The Global Climate 2001-2010: A Decade of Climate Extremes*, Summary Report, (World Meteorological Organization, Geneva, 2013), p.3.

339 "WMO Confirms 2017 Among the Three Hottest Years on Record," January 18, 2018, at http://www.latimes.com/science/sciencenow/la-sci-sn-global-temperatures-2017-20180118-story.html.

340 "Global Summary Information – July 2015," at https://www.ncdc.noaa.gov/sotc/summary-info/global/201507.

341 Stocker (et. al. eds.), as above, p. 63; Y. Kosaka and S.-P. Xie, "Recent Global-Warming Hiatus Tied to Equatorial Pacific Surface Cooling," *Nature*, vol. 501, 2013, pp. 403-407.

342 K. Cowtan and R. G. Way, "Coverage Bias in the HadCRUT4 Temperature Series and its Impact on Recent Temperature Trends," *Quarterly Journal of the Royal Meteorological Society*, vol. 140, 2014, pp. 1935-1944.

343 D. R. Easterling and M. F. Wehner, "Is the Climate Warming or Cooling?" *Geophysical Research Letters*, vol.36, 2009, L08706; doi: 10.1029/2009GL037810 cited p. 1.

344 A. Otto (et al.), "Energy Budget Constraints on Climate Response," *Nature Geoscience*, vol. 6, 2013, pp. 415-416.

345 The Geological Society, *An Addendum to the Statement on Climate Change: Evidence from the Geological Record*, (December, 2013), at http://www.geolsoc.org.uk/climaterecord.

346 P. J. Gleckler (et al.), "Industrial-Era Global Ocean Heat Uptake Doubles in Recent Decades," *Nature Climate Change*, (2016); doi:10.1038/NCLIMATE2915.

347 J-P. Gattuso (et al.), "Contrasting Futures for Ocean and Society from Different CO_2 Emissions Scenarios," *Science*, vol. 349, 2015, pp. aac4722-1 – aac4722-10.

348 S. Goldenberg, "Warming of Oceans Due to Climate Change is Unstoppable, Say US Scientists," July 17, 2015, at http://www.theguardian.com/environment/2015/jul/16/warming-of-oceans-due-to-climate-change-is-unstoppable-.

349 K. L. Ricke and K. Caldeira, "Maximum Warming Occurs about One Decade after a Carbon Dioxide Emission," *Environmental Research Letters*, vol. 9, 2014, 124002.

350 M. Le Page, "Earth Now Halfway to Warming Limit," *New Scientist*, August 1, 2015, pp. 8-9.

351 D. G. Victor and C. F. Kennel, "Ditch the 2°C Warming Goal," *Nature*, vol.

514, 2014, pp. 30-31.

352   J. Rockstrom (et. al.), "A Safe Operating Space for Humanity," *Nature*, vol. 461, 2009, pp. 472-475; https://www.theguardian.com/environment/2013/may/10/carbon-dioxide-highest-level-greenhouse-gas.

353   R. E. Kopp (et al.), "Temperature-Driven Global Sea-Level Variability in the Common Era," *Proceedings of the National Academy of Sciences*, February 22, 2016, at www.pnas.org/cgi/doi/10.1073/pnas.1517056113.

354   J. Hansen (et al.), "Ice Melts, Sea Level Rise and Superstorms: Evidence from Paleoclimate Data, Climate Modeling, and Modern Observations that 2° C Global Warming is Highly Dangerous," *Atmospheric Chemistry and Physics*, vol. 15, 2015, pp. 20059-20179.

355   See M. Le Page, "Superstorms Possible Even with 'Safe' 2 ° C Rise," *New Scientist*, August 1, 2015, p. 9.

356   P. Love, "OECD Environmental Outlook to 2050: We're All Doomed," *OECD Insights*, March 19, 2012, at http://oecdinsights.org/2012/03/19/oecd-environmental-outlook-to-2050-were-all-doomed .

357   D. Adam, "Amazon Could Shrink by 85% Due to Climate Change, Scientists Say," *The Guardian*, March 11, 2009, at http://www.guardian.co.uk/environment/2009/mar/11/amazon-global-warming-trees.

358   BP, Energy Outlook 2030, (January, 2013) at http://www.bp.com/content/dam/bp/pdf/statistical-review/BP_World_Energy_Outlook_booklet_2013.pdf.

359   International Energy Agency, *Redrawing the Energy-Climate Map: World Energy Outlook Special Report*, (International Energy Agency, Paris, 2013).

360   F. Montaigne, "An Influential Global Voice Warns of Runaway Emissions," June 11, 2012, at http://e360.yale.edu/feature/fatih_birol_iea_economist_on__risk_of_climate_change/2537.

361   "Clean Energy Process too Slow to Limit Global Warming – Report," April 17, 2013, at http://www.reuters.com/article/2013/04/17/carbon-energy-warming-idUSL5N0CX3I020130417.

362   Pricewaterhousecoopers LLP, *Too Late for Two Degrees? Low Carbon Economy Index 2012*, (PricewaterhouseCoopers, November, 2012), p. 1.

363   As above, p. 2.

364   G. A. Jones and K. J. Warner, "The 21st Century Population-Energy-Climate

Nexus," *Energy Policy*, vol. 93, 2016, pp. 206-212.

365   World Bank, *Turn Down the Heat: Why a 4° C World Must be Avoided*, (World Bank, Washington DC, 2012).

366   National Research Council, *Climate and Social Stress: Implications for Security Analysis*, (National Academy of Sciences, Washington DC, 2012).

367   National Intelligence Council, *Global Trends 2030: Alternative Worlds*, (Central Intelligence Agency, Washington DC, 2012).

368   J. D. Ward (et. al.), "High Estimates of Supply Constrained Emissions Scenarios for Long-Term Climate Risk Assessment, *Energy Policy*, vol. 51, 2012, pp. 598-604.

369   K. Aleklett, *Peeping at Peak Oil*, (Springer, New York, 2012), p. 253.

370   Richard Heinberg, *Snake Oil*, as above, pp. 123-124.

371   I. Cronshaw, "The Current and Future Importance of Coal in the World Energy Economy," Energy Policy Institute of Australia, Public Policy Paper No. 5/2014, at http://www.energypolicyinstitute.com.au/images/Policy_Paper_Jan2014_Ian_Cronshaw_5-2014.pdf.

372   K. Anderson, "What They Won't Tell You about Climate Catastrophe," November 12, 2012, at http://www.ecoshock.info/2012/11/kevin-anderson-what-they-wont-tell-you.html.

373   J. R. Schramski (et al.), "Human Domination of the Biosphere: Rapid Discharge of the Earth-Space Battery Foretells the Future of Humankind," *Proceedings of the National Academy of Sciences*, vol. 112, 2015, pp. 9511-9517.

374   M. S. Tom and J. Harte, "Missing Feedbacks, Asymmetric Uncertainties, and the Underestimation of Future Warming," *Geophysical Research Letters*, vol. 33, 2006, L10703; doi: 10.1029/2005GL025540.

375   https://www.jpl.nasa.gov/news/news.php?release=2014-148.

376   S. Connor, "Vast Methane 'Plumes' Seen in Arctic Oceans as Sea Ice Retreats," at http://www.independent.co.uk/news/science/vast-methane-plumes-seen-in-arctic-ocean-as-sea-ice-retreats-6276278.html. N. Shakhova (et. al.), "Extensive Methane Venting to the Atmosphere from Sediments of the East Siberian Arctic Shelf," *Science*, vol. 327, 2010, pp. 1246-1250.

377   Z. Carpenter, "Scientists: We Cannot Geoengineer Our Way Out of the Climate Crisis," February 10, 2015, at http://www.thenation.com/blog/197521/

scientists-we-cannot-geoengineer-our-way-out-of-climate-crisis.

[378]   A. J. Ferraro (et al.), "Weakened Tropical Circulation and Reduced Precipitation in Response to Geoengineering," *Environmental Research Letters*, vol. 9, 2014, 014001; doi: 10.1088/1748-93/26/9/1/014001.

[379]   A. Kleidon and M. Renner, "A Simple Explanation for the Sensitivity of the Hydrological Cycle to Surface Temperature and Solar Radiation and its Implications for Global Climate Change," *Earth System Dynamics*, vol. 4, 2013, pp. 455-465.

[380]   Clive Hamilton, "Climate Change Signals the End of the Social Sciences," February 7, 2015, at http://www.carolynbaker.net/2015/02/07/climate-change-signals-the-end-of-the-social-sciences-by-clive-hamilton.

[381]   As above.

[382]   Guillaume Faye, *Convergence of Catastrophes*, (Arktos Media, 2012), originally published as *La Convergence des catastrophes*, (Diffusion International Edition, Paris, 2004).

[383]   As above, p. 198.

[384]   D. Price, "Energy and Human Evolution," *Population and Environment*, vol. 16, 1995, pp. 301-319, cited pp. 315-316.

[385]   W. Stanton, *The Rapid Growth of Human Populations 1750-2000*, (Multi-Science Publishing Company, Essex, 2003), p. 193.

[386]   J. D. Heyes, "Economic Collapse in the USA to Cause 25-50 Million Deaths in the First 90 Days From Starvation, Rioting, Murder and More," June 10, 2016, at http://collapsenews/2016-06-10-economic-collapse-in-the-usa-to-cause-25-50-million-dead-.

[387]   http://www.collapse.news/2018-11-28-when-shtf-america-will-see-a-resurgence-of-disease.html.

[388]   http://www.survivaldan101.com/shtf-diseases-long-eradicated-developed-world-will-rear-ugly-heads-many-unprepared-will-die/.

[389]   https://www.naturalnews.com/2019-01-02-preview-of-the-chaos-to-come-in-2019-and-2020-if-you-dare-to-glimpse-reality.html.

[390]   https://www.businessinsider.com.au/stephen-hawking-humans-leave-earth-or-be-annihilated-2018-10?r=US&IR=T.

[391] https://www.youtube.com/watch?v=kVWx_Dqod_Q;https://www.youtube.com/watch?v=MoGAUeMz6fM.

[392] https://www.theorganicprepper.com/how-to-die-when-the-shtf/.

[393] P. San Giorgio, *Survive the Economic Collapse: A Practical Guide*, (Radix/Washington Summit Publishers, Whitefish, 2013).

[394] https://www.conservapedia.com/American_Redoubt; https://survivalblog.com/redoubt/.

[395] Boston T. Party, *Boston's Gun Bible*, (Javelin Press, 2002).

[396] Rather than put this reference information in the next few pages to footnotes, as it is at a high level of importance, full references for easier searching, are added to the main body of the text.

[397] https://www.theguardian.com/news/2018/aug/28/how-to-be-human-the-man-who-was-raised-by-wolves.

[398] https://bugoutbagacademy.com/free-bug-out-bag-list/

[399] https://urbansurvivalsite.com/100-items-to-disappear-first-in-a-panic/

[400] https://www.heart.org/en/healthy-living/healthy-eating/eat-smart/sodium/how-much-sodium-should-i-eat-per-day.

[401] https://survivalblog.com/water-treatment-options-avoid-poisoning-toxins-part-1-ajs/, and https://survivalblog.com/water-treatment-options-avoid-poisoning-toxins-part-2-ajs/.

[402] https://survivalforum.survivalmagazine.org/forum/wilderness-survival-camping/wilderness-medicine/212213-new-edition-survival-austere-medicine-3rd-edition.

[403] https://drjockers.com/root-canals/.

[404] John Michael Greer, *The Long Descent: A User's Guide to the End of the Industrial Age,* (New Society Publishers, Gabriola Island, 2008).

[405] John Michael Greer, *The Ecotechnic Future: Envisioning a Post-Peak World,* (New Society Publishers, Gabriola Island, 2009), and *Not the Future We Ordered: Peak Oil, Psychology, and the Myth of Progress,* (Karnac Books, London, 2013). Further references to this note are to *The Ecotechnic Future.*

[406]   J. M. Greer, *Dark Age America: Climate Change, Cultural Collapse, and the Hard Future Ahead*, (New Society Publishers, Gabriola Island, 2016).

[407]   Lewis Dartnell, *The Knowledge: How to Rebuild our World from Scratch*, (The Bodley Head, London, 2014); Leonard Read, "I, Pencil," *The Freeman*, December 1958.

[408]   Rob Hopkins, *The Transition Handbook: Creating Local Sustainable Communities Beyond Oil Dependency*, (Finch Publishing, Sydney, 2009), p. 79, and p. 224.

[409]   Rob Hopkins "Why the Survivalists Have Got it Wrong," September 4, 2006 at http://transitionculture.org/2006/09/04/why-the-survivalists-have-got-it-wrong. The article is a response to Zachary Nowak, "Preparing for a Crash: Nuts and Bolts," *Energy Bulletin*, at http://www.resilience.org/stories/2006-08-31/preparing-crash-nuts-and-bolts.

[410]   Meg Raven, "What is Survivalism?" At http://www.aussurvivalist.com/whatissurvivalismmeg.htm; Douglas Good, "What is Survivalism?" at http://www.aussurvivalist.com/whatissurvivalismgood.htm.

[411]   "Survivalism," at http://en.wikipedia.org/wiki/Survivalism.

[412]   Kurt Saxon, "What is a Survivalist? (1980), at http://www.aussurvivalist.com/whatissurvivalismsaxon.htm.

[413]   As above.

[414]   James Wesley, Rawles, *How to Survive the End of the World as we Know It*, (Plume/Penguin Books, New York, 2009); "Precepts of Rawlesian Survivalist Philosophy," at http://www.survivalblog.com/precepts.html.

[415]   Richard Heinberg and Rob Hopkins, "To Plan for Emergency, or Not? Heinberg and Hopkins Debate," May 28, 2009, at http://www.postcarbon.org/article/40535-to-plan-for-emergency-or-not.

[416]   As above.

[417]   As above.

[418]   Peter Sandman, "The Government is Preparing for the Worst While Hoping for the Best – Now it Needs to Tell the Public to do the Same Thing," at http://www.psandman.com/col/WashPost.htm.

[419]   Chris Martenson, *The Crash Course: The Unsustainable Future of Our Economy, Energy and Environment*, (John Wiley and Sons, New Jersey, 2011), pp.

258-259.

[420] See: Thorrfin Skullsplitter, *Zombie Apocalypse Now!* (Manticore, 2019); Max Brooks, *The Zombie Survival Guide: Complete Protection from the Living Dead,* (Three Rivers Press, New York, 2003); Roger Ma, *The Zombie Combat Manual: A Guide to Fighting the Living Dead,* (Berkley Books, New York, 2010).

[421] Chris Lisle, "Prepare for Peak Oil on a Budget," at http://ebookbrowse.com/how-to-plan-for-peak-oil-on-a-limited-budget-pdf-d230019877.

[422] James Ballou, *Long-Term Survival in the Coming Dark Age: Preparing to Live After Society Crumbles,* (Paladin Press, Boulder, Colorado, 2007).

[423] As above, p. 3.

[424] See James Ballou, *The Poorman's Wilderness Survival Kit: Assembling Your Emergency Gear for Little or No Money,* (Paladin Press, Boulder, Colorado, 2013).

[425] See further James Ballou, *Makeshift Workshop Skills for Survival and Self-Reliance,* (Paladin Press, Boulder, Colorado, 2009) and *More Makeshift Workshop Skills,* (Paladin Press, Boulder, Colorado, 2011).

[426] As above, p. 68.

[427] "Retreat (Survivalism)," https://en.wikipedia.org/wiki/Retreat_(survivalism);" Ragnar Benson, *The Modern Survival Retreat: A New and Vital Approach to Retreat Theory and Practice,* (Paladin Press, Boulder, Colorado, 1998).

[428] Piero San Giorgio, *Survive the Economic Collapse: A Practical Guide,* (Radix/Washington Summit Publishers, Whitefish, 2013).

[429] As above, p. 250.

[430] Mel Tappan, *Tappan on Survival,* (Janus Press, Rogue River, 1981).

[431] Fernando "Ferfal" Aguirre, *The Modern Survival Manual: Surviving the Economic Collapse,* (The Author, 2009).

[432] "4 Things Doom-And-Gloomers Got Totally Wrong," June 2, 2014, at http://ferfal.blogspot.com.au/2014/06/4-things-doom-and-gloomers-got-totally.html.

[433] Survival Mom, "13 Reasons a Rural Retreat May Not be the Safe Refuge You Might Think," September 26, 2015, at http://thesurvivalmom.com/rural-survival-retreats-not-safe-refuge/.

[434] https://www.usatoday.com/story/news/2018/02/19/homicides-toll-big-u-s-

cities-2017/302763002/, J. LaFond and J. J. Bowie, *Letters from the Fall; Civilization Decomposes*, (Independently Published, April 18, 2019).

[435]   Aguirre, as above, p. 37.

[436]   For a general discussion and criticism of alleged problems with the American redoubt concept see, "The Problem with the American Redoubt Concept," December 24, 2014, at http://ferfal.blogspot.com.au/2014/12/the-problem-with-american-redoubt.html.

[437]   C. Nyergen, "Thirty Years in the Jungle! Could You do It?" At www.primitiveways.com/jungle_30_years.html.

[438]   "Survivalist Retreat," at http://www.conservapedia.com/Survivalist_retreat.

[439]   Joel Skousen, *Strategic Relocation: North American Guide to Safe Places,* 3rd edition, (Joel Skousen Designs, 2011).

[440]   See http://www.joelskousen.com.

[441]   Joel Skousen, *The Secure Home,* 3rd edition, (Swift, 1999).

[442]   See http://www.joelskousen.com/Secure/reports.html.

[443]   James Wesley, Rawles, *Rawles on Retreats and Relocation,* (Clearwater Press, 2007).

[444]   James Wesley, Rawles, *Patriots: A Novel of Survival in the Coming Collapse,* (Ulysses Press, Berkeley, 2009) (4th expanded edition, originally published in 1990).

[445]   See http://www.survivalblog.com/retreatareas.html.

[446]   Max Brooks, *The Zombie Survival Guide: Complete Protection from the Living Dead*, (Three Rivers Press, New York, 2003), pp. 154-181.

[447]   Scott B. Williams, *Bug Out: The Complete Plan for Escaping a Catastrophic Disaster before It's Too Late,* (Ulysses Press, Berkeley, 2010).

[448]   As above pp. 101-269.

[449]   Fernando "Ferfal" Aguirre, *Bugging Out and Relocating: What to Do When Staying is Not an Option* (The Author, 2014).

[450]   As above, p. 23.

[451]   Cody Lundin, *98.6 Degrees: The Art of Keeping Your Ass Alive!* (Gibbs Smith,

Salt Lake City, 2003), p. 14.

452   Forrest Griffin and Erich Krauss, *Be Ready When the Shit Goes Down: A Survival Guide to The Apocalypse,* (itbooks, Harper Collins, New York, 2011).

453   As above, pp. 53-55.

454   As above, pp. 61-63.

455   Bob Cooper, *Outback Survival,* (Hachette Australia, Sydney, 2016).

456   As above, pp. 50-51.

457   As above.

458   The classic "shitting in the woods book" is Cathleen Meyer, *How to Shit in the Woods: An Environmentally Sound Approach to a Lost Art,* 3rd edition, (Ten Speed Press, Berkeley, 2011).

459   Les Stroud, *Survive! Essential Skills and Tactics to Get You Out of Anywhere – Alive,* (William Morrow, New York, 2008).

460   As above, p. 28.

461   As above (Stroud), pp. 21-38, 354.

462   *US Army Survival Manual FM 21-76,* at http://www.equipped.org/.

463   F. Kim O'Neill, *The Ultimate Guide to Surviving a Zombie Apocalypse,* (Paladin Press, Boulder, Colorado, 2010).

464   As above, pp. 86-87.

465   Michael Thomas and Nick Thomas, *Zompac: How to Survive a Zombie Apocalypse,* (Swordworks, United Kingdom, 2009).

466   Max Brooks, *The Zombie Survival Guide: Complete Protection from the Living Dead,* (Three Rivers Press, New York, 2003).

467   As above, pp. 101-102.

468   As above, p. 102.

469   As above.

470   "How to Start a Fire in the Rain: An Illustrated Guide," November 5, 2015, at http://www.artofmanliness.com/2015/11/05/how-to-start-a-fire-in-the-rain-an-

illustrated-guide/.

471   Kathy Harrison, *Just in Case: How to be Self-Sufficient When the Unexpected Happens,* (Storey Publishing, North Adams, 2008).

472   Peggy Layton, *Emergency Food Storage and Survival Handbook: Everything You Need to Know to Keep Your Family Safe in a Crisis,* (Three Rivers Press, New York, 2002).

473   Harrison, as above, p. 45.

474   For further bug out/survival kit lists see Albert Bates, *The Post-Petroleum Survival Guide and Cookbook: Recipes for Changing Times,* (New Society Publishers, Gabriola Island, BC, 2006); "Thoughts on Disaster Survival," at http://www.frfrogspad.com/disastr.htm.

475   Cody Lundin, *98.6 Degrees: The Art of Keeping Your Ass Alive!* (Gibbs Smith, Salt Lake City, 2003).

476   Cody Lundin*, When All Hell Breaks Loose: Stuff you Need to Survive When Disaster Strikes,* (Gibbs Smith Publishers, Salt Lake City, 2007).

477   See further, L. McCullough and S. Arora, "Diagnosis and Treatment of Hypothermia," *American Family Physician*, vol. 7, no. 12, 2004, pp. 2325-2332.

478   Chris Townsend, *The Backpacker's Handbook*, 4th edition, (McGraw Hill, New York, 2012).

479   Sergeant Survival, "Best Bug Out Bag Survival Foods: The Ultimate Guide to Picking the Perfect Food for Your BOB," at http://besurvival.com/guides/best-bug-out-bag-survival-foods-the-ultimate-guide-to-picking-the-perfect-food-for-your-bob.

480   Tess Pennington, "Do It Yourself: How to Make Nutritious Homemade Meals-Ready-To-Eat (MREs)," February 23, 2016, at http://www.shtfplan.com/headline-news/do-it-yourself-how-to-make-nutritious-homemade-meals-ready-to-eat-mres_02232016.

481   *US Army Survival Manual FM 21-76*, at http://www.equipped.org/fm21-76.htm.

482   Royal Australian Navy, *The Survival Manual*, (Navy Office, Canberra, 1968).

483   Royal Canadian Air Force Survival Training School, *Down but Not Out*, (Queen's Printer, Ottawa, 1970).

[484] John Wiseman, *SAS Survival Handbook: The Ultimate Guide to Surviving Anywhere*, (Collins, London, 2009).

[485] Barry Davies, *The Complete SAS Survival Manual*, (Skyhorse Publishing, New York, 2011); Colin Towell, *Survival Handbook in Association with the Royal Marines Commandos*, (Dorling Kindersley Ltd, London, 2012); Christopher Nyerges, *How to Survive Anywhere: A Guide for Urban, Suburban, Rural and Wilderness Environments*, 2nd edition, (Stackpole Books, Mechanicsburg, 2014).

[486] Chris McNab, *SAS and Elite Forces Guide: Wilderness Survival: Military Survival Skills from the World's Elite Military Units*, (Amber Books, London, 2011), *SAS and Elite Forces Guide: Prisoner of War Escape and Evasion: How to Survive Behind Enemy Lines from the World's Elite Military Units*, (Amber Books, London, 2012), and Chris McNab, *SAS and Elite Forces Guide: Preparing to Survive: Being Ready for When Disaster Strikes*, (Amber Books, London, 2012).

[487] Richard Graves, *The 10 Bushcraft Books*, (CreateSpace, 2015).

[488] See www.backwoodsmanmag.com.

[489] See Michael Pewtherer, *Wilderness Survival Handbook: Primitive Skills for Short-Term Survival and Long-Term Comfort*, (McGraw-Hill, New York, 2010); Dave Canterbury, *Advanced Bushcraft: An Expert Field Guide to the Art of Wilderness Survival*, (F + W, Avon, 2014).

[490] See in general: https://survivalpulse.com/top-50-survival-blogs/.

[491] Bob Holtzman, *Adventure Survival Handbook: How to Stay Alive in the Wild with Just a Blade and Your Wits*, (New Burlington Books, London, 2012).

[492] On the merits of a relatively thin-bladed knife for camp work (e.g. food preparation) see T. M. Trier, "Choosing an Outdoor Knife," at http://www4.gvsu.edu/trier/cache/articles/t1/outdoorknife1.htm.

[493] Amy Rost (compiler), *Survival Wisdom and Know-How: Everything You Need to Know to Subsist in the Wilderness*, (Black Dog and Leventhal Publishers, New York, 2007).

[494] John McPherson and Geri McPherson, *Ultimate Guide to Wilderness Living: Surviving with Nothing but Your Bare Hands and What You Find in the Woods*, (Ulysses Press, Berkeley, CA, 2008).

[495] Tom Brown with Brandt Morgan, *Tom Brown's Field Guide to Living with the Earth*, (Berkley Books, New York, 1984).

[496] Tony Nester, *The Modern Hunter-Gatherer: A Practical Guide to Living*

Off the Land, (Diamond Greek Press and Ancient Pathways, LLC, Flagstaff, AZ, 2009).

497   Nester, as above, p. 63.

498   Dr Arthur T. Bradley, *Handbook to Practical Disaster Preparedness for the Family*, 2nd edition, (The Author, http://disasterpreparer.com/2011).

499   Dr Arthur T. Bradley, *Disaster Preparedness for EMP Attacks and Solar Storms*, (The Author, http://disasterpreparer.com/).

500   Matthew Stein, *When Technology Fails: A Manual for Self-Reliance, Sustainability, and Surviving the Long Emergency*, (Revised Edition), (Chelsea Green, White River Junction, 2008).

501   Matthew Stein, *When Disaster Strikes: A Comprehensive Guide for Emergency Planning and Crisis Survival*, (Chelsea Green, White River Junction, 2011).

502   James Wesley, Rawles, *How to Survive the End of the World as We Know It: Tactics, Techniques and Technologies for Uncertain Times*, (Plume Books, Penguin, New York, 2009).

503   E. F. Schumacher, *Small is Beautiful*, (Harper and Row, New York, 1973).

504   Bruce D. Clayton, *Life After Doomsday*, (Paladin Press, Boulder, Colorado, 1992).

505   Bruce D. Clayton, *Life after Terrorism: What You Need to Know to Survive in Today's World*, (Paladin Press, Boulder, Colorado, 2002).

506   Cresson Kearney, *Nuclear War Survival Skills* (1986), at http://www.oism.org/nwss/.

507   US Armed Forces, *Nuclear, Biological and Chemical Survival Manual,* (Basic Books, New York, 2003).

508   Harrison, as above, p. 804.

509   Layton, as above.

510   Jack A. Spigarelli, *Crisis Preparedness Handbook: A Comprehensive Guide to Home Storage and Physical Survival*, 2nd updated edition, (Cross-Current Publishing, Alpine, Utah, 2002).

511   Holly Drennan Deyo, *Dare to Prepare!* (Deyo Enterprises, Pueblo West,

2006).

[512]   Spigarelli, as above, p. 52.

[513]   As above.

[514]   Survival Diva, "The Mother of All Food Storage Myths," September 13, 2012, at http://survivethecomingcollapse.com/1970/the-mother-of-all-food-storage-myths.

[515]   Lundin, as above, p. 239; "What You Need to Know about Eating Expired Food," November 18, 2015, at http://www.backdoorsurvival.com/what-you-need-to-know-about-eating-expired-food/;

[516]   Mike Adams, "Fifty Food Items to Stockpile Now: Health Ranger Releases Preparedness Foods Shopping Lists," August 22, 2012 at http://www.naturalnews.com/036907_emergency_foods_shopping_list_discounts.html.

[517]   Zachery Nowak, *Crash Course: Preparing for Peak Oil*, (Green Door via Bonazzi, Italy, 2008), http://www.greendoorpublishing.com/.

[518]   See Ted Trainer, *The Transition to a Sustainable and Just World*, (Envirobook, Canterbury, New South Wales, 2010) and the "Simplicity Institute" website at http://simplicityinstitute.org/ted-trainer.

[519]   Carla Emery, *The Encyclopedia of Country Living*, (Sasquatch Books, Seattle, 2012).

[520]   John Storey and Martha Storey, *Storey's Basic Country Skills: A Practical Guide to Self-Reliance*, (Story Publishing, North Adams, MA, 1999).

[521]   A. R. Gehring (ed.), *Back to Basics: A Complete Guide to Traditional Skills*, 3rd Edition, (Sky Horse Publishing, New York, 2008).

[522]   J. Cobb, *Pepper's Long-Term Survival Guide: Food, Shelter, Security, Off-The-Grid Power and More Life-Saving Strategies for Self-Sufficient Living*, (Ulysses Press, Berkeley, 2014).

[523]   John Seymour, *The Fat of the Land*, (Faber and Faber, London, 1961).

[524]   John Seymour, *The Self-Sufficient Life and How to Live It: The Complete Back-to-Basic Guide*, (Dorling Kindersley, New York, 2003).

[525]   John Seymour, *The Forgotten Arts*, (Angus and Robertson Publishers, North Ryde, New South Wales, 1984).

[526] The slasher is pictured on p. 53 and p. 74, as above. See also pp. 134-135 on blade making in John Seymour, *The New Complete Book of Self-Sufficiency: The Classic Guide for Realists and Dreamers,* (Dorling Kindersley, London, 2009).

[527] As above, p. 13.

[528] Stephen Scott and Kenneth Pellman, *Living without Electricity*, (Good Books, Intercourse, Pennsylvania, 1990), p. 8.

[529] For a positive evaluation of Amish agriculture practices and lifestyle see Wendell Berry, *The Unsettling of America: Culture and Agriculture*, (Sierra Club Books, San Francisco, 1977), *Amish Economy*, (Adela Press, Versailles, KY, 1996).

[530] "Physical Weed Control Methods," at https://www.business.qld.gov.au/industry/agriculture/land-management/health-pests-weeds-diseases/weeds-and-diseases/controlling-weeds-property/physical-weed-control-methods.

[531] See D. Cook, *The Ax Book: The Lore and Science of the Woodcutter*, (Alan C. Hood and Company, Chambersburg, 1999).

[532] On the hand-held slasher see Edward Mundie, *Go Country: A Troubleshooter's Guide to Successful Country Living*, (Hyland House, South Melbourne, 1994), p. 53.

[533] James Ballou, *Long-Term Survival in the Coming Dark Age*, (Paladin Press, Boulder, Colorado, 2007), pp. 29-63. On beginning blacksmithing see Alex Bealer, *The Art of Blacksmithing*, (Castle Books, Edison, 2009).

[534] Brett McKay and Kate McKay, "Measure Twice Cut Once: Applying the Ethos of the Craftsman to Our Everyday Lives," July 3, 2013, at http://www.artofmanliness.com/2013/07/03/measure-twice-cut-once-applying-the-ethos-of-the-craftsman-to-our-everyday-lives.

[535] Michael Drac, "Foreword" to Piero San Giorgio, *Survive the Economic Collapse: A Practical Guide*, (Radix/Washington Summit Publishers, Whitefish, 2013), pp. xx-xxi.

[536] https://townhall.com/tipsheet/briannaheldt/2019/01/07/american-psychological-association-labels-traditional-masculinity-as-harmful-n2538637; https://www.apa.org/monitor/2019/01/ce-corner.aspx.

[537] Jack Donovan, "Violence is Golden," http://www.jack-donovan.com/axis/2011/03/violence-is-golden/.

[538] https://www.energeticnutrition.com/vitalzym/xeno_phyto_estrogens.html.

539   https://www.rooshv.com/the-decline-in-testosterone-is-destroying-the-basis-of-masculinity.

540   D. Gillespie, *Sweet Poison: Why Sugar Makes Us Fat*, (Penguin, New York, 2013).

541   https://articles.mercola.com/sites/articles/archive/2015/02/18/processed-fructose-obesity-diabetes.aspx; https://www.mercola.com/infographics/fructose-overload.htm;

542   https://articles.mercola.com/sites/articles/archive/2010/06/19/richard-johnson-interview-may-18-2010.aspx; https://www.naturalnews.com/2019-02-14-excessive-sugar-consumption-dramatically-increases-your-risk-of-cancer.html.

543   http://www.natural.news/2018-11-01-blueberries-contain-a-specific-substance-that-can-prolong-your-life.html.

544   M. Lahtinen and A-K. Salmi, "Mixed Livelihood Society in Iin Hamina – A Case Study of Medieval Diet in the Northern Ostrobothnia, Finland," *Environmental Archaelogy*, vol. 24, 2019, pp. 1-14.

545   https://www.naturalnewsblogs.com/eat-fish-cheat-death/.

546   https://www.theorganicprepper.com/how-to-feed-your-family-when-youre-flat-broke/.

547   https://www.livescience.com/64454-belly-fat-brain-shrinkage.html.

548   https://www.zerohedge.com/news/2018-10-05/shocking-new-studies-find-young-americans-are-overweight-unhealthy-suicidal.

549   https://www.dailywire.com/news/22906/buzzfeed-guys-test-their-testosterone-levels-amanda-prestigiacomo.

550   H. I. Mencken, *Prejudices*, cited from A. R. Pratt, *The Dark Side: Thoughts on the Futility of Life from the Ancient Greeks to the Present*, (Citadel Press Books/Carol Publishing Group, New York, 1994), p. 210.

551   Victor Hugo, at http://classiclit.about.com/od/victorhugo/a/Victor-Hugo-Quotes.htm.

552   P. McAllister, *Manthropology: The Science of Why the Modern Male in Not the Man He Used to Be*, (St. Martin's Press, New York, 2009).

553   P. McAllister, "The Evolution of the Inadequate Modern Male," *Australasian Science*, May, 2011, pp. 19-21.

554   https://survivalblog.com/survival-fitness-health-part-1-jbh/.

555   https://www.oldtimestrongman.com/

556   https://web.archive.org/web/20120529122448/http://sandowplus.co.uk/Competition/Saxon/DPP/dppintro.htm.

557   http://www.wimsblog.com/2013/03/the-myth-of-military-hand-to-hand-combat-systems/

558   R. Miller, *Mediations on Violence*, (YMAA Publication Center, Boston, 2008), p. 138.

559   https://www.dailymail.co.uk/video/news/video-1833704/Video-Final-moments-hero-bouncer-fought-gatecrashing-mob.html.

560   https://guidedchaos.kartra.com/page/SteinerMythOfGrappling.

561   Sammy Franco, *Out of the Cage: A Complete Guide to Beating a Mixed Martial Artist on the Street*, (Contemporary Fighting Arts, 2013).

562   See: http://jameslafond.blogspot.com/p/ssurvival.html.

563   T. Larkin, *When Violence is the Answer*, (Little Brown and Company, New York, 2017).

564   M. MacYoung and J. Meek, *What You Don't Know Can Kill You*, (Carry On Publishing, Monument, 2018).

565   V. Freeborn, *Violence of Mind*, (The Author, 2018).

566   S. LeBlanc, *Constant Battles: Why We Fight*, (St. Martin's Press, New York, 2003).

567   https://cdn.ymaws.com/www.caceo.us/resource/resmgr/imported/documents/as14/Coopers-System-for-Awareness.pdf.

568   S. Begovic, *The Dark Secrets of SHTF Survival: The Brutal Truth about Violence, Death, and Mayhem that You Must Know to Survive*, (Daisy Luther Media, 2018).

569   L. Stroud, *Will to Live: Dispatches from the Edge of Survival*, (Harper, New York, 2011).

570   Cited from www.philosophyblog.com/2012/02/25/before-all-else-be-armed.

571   Sun Tzu, *The Art of War*, (Penguin, New York, 2002), p. 6.

572 https://mises.org/wire/bipartisan-support-new-federal-gun-controls-red-flag; http://www.shtfplan.com/headline-news/incoming-communists-ready-a-bill-that-will-criminalize-private-gun-sales_12182018; https://www.naturalnews.com/2019-01-27-oregon-democrats-push-new-bill-to-outlaw-self-defense-violent-crime.html.

573 https://en.wikipedia.org/wiki/Executive_Order_13603.

574 https://www.wsj.com/articles/gun-use-surges-in-europe-where-firearms-are-rare-11546857000.

575 https://www.theorganicprepper.com/defending-homestead-venezuela/.

576 M. Greenman, *The Zombie Shooting Guide: Survival Training for the Worst-Case Scenario*, (Ooda Media Group, Los Angeles, 2013).

577 R. Miller, *Meditations on Violence: A Comparison of Martial Arts Training and Real World Violence*, (YMAA Publication Center, Boston, 2008), p. 58.

578 Of interest: https://survivalblog.gunfighters-guide-lessons-learned-hard-way-part-1-grumpy-gunfighter, and https://survivalblog.com/gunfighters-guide-lessons-learned-hard-way-part-2-grumpy-gunfighter/; https://survivalblog.com/gunfighters-guide-lessons-learned-hard-way-part-3-grumpy-gunfighter/.

579 E. Keith, "The Best Home Defense Gun," *Guns & Ammo Guide to Guns for Home Defense*, 1975, pp. 42-44, at p. 44.

580 B. D. Clayton, *Life After Doomsday: A Survivalist Guide to Nuclear War and Other Major Disasters*, (Paladin Press, Boulder, Colorado, 1992).

581 M. Tappan, *Survival Guns*, (Paladin Press, Boulder, Colorado, 2009).

582 F. Rexer, *USA: The Urban Survival Arsenal*, (Delta Press, 1980).

583 https://survivalblog.com/weapons-systems-approach-firearms-training/; https://survivalblog.com/well-balanced-gun-collection/; http://www.survivopedia.com/top-6-survival-rifles/.

584 P. A. Kasker, "Terrible Reality," *American Survival Guide*, February, 1993, pp. 16-17; W. U. Spitu (et al.), "Physical Activity Until Collapse following Fatal Injury by Firearms and Sharp Pointed Weapons," *Journal of Forensic Science*, vol. 6, 1961, pp. 290-300.

585 https://www.naturalnews.com/2018-11-04-why-i-switched-from-glock-to-sig-for-concealed-carry.html.

586   J. Ballou, *Arming for the Apocalypse*, (Paladin Press, Boulder, Colorado, 2012).

587   http://jeffcoopersscoutrifles.blogspot.com/.

588   https://urbansurvivalsite.com/survival-bows/.

589   https://www.youtube.com/watch?v=BEG-ly9tQGk.

590   https://www.youtube.com/watch?v=6lf9q6OQseo.

591   https://www.youtube.com/watch?v=-CNaUbG54R8; http://insidearchery.com/coldsteel-cheapshot130/.

592   https://www.youtube.com/watch?v=P2WhUu15B5E; https://hiconsumption.com/2019/03/ek-archery-cobra-rx-adder-tactical-repeating-crossbow/.

593   https://www.youtube.com/watch?v=5qKP9TXHwrE.

594   https://www.youtube.com/watch?v=H8zitBN6iho.

595   https://www.youtube.com/watch?v=rdYjYnEOR_w.

596   https://www.livescience.com/2699-science-breaking-baseball-bats.html.

597   https://www.youtube.com/watch?v=pv4D8AjUT1w.

598   R. Ma, *The Zombie Combat Manual: A Guide to Fighting the Living Dead*, (Berkley Books, New York, 2010); A. Alasdair, *Weapons and Warfare in the Zombie Apocalypse*, (The Author, 2012).

599   See though for those wanting to acquire master of the fighting staff: D. C. McLemore, *The Fighting Staff*, (Paladin Press, Boulder, Colorado, 2009), and J. Varady, *The Art and Science of Staff fighting: A Complete Instructional Guide*, (YMAA Publication Center, Wolfeboro, 2016).

600   D. Tueller, "How Close is Too Close?' *S.W.A.T. Magazine*, March 1983.

601   https://www.buckeyefirearms.org/alternate-look-handgun-stopping-power.

602   https://www.youtube.com/user/ThegnThrand?pbjreload=10.

603   https://medievalshoppe.com.au.

604   J. Clements, *Medieval Swordsmanship: Illustrated Methods and Techniques*, (Paladin Press, Boulder, Colorado, 1988), p. 177; J. Kim Siddorn, *Viking Weapons and Warfare*, (Tempus Publishing, Gloucestershire, 2003).

[605] James LaFond, "Axes: A Brief Survey of the Barbarian's Best Friend," http://jameslafond.com/article.php?id=11993.

[606] J. Clement, "Echo of Steel," in S. Shackleford, *Spirit of the Sword: A Celebration of Artistry and Craftsmanship*, (Krause Publications, Iola, 2010), pp. 32-51; H. Withers, *The Illustrated Encyclopedia of Swords and Sabres*, (Lorenz Books, Leicestershire, 2012).

[607] https://www.manilatimes.net/juramentados-and-the-development-of-the-colt-45-caliber-model-1911/107609/.

[608] https://www.youtube.com/watch?v=8PQiaurIiDM.

[609] https://www.youtube.com/watch?v=8PQiaurIiDM.

[610] https://www.youtube.com/watch?v=_hfLZozBVpM.

[611] Miyamoto Musashi, *A Book of Five Rings*, (Overlook Press, Woodstock, 1974).

[612] https://www.machetespecialists.com.

[613] https://www.survivopedia.com/how-to-defend-against-a-machete-attack/.

[614] https://www.youtube.com/watch?v=rzbPdJEZw60; https://www.youtube.com/watch?v=EhUzkdntyqs.

[615] http://www.nononsenseselfdefense.com/knifelies.htm.

[616] R. Ryan, "Against the Odds," in R. Horowitz (et al., eds), *The Ultimate Guide to Knife Combat*, (Black Belt Books, 2007), pp. 239-241, at p. 241.

[617] As above.

[618] J. M. Ayres, *The Tactical Knife: Designs, Techniques and Uses*, (Krause Publications, Iola, 2010), *Survival Knives: How to Choose and Use the Right Blade*, (Skyhorse Publishing, New York, 2018).

[619] http://indigenousability.blogspot.com/2018/01/a-consversation-with-master-bladesman.html; http://www.jamesakeating.com/; http://www.jamesakeating.com/catalg3.html.

[620] See Donnie Be All Day, knife reviews, https://www.youtube.com/channel/UCyTdfiGszmuva7-Dq8mYWMQ.

[621] https://kailashblades.com/product/scourge/; https://kailashblades.com/product/sirupate/

[622]   J. M. Yumoto, *The Samurai Sword: A Handbook*, (Tuttle, Tokyo, 1989).

[623]   C. S. Lewis, *Rehabilitations and Other Essays*, (Oxford University Press, Oxford, 1939).

[624]   Oswald Spengler, *The Hour of Decision* (Part One), (Alfred A. Knopf, New York, 1963), p. 118.

[625]   K. Preston, "The Nietzschean Prophecies: Two Hundred Years of Nihilism and the Coming Crisis of Western Civilization," in T. Southgate (ed.), *The Radical Tradition: Philosophy, Metapolitics and the Conservative Revolution*, pp. 173-180.

[626]   See *Occidental Quarterly* vol. 13, no. 2, Summer 2013, Special Section.

[627]   G. Taunton, *Sophia Perrenis: The Return of Perennial Philsophy*, forthcoming 2020.

[628]   T Southgate, "Organising for the Collapse," in his *Tradition and Revolution: Collected Writings of Troy Southgate*, (Arktos, London, 2010).

[629]   G. Faye, *Convergence of Catastrophes*, (Arktos, London, 2012).

www.ingramcontent.com/pod-product-compliance
Lightning Source LLC
Chambersburg PA
CBHW031507270326
41930CB00006B/290